D0080772
DISCARDED
From Nashville Public Library

Democratic Religion

Recent titles in

RELIGION IN AMERICA SERIES

Harry S. Stout, *General Editor*

THE PRISM OF PIETY
Catholick Congregational Clergy at the Beginning of the Enlightenment
John Corrigan

FEMALE PIETY IN PURITAN NEW ENGLAND
The Emergence of Religious Humanism
Amanda Porterfield

THE SECULARIZATION OF THE ACADEMY
Edited by George M. Marsden and Bradley J. Longfield

EPISCOPAL WOMEN
Gender, Spirituality, and Commitment in an American Mainline Denomination
Edited by Catherine Prelinger

SUBMITTING TO FREEDOM
The Religious Vision of William James
Bennett Ramsey

OLD SHIP OF ZION
The Afro-Baptist Ritual in the African Diaspora
Walter F. Pitts

AMERICAN TRANSCENDENTALISM AND ASIAN RELIGIONS
Arthur Versluis

CHURCH PEOPLE IN THE STRUGGLE
The National Council of Churches and the Black Freedom Movement, 1950–1970
James F. Findlay, Jr.

EVANGELICALISM
Comparative Studies of Popular Protestantism in North America, the British Isles, and Beyond, 1700–1990
Edited by Mark A. Noll, David W. Bebbington, and George A. Rawlyk

RELIGIOUS MELANCHOLY AND PROTESTANT EXPERIENCE IN AMERICA
Julius H. Rubin

CONJURING CULTURE
Biblical Formations of Black America
Theophus Smith

REIMAGINING DENOMINATIONALISM
Interpretive Essays
Edited by Robert Bruce Mullin and Russell E. Richey

STANDING AGAINST THE WHIRLWIND
Evangelical Episcopalians in Nineteenth-Century America
Diana Hochstedt Butler

KEEPERS OF THE COVENANT
Frontier Missions and the Decline of Congregationalism, 1774–1818
James R. Rohrer

SAINTS IN EXILE
The Holiness-Pentecostal Experience in African American Religion and Culture
Cheryl J. Sanders

DEMOCRATIC RELIGION
Freedom, Authority, and Church Discipline in the Baptist South, 1785–1900
Gregory A. Wills

Democratic Religion

Freedom, Authority, and Church Discipline in the Baptist South, 1785–1900

Gregory A. Wills

New York Oxford
OXFORD UNIVERSITY PRESS
1997

Oxford University Press

Oxford New York
Athens Auckland Bangkok Bogota Bombay
Buenos Aires Calcutta Cape Town Dar es Salaam
Delhi Florence Hong Kong Istanbul Karachi
Kuala Lumpur Madras Madrid Melbourne
Mexico City Nairobi Paris Singapore
Taipei Tokyo Toronto

and associated companies in
Berlin Ibadan

Published by Oxford University Press, Inc.
198 Madison Avenue, New York, New York 10016

Oxford is a registered trademark of Oxford University Press

Library of Congress Cataloging-in-Publication Data
Wills, Gregory A.
Democratic religion : freedom, authority, and church discipline in
the Baptist South, 1785–1900 / Gregory A. Wills.
p. cm. — (Religion in America series)
Includes bibliographical references and index.
ISBN 0-19-510412-9
1. Baptists—Southern States—History—18th century. 2. Baptists—
Southern States—History—19th century. 3. Southern Baptist
Convention—Doctrines—History. 4. Southern Baptist Convention—
Discipline. 5. Authority—Religious aspects—Baptists.
6. Democracy—Religious aspects—Baptists. 7. Southern States—
Church history—18th century. 8. Southern States—Church
history—19th century. I. Title. II. Series: Religion in America
series (Oxford University Press)
BX6241.W55 1996
286'.175—dc20 96-20575

1 3 5 7 9 8 6 4 2

Printed in the United States of America
on acid-free paper

To Cathy

Preface

I came to this study unexpectedly. In 1992, I agreed to write a brief article on an early nineteenth-century Baptist preacher and intended only a short excursion into Baptist history. But the vistas that opened up while I studied the preacher's life were so surprising, so compelling, that I could not resist a closer look at early Southern Baptists.

Nineteenth-century Baptists were not what I anticipated. The brands of piety that flourished in the new American republic directed their appeals to the common people. In *The Democratization of American Christianity*, Nathan Hatch illustrated how the popular preachers altered their message to make it more appealing to the masses. They embraced the democratic ethos of the new nation and recast the gospel in a new, populist, individualist form—the gospel best suited to republicans was anticlerical, antiauthoritarian, anticreedal, and anti-Calvinist. In church as well as state, the ideals of democracy prospered.

In some ways, Baptists were no exception. Their churches were democracies. Their spirituality was egalitarian. But in the hands of nineteenth-century Southern Baptists, democratic religion meant a startlingly different kind of populism. Their democratic communities rejected much of the individualism that rose in tandem with the populist republicanism that swept the young nation. They honored their clergy, they were unashamedly authoritarian, they were stubbornly creedal, and they defended orthodox Calvinism. It was not until the early twentieth century that the values of political democracy reshaped Baptist piety.

From the colonial era until the early twentieth century, Southern Baptists resisted the Enlightenment's reconstruction of humanity. They rejected modernity's naturalism and opposed both evolution and biblical criticism. More important to this story, they rejected modernity's individualism. Baptist piety had individualist characteristics rooted in the Reformation doctrine of the priesthood of all believers—each person was accountable to God individually and received justification through the exercise of individual faith—but they repulsed the privatizing trend of democratic individualism. The church, they believed, had prerogatives that superseded those of individuals. The redeemed community determined corporately the meaning of the sacred text, the shape of Christian spirituality, and the regulation of virtue.

Although Southern Baptists privileged the congregational community, they were not advocates of an early form of postmodernism. They established structures and rituals that ensured that the community mediated the interpretation of scripture. However, they did not see this as an argument for the socially constructed nature of truth. To the contrary, they were quite certain that on a broad range of Bible topics they embraced eternal truth. They exercised communal authority not because modernity had corroded their trust in reason's ability to discover the unconditioned truths of the Bible. They exercised it because they had confidence in the interpretive powers of the pure community—not so much the power of objective reason or even of the chastened rationalism of the later Enlightenment, but the power of a community illumined through union with the same Christ who inspired the divine oracles. Southern Baptists established a spirituality that was at once democratic and authoritarian. Their democratic religion was as much medieval as it was modern.

I tried to let the Baptists speak for themselves. No historian attains objectivity, but attempting it improves the results. I tried to define and question the suppositions and sympathies that I brought to the task, in an effort to prevent them from distorting the history. Baptist historiography has many times suffered because the history is made to serve either denominational promotion or denominational polemics. Even in the strife about biblical authority, the arguments advanced were often historical ones. History is relevant in such debates, but sound historical judgment is often the victim.

My interests and views gave direction to this study. I state them here in the hope that they may further elucidate the argument. They may enable some to see inadvertent distortions that I missed. I have written as a Southern Baptist whose sentiments are not far from the tradition depicted here. I identify with the Reformed Protestant stream that flows from sixteenth-century Switzerland and southern Germany to seventeenth-century Puritanism to eighteenth-century American evangelicalism. I also identify with the Baptist version of that stream.

This book argues that one expression of that heritage established a precarious balance between premodern and modern cultural trends.

I relied primarily on sources from the Baptists of Georgia. Limiting the geographical scope of the study allowed me to attain depth that I would have sacrificed in a study of the South as a whole. Southern Baptists had some regional differences; Georgia was as close to the center of these differences as any state and harbored them all. Except where noted otherwise, churches and associations cited were located in Georgia.

I have retained the original spelling, punctuation, and capitalization when quoting material directly. In quotations from period print materials, I frequently omitted italics and block capitalization to be consistent with current usage. Brackets indicate material I have added for clarity or explanation.

I am deeply grateful to the many persons whose generosity made possible the completion of this book: Dave Edmondson, Jay and Barbara Farish, Johnny and Lynda Gresham, Bart and Vanessa Kaiser, John and Wilba McCoy, David and Paige Pattillo, Dave and Cindy Rawlins, Buddy and Kathy Rice, Clayton and Angela Slagle, Bill and Lynn Warren, and Mike and Nancy Wilkinson. Thanks are due especially for the frequent encouragement I received by special acts of kindness from Ferrell and Rhonwyn Ryan and from Jim and Sandy Wellman. The members and staff of Mount Vernon Baptist Church provided a spiritual home, the benefits of which are beyond reckoning.

Mary Overby and the staff of Mercer University's special collections department were most helpful in providing sources and advice.

R. Albert Mohler, editor of the *Christian Index*, and his staff deserve praise for kindly making their holdings available to me. This courtesy saved me considerable time and effort.

Jennifer West gave me the benefit of her research and sound judgment and suggested revisions to parts of this work. Tom Chaffin, Ernie Freeberg, Steve Goodson, and Mary Margaret Johnston-Miller shared their knowledge generously in many helpful ways.

Brooks Holifield's contributions were invaluable. His thorough criticism of its form and content made this book immeasurably better.

The support and encouragement of my mother, of Ingrid, and of George and Myrna cleared and smoothed the way. Without Cathy's love, patience, and sacrifice, this book could not have been completed.

Louisville, Kentucky G.A.W.
May 1996

Contents

Introduction: Religious Authority and the Democratic Impulse 3

1 Democratic Exclusivism 11

2 Democracies Primitive and Pure 26

3 Democratic Authority 37

4 Democracy, Race, and Gender 50

5 African-American Democracies 67

6 Freedom, Authority, and Doctrine 84

7 Associations, Creeds, and Calvinism 98

8 Democratic Religion Transformed 116

Conclusion 139

Notes 141

Index 185

Democratic Religion

Introduction: Religious Authority and the Democratic Impulse

In the late twentieth century, the Southern Baptist Convention, the largest Protestant denomination in the United States, suffered wrenching controversy. It differed from most earlier controversies in other denominations in that the moderate party lost control of the national organization to the fundamentalists. The fundamentalist victory was largely unexpected. Most Southern Baptists, though no theological liberals, appeared to be classic Protestant moderates—"conservative in theology, tolerant in spirit, and evangelistic in purpose."[1] Fundamentalist exclusivism seemed to cut against the grain of Southern Baptist individualism.

Most Southern Baptists subscribed to conservative theology—a divinely inspired Bible, the reality of the supernatural, the eternity of hell, the necessity of a spiritual rebirth for salvation, the obligation to evangelize the lost. When the fundamentalist party made the inerrancy of the scriptures their battle cry, they were counting on this commitment to rally the rank and file.

Many Southern Baptists subscribed also to tolerance. Throughout the twentieth century, they had placed the ideas of soul liberty and the priesthood of the believer near the center of Baptist theology. These doctrines, many Baptists urged, established the inviolable character of the individual conscience in matters spiritual: No person had a right to sit in judgment of another's religious convictions. They meant that each person was free to embrace Christianity according to individual judgment and that churches and denominational organizations should tolerate those diverse judgments. When the moderate party made freedom their battle cry, they were counting on this tradition of individualism.

Both sides raised the banner of evangelism. Southern Baptists were in the midst of aggressive overseas missions when the controversy exploded. Since the 1950s, they had expanded outside the Bible Belt, sending "home missionaries" to every state. Interest in evangelism appeared to be at an all-time high. The fundamentalists claimed that the churches committed to inerrancy were the ones that practiced evangelism, as evidenced by their growth and number of baptisms. The moderates claimed that the strife caused by inerrancy crusaders distracted the churches and placed obstacles in the path of evangelism. Furthermore, moderates argued, the churches leading the inerrancy crusade contributed paltry sums to the common fund that financed home and foreign missions.

Although moderates did not repudiate conservative theology and fundamentalists did not repudiate toleration, the antagonists correctly portrayed the struggle as a conflict between a particular understanding of toleration and a particular understanding of Baptist orthodoxy, with both sides claiming title to the evangelistic imperative.

Both parties saw the conflict as a struggle over the identity of the Southern Baptist denomination. Were Southern Baptists at heart moved by appeals to freedom grounded in the doctrines of soul liberty and the priesthood of the believer or by appeals to inerrancy grounded in fundamentalist orthodoxy? Many moderates believed that the fundamentalist challenge stood little chance of success.[2] They underestimated the influence of southern traditions of religious authority. In the final analysis, the heritage of exclusivism prevailed over modern forms of individualism.

Few could have predicted the fundamentalist victory, partly because Baptist historians had so frequently depicted eighteenth- and nineteenth-century Baptists as advocates of an intensely individualistic religion that embraced freedom as a sacred good. The counterpart to their commitment to freedom, historians said, was their rejection of authority. Historian Robert G. Torbet summarized the consensus view: Baptists "have ever sought to be free from ecclesiastical authority."[3] The history of moral discipline in early Baptist churches shows how gravely this conclusion misjudged the Baptist past.

This is the story of how one denomination fashioned a form of piety at once committed to religious freedom and to democratic authority. Its ideas of freedom and authority grew out of its conception of the church. Because Baptists saw the church as a voluntary democracy, they pursued spiritual egalitarianism. Because they saw it also as a bastion of purity, they excluded the impure and the false.

Indeed, the brands of American Protestantism that flourished after the Great Awakening shared an exclusivist temperament that rested on a vision of the church as separate from the world. These evangelicals insisted on conversion as prerequisite for church membership, on right belief, and on church discipline. Dissent from this vision fueled many a denominational controversy, and, as evangelical churches relinquished it for an inclusivist one in the twentieth century, the character of evangelical Protestantism changed.

In antebellum evangelical churches, the conversion experience defined church membership. Although Methodists, Presbyterians, and Congregationalists admitted the children of church members through infant baptism, and early Methodists admitted unconverted adults if they avowed a serious purpose to seek salvation, evangelical churches so accentuated the conversion experience as to make it effectively the only proper qualification of membership. To remain in an evangelical church without it was to remain a second-class member, subject to the special attentions and prayers of the pastor and converted members. The experience separated those within from those without. It formed the first support of evangelical exclusivism.

These churches also saw orthodox belief as intrinsic to Christian identity. Each denomination or church had a confession that defined the boundaries of belief. Theological commitments stood as fences separating church members from both unbelievers and believers of other denominations. Theological exclusivism made evangelical unity a distant hope. Although church union had long been the dream of both liberals and evangelicals, it made no headway until churches began to reject the exclusivist character of their doctrines.

Although not all church members were theological adepts—many knew little theology—the level of interest shown by the laity was remarkable. To claim that the laity ignored theology because the clergy surpassed them in knowledge is like describing patients as unconcerned about medicine because their physicians specialize in it. Though not always well informed, the laity often felt a keen interest in theology, especially in times of controversy. They took sides in public debates, formed factions in their churches, and expected sound theology from their ministers. Commitment to doctrine constituted the second support of evangelical exclusivism.

Evangelicals placed a premium on the purity of the church, which they endeavored to maintain through church discipline. This practice—the third support for the exclusivist vision—is central to the story of democratic religion. Evangelical exclusivism appeared most vividly in the principles and practices of discipline.

Among all the denominations, Baptists won the reputation of the strongest commitment to democratic principles and individual freedom. Yet they also demonstrated the most zeal for strict church discipline. They were religious populists—their churches democratic, their ministers needing only the call of the Spirit, their religion personal and fervent, their appeals addressed to the common person—but they combined their populism with authoritative Calvinism and unflinching church discipline. Prizing an independent, democratic government and employing a rhetoric of freedom, they expected their members to submit to a demanding corporate authority. These little democracies made their members conform.

They seemed to consider themselves set apart for perfecting an exclusivist church. When other evangelicals called them bigots, they found in the epithet a hidden compliment. They saw theirs as the only church properly ordered. Only they had a converted church membership; only they refused to baptize unconverted infants. Only they, moreover, understood baptism to mean immersion and refused membership to adults whose "baptism" consisted of sprinkling or pouring. To make things worse, most Baptists would not recognize what they termed *alien immersion*—immersion performed by non-Baptists—conceiving that no minister who believed in infant baptism could validly baptize even by immersion. And then they further provoked other evangelicals by refusing to take communion with them and withholding communion from their members. Baptists practiced close communion because they believed that baptism was prerequisite to participation in the Lord's Supper and that other evangelicals had never been baptized. Add to this their strict church discipline, and it is no surprise that other denominations scorned their exclusivism.

Baptists touted their allegiance to freedom and republicanism, for they alone, they said, truly advocated civil and religious liberty. They organized autonomous local churches free from tyrannical hierarchies, and they practiced a church government by democracy rather than by priests, bishops, or elders. However, they combined their populist democracy with ecclesiastical authority, and this was true nowhere more than in the South. Southern Baptists, like northern Baptists, identified themselves as champions of freedom, but they exceeded their northern counterparts in the rigor of their church discipline. They disciplined a far higher percentage of their members. The South proved amenable both to Baptists and to rigorists.

Southern Baptists descended from English Puritanism. The first English-speaking Baptist churches grew out of English Separatist churches in the early seventeenth century. These General Baptists rejected such Calvinist doctrines as limited atonement (the view that Christ died only for the elect) and unconditional election. By the 1640s, Particular Baptists organized churches that rejected any suggestion that

Christ died for all people; rather, he died for a particular people—the elect who had been chosen from all eternity. Particular Baptists were similar to other Puritans except that they baptized only professing believers and they baptized by immersion.[4]

Both Particulars and Generals established congregations in the American colonies. In 1639, Roger Williams and a few others formed a Particular church in Providence, Rhode Island. Other congregations followed in Rhode Island and Massachusetts. Some members were converts from colonial Puritanism; others migrated from Baptist churches in England, Wales, and Ireland. Although most of the early churches were Particular, General churches prospered in some areas.[5]

Baptist churches multiplied during the Great Awakening, growing from sixty congregations in 1740 to almost one thousand in 1790. Dozens of Separatist Congregational churches—congregations that separated from associations that rejected the methods and theologies of the revivalists—became Baptist. These revivalists were known as Separate Baptists, and a number of them became itinerant evangelists whose preaching created Baptist believers throughout the colonies.[6]

The first identifiable Baptist church in the South formed in Charleston, South Carolina, when a congregation of Particulars migrated from Maine in 1696. The awakening brought itinerant preachers like Shubal Stearns and Daniel Marshall, who separated from Congregational churches in New England and migrated to North Carolina in 1755 to establish Separate Baptist churches. The Philadelphia Baptist Association also sent to the South such evangelists as Morgan Edwards and John Gano, who established Regular (formerly known as Particular) Baptist churches, often by persuading the scattered General Baptist congregations to adopt Calvinist doctrine. The Regulars adopted the London Confession and looked askance at the Separates as agents of disorder. The Separates objected to parts of the London Confession and criticized the Regulars for tolerating luxury in dress and for retaining members who had received baptism before they were converted. Most Separates agreed with the Regulars' Calvinism, and between 1777 and 1801 the two united, state by state.[7]

In 1772, Daniel Marshall, who had been a deacon in a Congregational church in Connecticut for twenty years, planted a Separate Baptist church in Georgia. In 1773, William Botsford, an English immigrant, planted a Regular church. By 1784, these churches, along with three others, reconciled and formed the Georgia Association, with 223 members.[8] Although they healed the Separate-Regular divide, Baptists in Georgia and the South suffered other divisions. Early in the nineteenth century, some Baptists organized to support missions and other benevolent projects. Others saw no scriptural basis for benevolent societies, and they opposed these missionary Baptists, forming associations of Primitive Baptists in the 1830s. Between 1850 and 1900, a further controversy over Landmarkism disrupted the churches. The Landmarkists followed the teachings of Tennessee editor J. R. Graves, who contended that Baptists could not share pulpits with non-Baptists and that Baptist churches were the only true churches because they alone could trace an unbroken apostolic succession of true baptisms.[9] The issue created hard feelings, but it did not result in any schism.

In 1790, 67,000 Baptists worshiped in the United States. The South held 41,000 of them, 61 percent of the total. Half of these southern Baptists were in Virginia, but Georgia was becoming a Baptist haven as well; although the entire South is in view in this study, the practices of Georgia Baptist churches provide the backdrop before which most of this narrative unfolds. Georgia had only 3,245 Baptists in 1785, but eventually the Baptists and Methodists swept the field. Presbyterians could boast members of prominence, but they had only a small minority of the state's Christians. In 1827, the state harbored some 20,000 Baptists, 17,181 Methodists, and about 2,200 Presbyterians. All the Christian denominations totaled barely 10 percent of the state's residents, though many more people attended than joined. By 1850, the South held 59 percent of the nation's 715,000 Baptists. More than 52,000 of them dwelt in Georgia. By the onset of the Civil War, total church membership in the state climbed to about 20 percent, with Baptists accounting for 96,000 church members, Methodists 85,000, and Presbyterians 6,200.[10]

After the war Georgia became one of the most Protestant states in the nation. By 1906, 41 percent of Georgians claimed membership in a Protestant church, second only to South Carolina's 45 percent. Georgia also became the most Baptist of all the states. In 1906, one in every four Georgians was a Baptist communicant, a higher percentage than in any other state. Numbering 596,319, white and black Georgia Baptists outstripped the next largest Baptist state by more than 150,000 members.

The story of religious authority in Georgia Baptist churches provides the narrative for this book. They placed discipline at the center of church life, filling their monthly conference meetings with disciplinary matters and viewing the church as a bench of judges. Not even preaching the gospel was more important to them than the exercise of discipline. They were disciplined democracies.

Through discipline, Baptists sought to repristinate the apostolic church and to stake their claim to primitive Christianity. Through discipline, they would, moreover, sweep the nation, for they believed that God rewarded faithful pruning by raining down revival. So they required of every member submission to church discipline and demanded from everyone—saint and sinner alike—an acknowledgment of the church's right to censure and an acceptance of what they considered the orthodox tenets of Calvinist theology. Clergy and laity alike cherished and protected the doctrines of Calvinism with an intensity that some twentieth-century historians—accustomed to thinking that only an elite few cared about theological complexities—have found hard to fathom.

They combined a hierarchical view of society with an egalitarian view of the church. Their ideology of hierarchy meant that churches in some ways treated female and black offenders with greater severity than male and white offenders. Their egalitarianism meant that they treated male and white offenders in other ways with greater severity than female and black offenders. But by all appearances, women and blacks were at least as committed to the church's pruning knife as white men were. After emancipation, the African-American Baptists established in their churches similar forms and doctrines to those of the white churches, including the discipline.

After the Civil War, Baptist observers began to lament that church discipline was foundering, and it was. It declined partly because it became more burdensome in larger churches. Young Baptists refused in increasing numbers to submit to discipline for dancing, and the churches shrank from excluding them. Urban churches, pressed by the need for large buildings and the desire for refined music and preaching, subordinated church discipline to the task of keeping the church solvent. Many Baptists shared a new vision of the church, replacing the pursuit of purity with the quest for efficiency. They lost the resolve to purge their churches of straying members.

No one publicly advocated the demise of discipline. No Baptist leader arose to call for an end to congregational censures. No theologians argued that discipline was unsound in principle or practice. No "freedom" party arose to quash the tyranny of the redeemed. It simply faded away, as if Baptists had grown weary of holding one another accountable.

Attention to the meaning of church discipline should temper the notion that its significance resided simply in its function as a device of social control. It is true that evangelical churches were "moral courts of the frontier," enforcing standards of conduct amidst the lawlessness of frontier society.[11] But viewing discipline as social control goes only a short way in explaining its place in the lives of churchgoers. The faithful did not exercise discipline in order to constrain a wayward society. That was the task of families, communities, and governments. Churches disciplined to constrain confessing saints to good order and to preserve their purity. Church discipline was not about social control but about ecclesiastical control.

Until about 1830, much of Georgia was a frontier society, with all of the lawlessness, vice, and social chaos frontier conditions could engender. Even after 1830, Georgians, like other southerners, were prone to frequent outbursts of drunken brawling, replete with eye gouging and knife play. People in the churches disliked the disorder as much as other law-abiding Georgians, but they did not see it as their chief duty to do the sheriff's job. They had the Lord's work to do.

In fact, the more the churches concerned themselves with social order, the less they exerted church discipline. From about 1850 to 1920, a period of expanding evangelical solicitude for the reformation of society, church discipline declined steadily. From temperance to Sabbatarian reform, evangelicals persuaded their communities to adopt the moral norms of the church for society at large. As Baptists learned to reform the larger society, they forgot how they had once reformed themselves. Church discipline presupposed a stark dichotomy between the norms of society and the kingdom of God. The more evangelicals purified the society, the less they felt the urgency of a discipline that separated the church from the world.

1

Democratic Exclusivism

In 1806, William Barnes, estranged from some of the members of the Savannah First Baptist Church, requested letters of dismission in order that he and his family might join another church. The church, believing that Barnes had neglected his religious duties, charged him with "continued absence from the Church, and from the Table of the Lord, at our communion." On the advice of pastor Henry Holcombe, they voted to deal with him gently, pronouncing against him "the lowest Censure of the Church, to wit, Rebuke," but he ignored them.

One month later, the church again cited him to answer for his absence. Interpreting his actions as rebellion against their authority, they expressed their grief at "the apparent contempt with which Brother William B. Barnes has for a long time treated us, by his perpetual absence from our days of Discipline, as well as from our Communion seasons, not partaking with us of the Lords supper."

When Henry Williams delivered the church's message, Barnes exploded in frustration. His attempts to cast off ecclesiastical control had failed. According to Williams's account, Barnes "appear'd very angry, expressed dissatisfaction with some of the Brethren, & at length swore profanely that he would not appear at any Ecclesiastical court, for that he hated them, and always had hated them, &c." When Barnes did not appear as summoned, the church raised the stakes, disbarring him from the privileges of membership, including the Lord's Supper, and resolved "that Bro. William B. Barnes, not only for his repeated contempt of this church, but also for the horrid sin of profane swearing, be suspended."

The church's forbearance extended two months more.

> Our beloved Pastor [Holcombe] stated to the Church that it was long since the Church had expected that our Brother William B. Barnes would have been publickly expelled by excommunication from the special priviledges of this Church, that he however had thought proper to write to him, & had usd every argument to induce his return to his duty and to Order, hoping thereby to gain him by love, that he had also received letters from him, but that he was sorry to inform the Church that there was no reason, from the spirit in which he wrote, to hope for his wished for restoration. The Church, after expressing much sorrow, for the necessity which impelled them, unanimously resolved to Excommunicate the offending Brother from this Church, but in order that the cup of forbearance should, as it were, be drained towards him, they agreed that his Sentence should not be made public till next Lords Day a week, that he may have opportunity to seek restoration on Gospel principles.

When the church informed Barnes, he "said he was willing they proceed to his excommunication." On Sunday, pastor Henry Holcombe, "towards the latter part of his forenoon sermon in a very moderate and delicate manner pronounced the Church's act of excommunication against Mr. William B. Barnes." In the final action of this four-month drama, Savannah Church unceremoniously demoted "Brother Barnes" to "Mr. Barnes."[1]

If he did not know it before, Barnes discovered the hard way that Baptists accepted no opposition to the principle of ecclesiastical authority. To an antebellum Baptist, a church without discipline would hardly have counted as a church. For this reason, Savannah Baptists refused to permit Barnes to absent himself from the "days of Discipline." For the same reason, the church refused to allow Barnes's "contempt" to go unrebuked. Installing discipline at the center of church life, Baptist churches required their members to submit.

In a sacred drama that alternately wooed and chastised straying members, the Baptists manifested their core convictions. Because they believed it a divine drama, carried out under the directions of the heavenly Christ and replete with eternal implications, they exercised their discipline with emotion and ardor. With varying outcomes, the Baptists of the nineteenth-century South repeated the Barnes affair ad infinitum. By the time of the Civil War, the democratic Baptists had excommunicated more than forty thousand members in Georgia alone.[2]

Separation from the World

Antebellum southern Baptists found nothing remarkable in excommunication. They found it in the New Testament, in Jesus' command to cast unrepentant sinners out of the church and in Paul's command to "expel the immoral brother." The early church expelled those who sinned or denied church teaching. By the fourth century, churches allowed transgressors only one repentance after baptism; subsequent lapses could not be forgiven. Transgressors had to endure years of faithful observance before bishops restored them to membership.[3]

Medieval churches swept aside the once-only rigor of the early church and substituted a system of private penance. Local priests directed the discipline of the faithful in a life-long practice of confession, penance, and forgiveness. The Fourth Lateran Council endorsed this system in 1215.

Luther and other Protestant reformers objected to the medieval practice and its implicit denial of justification by faith. Protestants tried to reform discipline. Although they sometimes insisted that discipline was a mark of the true church, in most areas civil authorities limited their power to exercise it. In Geneva, Protestant leader John Calvin eventually prevailed in the struggle to grant the church some independence to discipline.[4]

English and American Puritans, from whom Baptists came, objected to the Church of England as being defective not "so much in *Doctrine* as in *Worship and Discipline*." They sought to perfect the Reformation by restoring "Primitive godly discipline." Separatists, Baptists, and New England Puritans remedied the defect and cast out the wayward in their churches. The southern Baptists identified themselves with the English dissenting tradition and proclaimed a gospel that divided the world into sinners and saints. God required Baptists to establish churches purified by discipline.[5]

Southern evangelicals constituted only a small percentage of the southern population, but they made their presence felt. In 1800, Baptists, along with Methodists and Presbyterians, were outspoken critics of all forms of worldliness, which, they thought, found its clearest expression in the pleasures and customs of the wealthy. The southern gentility, in turn, despised the Baptists especially as poor, uneducated, and lacking culture. Baptist social criticism and Baptist discipline exemplified not only opposition to sin but also a separation of social worlds.[6]

At midcentury, evangelicals remained a minority, and Baptists remained suspect in the eyes of the southern social elite. Although the values of evangelical religion were preparing the way for Victorian culture in northern cities, southern values still revolved around the notion of honor. Swearing, gambling, drinking, wenching, and defiance of Sabbath customs, wrote southerner William Grayson in 1853, were permissible pursuits for a "man of honor." Baptist discipline continued to oppose such genteel pastimes even as Baptists aspired to finer education and culture.[7]

After the Civil War, evangelicals were more at home in society. As their numbers grew, they built exquisite churches and established schools and colleges for their children. Yet they could not relinquish their suspicion of the "world." Their minority status and their social history conspired with their beliefs to confirm their separatist identity. Requiring believers to subordinate their individual moral autonomy to the judgment of the whole, Baptist churches strove to be exclusive. Only in the late nineteenth century did the discipline wane.

Though an otherworldly drama, the discipline of the saints played before a larger public. Many who did not belong to any church watched the rituals by which evangelical churches protected their citadels of purity. To some, it appeared an uncivilized spectacle—a Savannah resident described a local excommunication process as "a relic of barbarism, of which only puritanism could be guilty." To others, it was an admirable bulwark of the virtue essential to the American republic. For church members, the liturgy of church discipline set before the world a tableau depicting their moral and doctrinal separation. Baptists kept their discipline meetings public, the Georgia Baptist Association explained, in order to "let your light so shine before men, that they may see your good works."[8]

The effects of church discipline thus reached beyond the membership of the antebellum churches. Like the Methodists and Presbyterians, Baptists gained such a reputation for spiritual exclusivism that even religious southerners hesitated to join. Many attended regularly without seeking membership. In 1791, John Asplund, a Baptist pastor who traveled up and down the eastern seaboard gathering statistics on American Baptists, estimated that the "congregations," those who attended church but were not members, totaled several times the number on the membership rolls. "There is in reality more baptists than on this list, when we consider those who have not joined any church, excommunicated, &c. and a large number attend the meetings, at least three times as many as have joined the church." A generation earlier, the clerk of the Philadelphia Baptist Association reported "partly from their [the churches'] letters to the Association, and partly from private information," that the churches of the association had 4,018 members and 5,970 "Hearers." The total number of people who participated in Baptist congregations was thus some ten thousand, two and a half times the number of church members. Jesse Mercer, longtime president of the Georgia Baptist Convention and editor of the weekly *Christian Index*, estimated in 1835 that Baptists in the United States numbered 400,000, with "certainly not less than twice that number of persons attached to our congregations, who are not church members," making the total number of adherents 1.2 million, three times the number of church members.[9]

The congregations were frequently much larger than the membership. In 1830, one church in southeastern Georgia reported that "the congregation is good and attentive," but they had only eleven members. Another church in the same area reported that "our meeting house is generally crowded with an attentive audience," although their membership numbered only thirty-five.[10]

The congregation might include excommunicated members, friends and family of members, and members of other area churches not meeting that day. When the members of one church desired to improve the quality of hymn singing in their worship services, they resolved that "the church & congregation (& the church in Particular) be respectfully recommended to become members of the singing society." When another church called William H. Stokes to become their pastor, they had separate ballots for each group, so that he "received the unanimous call both of the church and congregation." New members frequently received baptism in the presence of sizable crowds, "the Church and congregation having repaired to the Pool." Although congregations could not participate in the Lord's Supper, they customarily remained in their seats as spectators in the antebellum period.[11]

In distinguishing the congregation from the church—a distinction characteristic of English dissenting Protestantism—Baptists expressed their adherence to the ideal of a pure church gathered out of the world. Undergoing baptism was a radical step, for it meant crossing the wide chasm from a life of moral autonomy to a life of submission to the moral authority of the church, and Baptists made that passage narrow, admitting only those who fulfilled a list of conditions, which the demographer Asplund summarized in 1794:

> 1st. An experience of Gods grace upon their souls, viz. conviction and conversion, is required, which must be verbally delivered before the church, together with a testimony from serious persons, that a reformation in practice has taken place.
>
> 2dly. They must have faith in, and submit themselves to the holy ordinance of Baptism.
>
> 3dly. The mode must be attended to. . . . The person must be dipped or immersed in water.
>
> 4thly. The element must be observed, viz. water. . . .
>
> 5thly. The administrator must be a qualified person for that work, viz. 1st. Converted or regenerated. 2ndly. He must have faith in the ordinance of Baptism or Immersion. 3dly. He must have been baptized by a qualified minister of our denomination, and in good standing. 4thly. He must be duly ordained by a presbytery by laying on of hands. 5thly. He must be a member of an orderly Baptist church. 7thly. [*sic*] In good standing viz. orthodox in judgment and moral in practice.[12]

These gathered communities made a great deal of their exclusivism, making the rite of passage from the world to the church an affair of unusual interest both within and without the church.

Baptisms were public affairs, transacted outdoors. Bethesda Baptist

Church, for example, received three converts, who "Submitted to the ordinance of Baptism and was immerced in Little river by Br. Jonathan Davis in the name of the Holy Trinity in the presence of a vast concourse of Weeping Spectators." When Baptist pastor Henry Holcombe baptized ten converts in the Savannah River, "the spectators on this solemn occasion were more numerous than on any former occasion, a great number of distinguished personages were present, and joy in many countenances seemed visible." Athens First Baptist Church baptized several persons in the Oconee River "in the presence of an audience, supposed to contain fifteen hundred or two thousand persons." Augusta's twelve-hundred-member Springfield African Baptist Church turned out for winter baptisms, the clerk reporting that "while the whole earth, house tops and trees were draped in raiment of white snow, the church withe Ten candidates, . . . Wended their way to the river and were baptised by the Pastor." When some urban southern churches talked in the 1840s of building indoor baptistries, W. H. Stokes, editor of the *Christian Index*, complained that "this is a sort of refinement we hope never to see carried out."[13]

The "weeping spectators" attending public baptisms were forceful reminders of the radical character of the separation inaugurated in this ritual. At an 1837 protracted meeting in Eatonton, Georgia, a young woman named Caroline, having experienced conviction and conversion, expressed the exclusiveness of baptism and church membership with unusual force. Seeking admission to the Baptist church, she "related a most interesting experience," confessing that she had struggled with the need "to give up worldly amusements of a sinful nature, especially dancing." The struggle having ended, Caroline testified: "I desire to be even more devoted to my Savior than I have ever been to the world." A longtime friend later described her baptism in a creek the following night, an event that gave new impetus to the revival there:

> Of course everybody was there. The banks of that little stream were lined with crowds of interested spectators. . . . Julia, of Monticello, her bosom friend and companion in her worldly course, seemed loath to leave her even for a moment, and clung to her till she reached the water's edge. A hymn was sung, [minister C. D.] Mallary made a few remarks and offered prayer, when [minister John] Dawson took Caroline by the hand and led her down the shelving bank into the limpid stream. They had attained about half the desired depth, when she requested him to stop a moment, and, turning to those on the bank, waving her hand, she said, *"Farewell, young friends! Farewell, Julia!"* The effect was electrical. The whole audience convulsed, and tears rained from eyes unused to weeping. . . . Upon coming up out of the water, Julia rushed forward to meet her friend, embracing her, and crying out in agonizing tones, *"Oh, Carrie, you must not leave me! Mr. Dawson, pray for me! Mr. Mallary pray for me?"*"[14]

Baptized in the Oconee, converts crossed a spiritual Rubicon.

Mere members of the congregation could not vote in the election of officers or in the trial of members or receive communion. But they were aware that they retained one advantage over church members—they were not subject to ecclesiastical discipline. They needed not fear that they would be judged or censured for their moral offenses. The churches reserved this privilege to members alone.

Baptist Exclusivism

As Baptists saw it, both the preaching of the gospel and the exercise of church discipline served the vision of the pure church by separating the righteous from the unrighteous. An 1837 Baptist ministers' meeting resolved that the two most important things that preachers could do to foster the purity of the churches, after setting a godly example themselves, were to "preach the word, faithfully," and to "excite and enforce in the Churches, a godly discipline." Pastor B. H. Whilden, comparing the two tasks to emetic and stimulant medicines, asserted that discipline "is as necessary to the spirituality of the church as the pleasant ministrations of the Word."[15]

Espousing a thorough Calvinism, Baptists held that preaching separated the elect from the world, the Holy Spirit creating faith in the gospel. The gospel of "distinguishing grace" functioned as a sieve, fanning away the chaff. Discipline likewise would "purge and scourge the wicked from among the righteous, so that a clear distinction should be made between the godly and ungodly, the chaff and the wheat." The highest honor that Baptists could bestow on a church was that "you have endeavored to keep yourselves unmixed with, and unspotted from the world."[16]

With other Calvinists, Baptists held not only that God had predestined the elect to salvation but also that he would grant them perseverance in the faith until death. When saints strayed from moral duty, Baptists believed, discipline would restore them. Baptists never had to fear that discipline might cause one of the elect to reject God and the church, for the excluded "brother[,] if he is a true child of God[,] will repent and never rest until he gets back into the fold."[17]

Even as discipline restored straying saints, it extruded unregenerate, hypocritical members. Because each church was "designed to be a Society of true genuine believers," whenever an unconverted person entered the fold, it was the church's "duty, however painful, to exclude him from their fellowship as soon as his true character was discovered." True saints would survive the ordeal of discipline, but false ones would not. The Spirit gave the elect the humility to submit to the church's judgment. Hypocrites retained the pride of their fallen state and would rarely suffer the humiliation of judicial control.[18]

Henry J. Ripley, a Baptist pastor in southeast Georgia, explained that the churches did not need to fear using the "knife" of discipline: "Real christians, when rebuked for a fault actually committed, will immediately or when the ebullition of passion has subsided and reason resumed her throne, make frank and ingenuous acknowledgements, and crave restoration to the fellowship of the church. But an unconverted man will view all attempts to deal with him as resulting from a spirit of resentment and a meddlesome infringing on his liberties. His faults will be metamorphosed into mere venial peccadillos, while others of his own stamp will vociferate, 'persecution of an innocent man.'" Basil Manly Jr., while serving both as a pastor and as president of Georgetown College in Kentucky, exhibited a similar view in a discussion of a case of discipline involving a couple who had committed fornication and were married after the birth of a child. As the disciplinary proceedings of the church neared their culmination, Manly reflected upon discipline's effect on the man: "If he is a good man, but has been overtaken in a fault, he will adhere to her, & try to maintain a correct course in quiet hereafter. If he is a bad man, he will probably deny his guilt altogether, perhaps abandon her, & betake himself to some far country." Discipline improved the converted and exposed the hypocrite.[19]

On their "days of Discipline," the saints sat in judgment upon one another in an exercise fully as important as the preaching of the gospel. Only by purging the wicked could the churches remain pure and separated from the world. When William Barnes absented himself from disciplinary meetings, he jeopardized a sacred ritual. Railing against the church as an "Ecclesiastical court," he recognized how important the ritual remained in the church's identity. Baptists found unexceptional Georgia pastor James Perryman's affirmation that "a Church is a sort of bench of Judges."[20]

The Conference Meeting

At the heart of Baptist democratic religion were gatherings called "conference days" or "conference meetings," although the less common name "days of Discipline" was more descriptive. Church members came together once a month for their conference meeting. Pastors, having charge of three or four churches, conducted the conferences on a weekend, with pruning of the congregation done on Saturday prior to worship on Sunday.[21]

Churches required their white male members to attend on pain of excommunication. So highly did Baptists esteem this day that any sign of diminishing loyalty to it evoked unease. On one occasion, a church clerk noted his dejection: "Being the regular day for Conference meeting, I repaired to the Church, at 10 oclock, in the forenoon, and remained there, till after 11 oclock; when no other person being in attendance— I left the church with a sad heart."[22] Not only white men, but also female and slave members and friends of the church often attended. The pastor acted as moderator, unless absent, in which case the church elected a leading layman or a visiting preacher. After singing and a devotion or sermon, the business of the day began.

Although churches filled their conferences with disciplinary activity, they transacted other kinds of business as well. They elected pastors and deacons, received and dismissed members in good standing, admitted new converts, and resolved questions about church policy, property, and finances. The examination of new converts was a common event. Granting membership only to applicants who gave sufficient evidence "whether there is a genuine work of the Spirit" in their hearts, the churches required candidates to relate a narrative of their conversion experience and to confirm it by a holy life. A genuine conversion experience, as Baptist editor William H. Stokes summarized, conformed to Baptist theology:

> When I was brought to a knowledge of my condition, I determined to reform, and go through with the prescribed round of duties. I wept for my sins, but found no relief in tears—I read my Bible to find consolation there, but saw condemnation on every page. The more I prayed the worse I felt, until I was brought to believe that, surely there was no hope for me. I determined to retire yet once more, and throw myself, unreservedly, on the Lord Jesus Christ; feeling, that if he rejected me, I was utterly undone. I did so; and while I was on my knees, I felt the blessed light of God's countenance break into my heart, and heard God's voice speaking peace to my troubled conscience.

In accordance with Calvinist theology, Baptist conversion narratives attributed everything to the work of the Holy Spirit, from the conviction of sin to the faith that brought peace. When new converts related their experiences, members rejoiced at the simple pageant of redemption, sinners transferred from the iniquitous world into a haven of purity.[23]

Admitting only those whom "in the judgment of charity" the members esteemed truly converted, churches also rejected applicants. If candidates persisted in an immoral practice after professing faith in Christ, the church deemed them unconverted and rejected their petition for membership. When a slave named Charles sought admittance to a church, having "previously related his experience [of conversion] and some objections having been made to his moral character he was refused admittance into the church."[24]

Likewise, when candidates inadequately expressed their feelings of condemnation before conversion or of joyous acquittal after it, churches might reject their petition. Yet it was not feeling alone but theological assent that the churches expected. Powelton Baptist Church rejected slave applicant Tom Askew, explaining that "they were not satisfied with his relation." Pastor Jesse Mercer convinced a church to reject an applicant for failing to connect his feelings to the doctrines of grace. The candidate having said a great deal "about his tenderness and feeling," Mercer delicately rebuked him: "When I was a boy, . . . my father sent me out into the woods to call up the stock. I took my wallet of corn, and to amuse myself, called up the swine in a very sad and melancholy tone. As I proceeded in this way, the first I knew I found myself weeping at the mournful sound of my own voice." Baptist churches sat in judgment to discriminate the true from the false conversions.[25]

By 1640, New England Puritans had introduced the practice of requiring candidates to give a narrative of their conversion before admission to membership.[26] It aided their effort to admit only converted persons to the churches. The revivals of the two awakenings, with their emphasis on the new birth, further encouraged the practice. Continuing this tradition, the Baptists filled their conference meetings primarily with "matters of fellowship" that established the boundaries between iniquity and purity. Here they decided when to receive members from other Baptist churches and when to dismiss their own. Here they decided whether candidates had been converted and made fit for baptism. And here they decided the gravest of all issues of fellowship: whether to retain or to expel transgressing members. The conference meeting and the practice of discipline remained intertwined; later, they would wane in tandem.

The Ritual of Baptist Discipline

Baptist doctrine gave each church authority to manage its fellowship and adopt its own constitution, consisting of a covenant, articles of faith, and a decorum. In their covenants, church members pledged themselves to submit to the laws of Christ. In their articles of faith, they declared their commitment to Calvinist theology, antipedobaptism (opposition to infant baptism), and congregational church order. In their decorums, they set down rules for conducting business in church conferences.[27]

English dissenters introduced covenant-based churches during the reign of Mary Tudor. The English exiles in Frankfurt established their church upon a covenant in 1554, as did Robert Brown's Separatist church at Norwich, formed in 1580.[28] Church covenants were a natural development of the Puritan move to the voluntary church. Pure churches could not admit persons based on parish boundaries, for that would mean admitting many unconverted persons. They could admit those only who were converted and who voluntarily pledged to separate from the world. This voluntary pledge was also the basis of strict discipline.

The Scottish Presbyterians and English Independents employed covenants widely. Although some English Baptists did not employ covenants, most Particular Baptists followed earlier Separatists in their use. Methodists similarly pledged to follow a covenant-like "Rule" and held "covenant services." American Puritans and Baptists uniformly employed church covenants and taught their apostolic origin.[29]

Baptist covenants committed church members to discipline. In the covenant common to most antebellum Baptist churches in Georgia, church members renounced considerable independent action and individual freedom. Announcing their separation from "the World," they declared themselves "henceforth to be his [Christ's] and no longer our own." Members then professed to give themselves to one another, "meaning hereby to become one body jointly to Exist, and jointly to act by the Bands and Rules of the gospel, Each Esteeming himself henceforth as a member of a Spiritual body, accountable to it and Subject to its Control, and no otherwise seperable therefrom than by Consent first had or unreasonably Refused."[30]

More than anything else, Baptists understood mutual submission to mean voluntary subjection to church discipline. Church members promised "to Keep up a Godly Dicipline, and to Deal faithfully and tenderly with those if any, who shall Depart from the faith which was once Delivered to the Saints, Either in principle or practice."[31] Baptist pledges to submit to one another therefore achieved fullest expression in conference meetings, where the Baptist churches entertained confessions of wrongdoing, invited accusations and reports of illicit behavior, received avowals of repentance, and voted to forgive, restore, or excommunicate. Their members submerged their individualism under a sea of ecclesiastical authority.

Churches initiated disciplinary proceedings in two different ways. When the time arrived in the course of the conference for new cases of discipline, transgressors frequently stood up and offered an unsolicited confession, requesting forgiveness. If members were satisfied, they voted to forgive, retaining the offender in membership. If the church thought the confession unsatisfactory, they could vote either to excommunicate the transgressor or to initiate an investigation.

Church members also accused each other. If the accused confessed, the church voted whether to forgive the offender and retain fellowship. If the accused failed to attend or denied the charge, the church initiated disciplinary proceedings, ordinarily by appointing two or three members as a committee to "labor with" defendants, "citing" them to appear at the next conference. If defendants denied the charges, the church charged the committee to investigate. Thus, when a defendant "denies the charges preferred," the church voted that the investigating committee "is again ordered to site [cite] her to next conference and to notify the witnesses in the case to appear also."[32]

In difficult cases, discipline committees might busy themselves for months, meeting with witnesses and with the accused, citing interested parties to attend conference, and preparing a report for the church. To add formality, Atlanta First Baptist Church ordered that "all Charges brought before the Church in future shall be presented in writing and after a Committee is appointed to investigate such Cases it shall be the duty of the Clerk to furnish the Chairman with a Copy of the Charge and the names of the Committee. It shall then be the duty of the Chairman to Call his Committee together, and after careful investigation of the matter Submit their written Report."[33]

Some antebellum churches chose to establish standing rather than ad hoc discipline committees. Poplar Springs Baptist Church in Stephens County established an "Annual Standing Committee" of seven men "to Settle temporal matters," for the church's decorum prohibited members from seeking redress of grievances among one another in civil courts. More often, such committees were "to arrange all matters of church dealings," investigating the full range of offenses.[34]

Churches frequently gave their deacons these unenviable duties, as when Penfield Baptist Church "ordered that the Brethn. Green, Reeves & McDaniel, deacons of the church be appointed & considered a standing committee and that it be considered their duty to inquire into any prejudicial reports against any member or disorderly conduct of any member and prepare the same for the hearing and action of the church." Having the full burden of a church's disciplinary activity, standing discipline committees endured considerable trouble. The Penfield committee, for example, at one conference received three cases to investigate, one involving travel to the county seat. The church ordered that "the Deacons use their endeavors to ascertain as many of the facts in these cases as they may be able to do before the next conference and submit them accordingly."[35]

The church expected the committee's work to culminate in a report and a recommendation. In the report, the committee paraded the relevant evidence and testimony, including the demeanor of the accused and a résumé of the course of the investigation. When churches concluded that the committee had neglected evidence or exercised insufficient diligence, they might reject the report and order the committee to continue its work.

If the church accepted the committee's report, then it considered its recommendation. The committee might recommend acquittal, forgiveness (usually with a public rebuke from the pastor), or excommunication. Churches generally adopted the recommendation of the committee but sometimes rejected it in favor of some other course of action. Some Baptist churches kept a portion of their membership in constant activity by perennial appointment to discipline committees.

Antebellum southern Baptists excommunicated nearly 2 percent of their membership every year. Achieving excommunication rates nearly 60 percent higher than their northern colleagues, they fully exemplified their professions of allegiance to discipline. Episcopalians abjured such rigor and found little occasion for discipline. Presbyterians disciplined members far below the Baptist rate and preferred to suspend offenders rather than excommunicate them. Methodists came closest to Baptist rigor, expelling members at about one-third the Baptist rate. In their "days of discipline," Baptists displayed their commitment to democratic spiritual authority.[36]

Trials of Church Members

When Baptist churches entered into disciplinary proceedings against members, they referred to the process as "dealings," "church dealings," or "trials."[37] The trials of those "under dealings" involved every group in the church in one way or another. Each group in its own way affected the texture of discipline.

Whether men or women, blacks or whites, the Baptists conducted the discipline informally, and it can be misleading to refer to the proceedings as trials, but the churches did demonstrate a concern for fairness and justice. When churches determined that "the charges was proven," a clerk might record that the verdict came "after hearring the evidence" or "after hearing Testamoney."[38] The clerks left ample evidence that churches called witnesses and evaluated evidence, as when the clerk of Poplar Springs Baptist Church recorded that "Bro Jos. Stovall states that Sister Sarey Denman has had a Base begotten Child and the same being proven by two witnesses, the Church Excludes her."[39] Although they may have sometimes decided cases in summary fashion, they could look as carefully into evidence and testimony as any secular court.

One church in north Georgia adopted a decorum in which they agreed that "no Evidence Shall be Received in this Church from the world on Tryal of aney Member." This meant that they would receive no evidence from persons outside the church. Fearing contamination and recognizing their powerlessness over nonmembers, the churches protected themselves in this way against perjury and slander by unbelievers. The Tugalo Association reasoned that, "as the church of Christ is separate and distinct from the world, having no power over non professors, we therefore consider worldly testimony not admissible, only [except] as it may cast light in corroberation with gospel [believers'] testimony."[40]

Most churches and associations, however, accepted testimony from outsiders. "The object for which testimony is received at all," Jesse Mercer argued, "is to ascertain the truth; but if a church refuse all testimony from without, she will in many cases refuse valid evidence, and so obscure the truth, and injure the cause of union and fellowship in herself."[41] When the purity of the church was at risk, the testimony of the impure was the lesser threat.

The churches did not pattern their proceedings after the forms and rules of civil courts. State laws in the South, for example, prohibited slaves from testifying in civil courts against whites. In church courts, slave members could testify against whites. The Hephzibah Association refused even to consider whether it was "right according to the Scriptures to hear evidence of a slave, who is a member of the Church, against a white member," evidently because they could conceive of no basis for rejecting slave testimony.[42]

Two slaves testified in Savannah First Baptist Church against a white who was a slave driver accused of killing a slave under his supervision. The verdict was guilty. When Atlanta First Baptist Church excommunicated a white woman for telling fortunes, a male slave testified that she had told him that she used a deck of cards "to tell fortunes with when her demon came." Churches could ignore the protocol of southern society when it stood in the way of church purity.[43]

Due process and individual rights took a subordinate position to the goal of ecclesiastical purity. A church might show due regard to a procedural request from a troublesome excluded member. When excommunicant John Cooper asked the church to give him a bill of his faults and a list of the witnesses, the church granted his request. Even under aggravating circumstances, churches could strive for what they considered fairness, as when a slave accused of absconding, disobedience, and slandering his owner, who happened to be the pastor, convinced the church to give him a delay in the trial. Sometimes churches ruled that charges did not refer to moral transgressions and therefore did not fall under their jurisdiction. Churches would not reprosecute a case except by appeal of the accused. The Bethesda Baptist Church expressed the consensus when it asserted that "a member can not again be arrained before the church for the same offense unless subsequently convinced of illegal proceedings." Yet churches did grant appeals from offenders for new trials, if necessary calling in "helps," leaders from nearby churches who could offer advice. When Josiah Carter, excommunicated from Powelton Baptist Church, requested a new trial, the church invited helps from three other churches to assist them. His appeal failed, but when "Gabriel, a man of colour," pleaded for another hearing, he won a reduction of his sentence from excommunication to suspension from the Lord's Supper.[44]

The most frequent issue of due process, however, had less to do with fairness than with scripture. In some churches, when members brought a "private" offense before the conference without first reproving the offender in private, the charge was ruled out of order. Churches could refuse to recognize charges if the accusers had neglected the "gospel steps," the triple warning formula of Matthew 18. When Sister Cheves accused Mary Wilson of "swindling," Benevolence Baptist Church threw out the charge "because the Gospel steps were not taken by Sister Cheves." However, appeals to this duty of due process did not always succeed. Brother Marshall, accused of allowing card games in his store, tried to avoid censure by claiming that "the case was not brought according to Gospel Order." The church disagreed, appealing to "the Jeneral rule of church Government." Few churches would allow an accusation to go unnoticed merely for reasons of procedure.[45]

Along with orthodox preaching and an evangelistic mission, discipline defined the nature and purpose of Baptist churches. Establishing communities separate from the world, they protected their purity through the exercise of democratic authority. Driven by the exclusivist agenda, their monthly "days of discipline" uniquely expressed their democratic religion.

2

Democracies Primitive and Pure

In 1817, an eyewitness recalled, "brother Lancaster," a member of Powelton Baptist Church, "rendered himself obnoxious to discipline" by allowing the young people at his house to dance at his daughter's wedding. The dancers conducted themselves with decorum, and Lancaster saw no harm in celebrating the occasion with fiddling and dancing. The church saw the matter differently. On conference day, "after singing and prayer, the ecclesiastical court was opened, the Rev. Jesse Mercer, the pastor of said church, presiding as moderator." A large crowd attended, some for and some against Lancaster. Mercer introduced the case to the congregation, explained the rules of "the judicatory," and delineated the reasons why fiddling and dancing should be considered immoral: Modern dancing was sensual and lascivious, and it would be impossible for Christians embarking upon a dance "to invoke the blessing of God by prayer." He urged the church to settle the "vexed question" of dancing once and for all.[1]

Mercer, president of the Georgia Baptist Convention from 1822 to 1840, gained fame as a pastor, preacher, and denominational leader. Crowds turned out to hear his sermons, which explained in rustic metaphors the theological arguments aimed at the intellect as much as the heart. W. B. Johnson, founding president of the Southern Baptist Convention, judged that as a preacher Mercer was "the most interesting man that I ever heard without exception." He was a zealous evangelist and missions advocate, serving as president of the Baptists' foreign mission board from 1830 to 1841. He promoted ministerial education and led the effort that established the university that bears his name. As editor of the *Christian Index,* the first enduring Baptist paper in the South, he exercised wide influence. Benevolent agents sold an engraving of his likeness to raise money. Lay persons sought his counsel: "As your views on Church discipline are considered good, and generally received, you will please give your opinion on the following case." Colleagues lionized him: "Jesse Mercer, the able expounder of gospel discipline." His ability to manage discipline proceedings was reputedly without equal—he rarely failed to carry his point—and the Lancaster trial was no exception.[2]

Lancaster rose from his seat and admitted that the accusation was true, "but never until now have I been prepared to confess its guilt." Mercer's "learned and lucid address" convinced him that he was a transgressor. Normally at this point in the trial, the offender would have requested forgiveness, and the church would have granted it, but now the accused turned accuser, and some of the members egged him on: "Let him go on! Let him go on!" Mercer thought Lancaster out of order but agreed to allow it: "Let us have a thorough winnowing of the wheat and get rid of the chaff."

Lancaster charged that the church cried out against dancing and fiddling when more serious offenses passed without censure. Turning to the assembled members, he indicted them for Sabbath breaking, partiality, worldliness, and gossiping. The church stigmatized the tunes of $5 fiddles in the cabins of the poor as worldly, Lancaster insinuated, but blessed the notes of $800 pianos in the mansions of the rich as an "innocent recreation." The women of the church, his chief accusers, had refined away their piety, lavishing praise on the "frothy" discourses of important preachers, but showering contempt on the simple sermons of plain, rustic ministers.

When Lancaster's courage failed, Mercer encouraged him to continue, saying that it was good "that our faults be exposed, and that we ought to submit to have them whipped in the proper spirit of charity." The women likewise shouted "Go on! Go on! We want to know what it is that sticks in your throat." When Lancaster finished, he asked forgiveness for the frolic. Mercer "rose in tears," offering prayer that God would make the trial an "occasion of a gracious outpouring of his Spirit, of burying all animosities and ill feelings." The church then "rose up to greet and shake hands with the offending brother, and to sing and rejoice together;—and that was the commencement of the most signal revival ever had in that church."[3]

Beginning in transgression and ending in revival, the Lancaster trial illustrates the spiritual power of discipline in Baptist piety. The congregation was paramount; discipline was an affair of the entire church, which sat as a judicatory of Christ with dreadful authority over the moral behavior of the flock. It gathered its moral tribunal for the purpose of purifying the congregation of impiety, and it trusted that the faithful exercise of discipline would result in spiritual blessings, especially revival. According to Baptists like Mercer, "a thorough winnowing of the wheat" resulted in a harvest of souls and renewed devotion to God.

Primitive Democracies

Bent upon reproducing churches on the apostolic pattern, Baptists frequently rehearsed the outlines of their ecclesiology. They sought to repristinate both the worship and the government of the primitive church. The apostles, Baptists held, had organized churches according to the commands of Christ. The form of the primitive church was binding on all subsequent history. "This apostolic example," wrote Jesse Mercer, "forms the true pattern for the constitution of all after churches."[4]

Not merely the commands of the New Testament, but also "the practices of the first churches . . . are the rule for us to follow; . . . a complete system, adapted to every age." Recognizing that some preferred Episcopal or Presbyterian government, Baptists said that to consider church government "a matter of taste, or of expediency," was a "radical, mischievous error." Everything about a church was determined by "pure revelation." Baptists strove for "conformity to the primitive church of Christ," and they boasted of their success, convinced that "in our denomination there are no splendid innovations."[5]

The primitivist impulse has always been near the heart of Protestantism. The Reformers proclaimed a scripture-only religion in opposition to ten centuries of human innovations. Passing over the Dark Ages, Protestants sought to restore the practices and beliefs of the apostolic church. They valued the noncanonical writings of the early church for what they revealed of the practices of the first churches. They sought to reestablish the simplicity of the apostolic era by freeing their churches of unwarranted accretions to the divine pattern. The primitive was normative. Puritans developed primitivist theology further in their long struggle against the "innovations" of Anglican ecclesiology. New England Congregationalism arose on this model, as did American Baptist and Presbyterian churches.

New primitivist impulses arose in the context of American religious freedom and denominationalism. The most successful was the Restoration movement of Alexander Campbell and J. Barton Stone. They eschewed denominational labels as unscriptural and refused any name but "Christian" or "disciple of Christ." Because the New Testament church had no creeds or systems of church government, neither did they.[6]

Southern Baptist churches also followed the divine law embodied in the practices of the primitive churches. Because the first churches admitted only those who experienced conversion, professed faith in Christ, and underwent baptism by immersion, they insisted that they were bound to do the same. Churches that baptized infants might be true churches, most Baptists judged, but they were "in disorder," irregularly constituted of both qualified and unqualified persons.[7]

The primitive charter also defined church authority. True churches had no right to make new laws. Because Christ was "the only lawgiver in Zion," the functions of a church were merely executive and judicial. In discipline as well as doctrine, the Bible was the only legal rule. Church power, moreover, inhered in all the members of a church, and it could be delegated to no other individual or group. Baptists eschewed monarchical and aristocratic models for local church government because Jesus commanded the entire church to expel the sinner (Matt. 18:17) and the church at Corinth expelled an immoral man by vote of the majority (2 Cor. 2:6). They established pure democracies because "the first converts were democrats, in regard to their ecclesiastical polity."[8]

The apostolic charter decreed that ecclesiastical authority resided in the local church alone. Church government was congregational, Baptists taught; each church was autonomous, possessing full power to exercise its rights and duties, whether exercising discipline, admitting members, appointing officers, or observing ordinances. "Every Baptist Church is a republic in miniature," wrote Baptist preacher and educator Adiel Sherwood, who argued that church authority was "not committed to church wardens, the preacher in charge, the Bishop, ruling elders, Presbyteries, Conferences, Associations, Conventions, or anything of the kind." Jesse Mercer summarized the doctrine:

> Our Lord has laid down a few plain rules of government, and established a tribunal in his Church, at which all offences are to be tried and decided; and from which there is no appeal. I believe it is adopted by all regular Baptists as the doctrine of Christ, that his Church is his kingdom on earth; that he sits in judgment there; and that when a Gospel Church is sitting, in Gospel order, for the transaction of disciplinary business, there is not a higher court on earth; and that such church is arraignable at no other, or foreign bar; because her judge is in her midst, and has commanded her implicit obedience. Now any departure from these rules, and any appeal from this authority and tribunal, will, can do no other than produce amongst Baptists, strifes and divisions.

Mercer's colleagues honored his defense of primitive ecclesiology by giving him a silver medal inscribed, "Government is in the Church."[9]

The charter mandated for each church three essential functions. Its members had to assemble for the divinely sanctioned worship of God; they had to uphold orthodox teaching, "to keep the faith which was once delivered to the saints"; and they had to maintain the moral oversight of the membership, "to keep up a Godly discipline." In practice, however, the exercise of discipline defined scriptural churches. One gathering in 1785 "concluded that it would be best for us to be constituted in order to Keep up a Godly Gospel Disipline for Gods Glory and our happiness." The Georgia Baptist Association, organized in 1784, adopted a confession later accepted by other associations. It defined the church in terms of its disciplinary function: "We believe that the visible Church of Christ is a congregation of faithful persons, who have gained christian fellowship with each other, and have given themselves up to the Lord, and to one another, and have agreed to keep up a Godly discipline, agreeably to the rules of the Gospel."[10]

Scripture's "perfect code of discipline" provided the rules for censure. Baptists understood the New Testament code to distinguish two classes of offenses. Public offenses were of a "general character, and of a heinous nature," bringing scandal on the reputation of Christ and the church. Churches responded severely to such offenses as sexual immorality, murder, theft, idolatry, or heresy. They found precedent in the case of incest in the Corinthian church: Paul commanded the church to expel the offender peremptorily (1 Cor. 5:1–5). Private offenses were of lesser gravity. They frequently involved disputes among members or neglect of some duty, especially church attendance. Private offenses called for the gospel steps outlined in Matthew 18:15–17, three stages of increasingly grave admonitions, delivered first privately, then by two or three members, and finally by the church. If offenders did not repent at some point along the way, the church excommunicated them.[11]

The apostolic code also distinguished two kinds of censure. The first was admonition or rebuke, which the moderator delivered to a repentant offender whose offense did not lead to expulsion. The second was excommunication, the loss of all rights and privileges of membership. Despite frequent recourse to it, antebellum Baptists considered excommunication a drastic action. They expected members to limit social interaction with the offender to what was absolutely necessary. By excommunication, the church remanded offenders to the care of the world. Only by repentance and continued piety could they reclaim a place among the redeemed. Indeed, the guilty frequently came before the church requesting restoration, and the churches usually restored the penitent to full membership.[12]

Most churches required unanimous votes to admit members and forgive offenders, but they deemed a simple majority sufficient to exclude an offender. They believed that the ideal of unity required all members to be "in fellowship." Offenders broke fellowship by transgressing and were obligated to restore a perfect fellowship. If even one member objected to forgiveness, the church would not grant it, for the objection meant that the united fellowship was not yet recovered.[13]

The primitive charter, finally, revealed the purposes for which God designed discipline. Its exercise rendered glory to God. Discipline, pastor Benjamin Roberts asserted, "must be faithfully kept up for God's glory." Sometimes, in difficult cases, a decision about excommunication turned upon this consideration: "Do you think it would be more for the benefit of the glory of God to retain him in fellowship? or cut him off from us?" It was not unusual for a church to resolve that "for the glory of god & good of the cause of religion," one or another erring soul had to be extruded from the fellowship. Discipline redounded to the honor of God.[14]

God also designed discipline for the good of the offender. It was the medicine prescribed by the divine physician. Private reproof, public admonition, and even excommunication brought spiritual benefits to the elect. God used these moral censures to produce humility before the moral law, repentance, and a desire for holiness. "The first thing to be attempted, in all cases," wrote Jesse Mercer, "is the restoration of the affected member."[15]

But the chief purpose of discipline, Baptists constantly proclaimed, was the purity of the church. "The design in Discipline," urged preacher Sylvanus Landrum, "is to keep the church pure, and if practicable restore the offender." Reclaiming the straying was a noble purpose, but first "churches are bound to maintain a godly discipline, for the purity of the body." The great object of Baptist church discipline was holiness and the preservation of purity.[16]

Purity, Unity, and Freedom

The commitment to purity as the primary goal of discipline derived from the Baptist vision of a church separate from the world. Jesse Mercer excoriated Georgia Baptists in 1801 for conceiving "an eager lust for the flesh-pots in Egypt." They had lost so much of their purity, Mercer judged, that "it has become extremely difficult to distinguish you, as a body or as individuals, from a surrounding wicked world." An apostolic church would exemplify "the duty of being separate, and abstracted from the world in all its ramifications." At this time, southern Baptists stood at the bottom of the social order. Although congregations in plantation districts often had one or two planters of some wealth, most Baptists were poor and illiterate. The planter aristocracy pursued dancing, gambling, and luxury and made them marks of respectability or refinement. But worldliness did not have to be expensive. Rich or poor, Baptists who lusted after Egyptian fleshpots often found their way to the church's defendant chair. The Baptists responded to calls for purity and separation from the world.[17]

In the wake of the 1827–1829 revival, in which thousands of converts joined Baptist churches in Georgia, Baptists expected a revival of discipline. Savannah pastor H. O. Wyer expressed grief at the "disorder" in many churches but found consolation in the knowledge that "the great ingatherings, by which they have been blessed, will, no doubt, be followed by winnowings and siftings. I hope there will be found after all much good wheat which the great & good Husbandman will put away in the garner." Even revivals could not diminish the thirst for the purity won by tireless pruning.[18]

The fruit of purity was the unity of the church, which had to rest on a foundation of purity because impure members would cause divisions and strife. Churches that harbored an immoral member were "not in union" but divided. Without discipline, they might outwardly profess unity but inwardly they were torn asunder. Such "outward pretention," Jesse Mercer wrote, "is special hypocrisy."[19]

Discipline was also the practice that made freedom necessary. Such Revolutionary War–era leaders as Isaac Backus in Massachusetts and Silas Mercer in Georgia interpreted religious liberty as the freedom to exercise discipline. Backus objected to governmental establishment of the churches in large part because it obstructed "discipline in the church." Mercer scorned state churches as the beast of the Antichrist because they "destroyed the liberty of the laity, and reduced them to a state of vassalage, so that they had no power to choose their own pastors, nor carry on any discipline." A large part of religious liberty, early Baptists contended, was the freedom to establish pure churches by means of discipline.[20]

In early colonial Georgia, as in the other four southern colonies, the Anglican Church enjoyed exclusive state establishment, but Georgia's 1777 constitution permitted an establishment of multiple denominations, granting the legislature power to levy taxes to support ministers of the taxpayer's choice. By 1798, the state constitution prohibited taxation for the support of religion, but Baptists continued their rhetoric against state churches. The memory of having once been dissenters in a state establishment still colored the Baptist temperament.[21]

Many Baptists were suspicious of any supralocal agency. This was the great era of American voluntary societies. Many societies, like the Baptist Board of Foreign Missions, were national in scope. To all such societies, Primitive Baptists were especially resistant. They rejected benevolent societies, they said, because they embodied a hidden justification-by-works scheme and because New Testament churches did not have them. They also resented the college-educated northerners who raised money for distant causes. Poorly educated and poorly paid Baptist ministers felt themselves fleeced by the more polished agents of missionary societies.[22]

The disagreement over benevolent societies produced schism in the 1830s, when Primitive Baptists declared nonfellowship with churches and associations that supported "the Systems of the day, benevolent so called, such as Bible, Missionary, Temperance and Tract Societies." In some instances, the Primitive churches insisted that associations had authority in matters of discipline. Missionary Baptists objected that such a position entailed "improper interference with the rights of the churches." They thought that each local church must be free to exercise discipline unhindered by any other agency. Jesse Mercer reserved his strongest condemnation for infringements on the freedom of congregational discipline: "If then any [other] body attempts to use this right, to exercise this power, he so far makes himself an Anti-Christ." The actions of Primitive Baptist associations threatened the freedom of congregational discipline, Mercer judged, jeopardizing "the pure democracy of the New Testament" by means of "imposing appearances of splendid national forms of church government."[23]

Just as church purity stood on the foundation of religious liberty, so also it established the limits of individual liberty. Baptists were religious populists, but they were suspicious of individualism. The American Revolution gave impetus to individualism—"the principle that all values, rights, and duties originate in the individual." Populist religious leaders touted private judgment, personal autonomy, and individual conscience over creedal systems. But when John Leland, the most famous Baptist exponent of individual autonomy, exercised his right of private judgment in scripture interpretation, his association disfellowshiped him. Baptists opposed this kind of individualism. Conscience was not supreme.[24]

When one John Cooper wrote Jesse Mercer that churches were too strict, Mercer placed firm limits on individual freedom. Cooper argued on republican grounds: "My sense of republicanism is equal rights to all. . . . My principle is equal rights to all, and a republican form of church government." Mercer chided him:

> We hope our brother does not intend to push his republicanism into licentiousness, or to insinuate [that] the churches have no disciplinary control over their members, so that after all proper efforts have been made to persuade them to desist from the offensive pursuit, they have the right still to persist in their own chosen course, and defend themselves on the ground of equal rights. No, we will not believe it; for equal rights must cease when iniquity begins. . . . That it is the duty of the churches to discipline their members in case of immorality none will deny. And that the members are bound to submit themselves to this authority in the Lord, will as readily be acknowledged.

The only Christian freedom worth contending for was one built on the purity secured by discipline.[25]

Discipline and Revival

Baptists saw discipline as a source of spiritual revival. A church with no discipline was no church. "When discipline leaves a church," Baptist theologian John L. Dagg contended, "Christ goes with it."[26]

The revivals of the 1740s and 1750s produced Baptists by the thousands, and the experience indelibly shaped Baptist piety. Since the days when the preaching of such itinerants as Shubal Stearns and Daniel Marshall spread revival from Virginia to Georgia, Baptists looked expectantly for heaven-sent awakenings. In these revivals, they experienced renewed zeal for personal devotion and self-denial. They received new assurance of their own salvation and rejoiced at the testimonies of sinners finding grace.

Early Baptist revivals were not much planned. Although regular ministers often itinerated on three-month "missionary" tours and gave impetus to revival, most pre-1820 revivals grew out of the regular meetings of the church or association. In churches, the monthly two-day conference meetings, the quarterly communion meetings, and the "annual meeting" were particularly suited to outbreaks of revival. When these meetings "became interesting" because of God's "pouring out his Spirit," they were protracted for days. Other revivals occurred when preachers meeting at the annual association or convention preached salvation to the crowds of people that gathered.[27]

By the late 1820s, Georgia Baptists frequently employed the "new measures" popularized by the northern Presbyterian evangelist Charles G. Finney. Preachers planned "protracted meetings," invited convicted sinners to the "anxious" or "mourners'" bench, and prayed individually over "mourners." In less settled areas, Baptists sought revival through camp meetings, a method made popular at the 1801 Cane Ridge revival in Kentucky, where people camped at the meeting site for several days. Several thousand people could gather at camp revivals, with hundreds of mourners rushing to the altar at the invitation. By 1833, one Baptist felt that camp meetings were "becoming a permanent and integral link in the chain of means amongst the Baptists." Provided that preachers employed the new measures as God's appointed "means" and not as human causes of salvation, Calvinist Baptists praised them. Revivals had a populist character—the Spirit might fall on anyone and produce the required individual conversion—and were central to southern Baptist identity. Lax discipline threatened it.[28]

Mississippi Baptist Elias Hibbard, who worried about excessive discipline, conceded its benefits: "I am aware that discipline when exercised in a proper manner is the life of our churches, and often precedes the blessings of the Almighty." Mercer went so far as to proclaim that discipline vivified a church: "A well executed discipline is the ecclesiastical life of a Gospel Church." He exhorted the churches "to be promptly active in the execution of discipline . . . —discipline, which, in its right use, is the church's ecclesiastical life—bond of union and peace—spring of order and fellowship—and great source of harmony and love."[29]

When churches gathered for days of discipline, their spiritual vitality hung in the balance. Editor Joseph S. Baker expressed the common conviction that "without a correct understanding of church discipline, and proper exercise of it, no church or association can expect to be blessed or prospered." Even with "the elegant preaching and the eloquent prayers and the splendid appearances," Baptists reasoned, "no church can prosper spiritually if there is no discipline." In varying forms, the adage resounded in Baptist gatherings that "nothing is more essential to church prosperity than the maintenance of faithful discipline."[30]

This belief in the vivifying power of discipline long survived in Baptist churches, due in part to Jesse Mercer. Pastors for decades would repeat the refrain identifying discipline as the source of church life. Sylvanus Landrum, who served large congregations in Macon, Savannah, Memphis, and New Orleans, wrote in 1858 that "it was, we think, Jesse Mercer, who said in a Circular upon this subject:—'Discipline is the life-blood of the church.'" A generation after Mercer's death, one of the churches that Mercer planted continued to intone that "correct discipline is the life of the Church, without it the Church is despised by the world, shorn of its power & will soon fall to pieces."[31]

When discipline waned in the late nineteenth century, stagnant churches received the same program of church growth: "The condition of all the churches would be greatly improved by the faithful and fearless administration of discipline." Churches prospered not by hiring a noted evangelist, Georgia pastor J. H. Kilpatrick argued in the 1885 commencement sermon of the Southern Baptist Theological Seminary, but by means of the old plan that "enforces a thorough and godly discipline" motivated by zeal "for the maintenance of the purity of the church." In 1874, the Stone Mountain Association, exulting in a record number of baptisms, sought to explain why "the exclusions of this year also exceed those of the last 17." It concluded that renewed disciplinary zeal was "a strong indication of increase rather than decrease of spirituality of the churches." Purity produced spiritual vigor.[32]

When churches encountered troubles, ecclesiastical detectives could be counted on to round up the usual suspects—first among them being neglect of church discipline. Mercer believed that "most of our church difficulties grow out of neglected church discipline" or discipline improperly administered. As the debate over benevolent societies wrenched the churches in the 1830s, Mercer assigned the blame to the neglect of discipline. "I consider the causes of these divisions, which have rent our Churches and spoiled our beauty, as a denomination, are to be found in the neglect of a Godly discipline, and the consequent results." Without discipline, there could be no order, peace, or vital fellowship in the church.[33]

Baptists believed that churches with impure members suffered in reputation, which undermined their evangelistic mission. But the neglectful church could encounter even harsher realities: God "invariably chastised" them with "declension and destruction." A church negligent in discipline "tolerates or connives at the sinful conduct of her members" and brought a curse not only upon itself but also upon the community.[34]

Proper tribunals, however, brought showers of blessing. "The sacred rules laid down by Christ, followed out in the proper time and spirit," Mercer wrote, "we think would preserve peace and further godliness in all the churches of the saints. Nothing is necessary, but due attention to scriptural discipline." When churches attended to moral correction, God granted them prosperity. Disciplined churches were shining cities on a hill whose light drew unbelievers to God.[35]

Pastor T. H. Stout took the occasion of a revival to inculcate the doctrine. The members of Bethel Baptist Church became zealous for discipline and excluded two offenders. Stout recounted the result:

> Very soon, a perceptible improvement was seen in the church. Brethren began to take up their crosses. They met and conversed on the condition of Zion, confessing and bewailing their coldness. Brethren, discipline is the life of our churches. We have no right to look for the blessing of our precious Savior unless we "come out from the world." Be "ye separate," says God. . . . May not many of our churches be incurring the displeasure of the "Great Head of the Church" by laxity of discipline? During July . . . the church was greatly revived. . . . Quite a number of brethren prayed [publicly] who had never done so before. . . . Twenty-four were added to the church; 12 by experience and baptism, and 12 by letter.

Discipline brought revival.[36]

Baptists had good reason to believe this. They maintained high rates of discipline at the same time they experienced rapid growth. Nationally, Baptists grew 1.9 times faster than the population, from 67,000 in 1790 to 1 million in 1860. In Georgia, they grew 2.3 times faster than the population, from 3,340 in 1790 to 99,149 in 1860. In southern democratic religion, discipline and revival appeared to go together.[37]

3

Democratic Authority

The Southern Baptist maxim "Correct discipline is the life of the church" conveyed primarily the idea that discipline was the source of vitality and progress. Yet discipline constituted the life of the churches in another sense, for to a great extent it shaped their month-to-month activity. In most churches, virtually every conference meeting brought accusation, confession, repentance, forgiveness, excommunication, and restoration. At the heart of this drama was the notion that piety required submission to ecclesiastical authority.

Accusation and Confession

The genteel arbiters of southern society valued honor, not accusation and confession. The southern ideal of honor exalted violence and revenge, the sanctity of one's reputation, an indomitable will, and exaggerated masculinity. Baptist churches turned the system of honor on its head.[1]

Public discipline began with accusation or confession. In most instances, one member accused another in public conference. The church clerk usually noted only that the member stood accused, omitting the name of the accuser: "Brother Daniel Servant of Brother V. R. Thornton is charged with the sin of Adultery" or "Brethren Jeptha Davis Wm. Greene J. Holtsclaw L. B. Tuggle M. W. May were charged with watching in the night time Brother Bowles house & premises."[2]

Common fame frequently served as the accuser: "It being reported to the church that Br. L. B. Freeman of late has been guilty of drunkenness," "Unfavorable reports being in circulation relative to the pious walk of our brother Lester," or "It being notorious to many of our church that Br. Robt. Porter has of late been guilty of repeated drunkenness." Churches considered these "unfavorable reports" perfectly admissible in their disciplinary hearings, taking the opportunity to question the alleged offender and to initiate an investigation.[3]

When church clerks troubled themselves to identify the accusers, white men appeared most frequently, even though they constituted a minority of most churches: "Br. Newsom reported that Br. Jack belonging to Br. W. Tuggle has been guilty of Drunkness," "Brother Thornton prefered some charge against Brother Vason," or "A charge was brought by Brother John Mercer against Sister Rachel servant of Esqr. Hatchett for absconding." Most Baptists considered this appropriate enough, for they expected men to take leadership in the churches and in some instances expected women to keep silent.[4]

Women nevertheless sometimes presented accusations in conference, without hint of resistance. Even churches that restricted suffrage to men granted standing to women in disciplinary procedures: "Female members may, when called upon, act as witnesses in a church and, when aggrieved, are to make known their case, either in person or by a brother, and must have a proper regard paid them." Clerks only occasionally noted that a woman introduced an accusation.[5]

Most black members were slaves who could rarely attend regular Saturday conferences. Some did, however, and even more attended the occasional or standing Sunday conferences. Whites were liable to construe any black leadership or initiative as an overstepping of proper social boundaries, but as members they had standing before the ecclesiastical bar. Hence, clerks recorded that slaves ventured to accuse, as when "a complaint was laid in by Br. Abram the Property of John Ramsey against Br. Peter the Property of Isaac Ramsey Esqr. for Leaving his wife and taking up with another woman." Their status was precarious, and with rare exceptions they accused only other slaves.[6]

In civil courts in the South, slaves could not be party to any legal proceeding involving whites except as defendants. In the churches, a slave member might occasionally accuse a white member, and allegiance to democratic purity could overpower scruples about social improprieties. Without discomposure, one church excluded a white woman upon accusation by a slave, the clerk noting that "Mr. Wilkinsons Frank makes report that Sister Charity Finch has been drinking too much Spirits."[7]

Another common form of accusation was self-accusation: 28 percent of all cases between 1785 and 1900 arose this way. Although offenders occasionally accused themselves by letter or by proxy, they generally did it in open conference. Sometimes they confessed grave offenses after the church charged them with minor ones. Sometimes they accused themselves because others already knew about the offense and might reveal it. By preempting the church's action, offenders could certify their repentance: "Brother Council Phillingame made known to this conference that report had charged him with being drunk at Mr. Callaways, he confesses that he drank too much, & he shews considerable Penitince for the same."[8]

In other cases, members accused themselves out of a guilty conscience or from a sense of duty to submit to moral oversight. Self-accusation did not render offenders immune from punishment. "Brother Joseph Taylor before the conference charged himself with becomeing Irritated with his Wife & that he gave her some slight abuse[,] that he and wife were perfectly reconciled at the present & that he was sorry that he had acted so ungarded & hoped forgiveness by his Brethren." Taylor suffered rebuke but received forgiveness. His fellow member, Archibald Watts, had less success. Watts "in open conference acknowledged himself guilty of acting in a very unchristian like manner in the town of Greensboro on the first monday night of this month by drinking spirits too free, and having been guilty of gambling, &c., for which he professed to be truly sorry." The church excluded him.[9]

The large number of self-accusations suggests that members accepted the authority of the church to judge their behavior, as does the fact that most who faced accusation confessed their crime, regardless of whether they desired forgiveness from the church. In cases in which the plea of the defendant was recorded, fully 92 percent of defendants between 1785 and 1860 acknowledged their guilt. The pattern was not one of antiauthoritarian populism but of submission to a populist religious authority.[10]

Forgiving the Penitent

When Henry Smith, for twenty years the clerk of Mount Olive Baptist Church in southwest Georgia, died in 1877, the church praised his exemplary piety, eulogizing that "he was kind and forgiving towards those that er[r]ed yet he loved strict deciplin." Mildness tempered the severity in Baptist discipline—a mildness that appeared in the willingness of churches to forgive and retain some transgressors, and to restore others to full membership. Even in extending the mercy of forgiveness, however, they upheld the ideal of democratic religion.[11]

Members accused of moral offenses could plead that they were innocent, but this was neither a popular nor an effective defense. Of 6,300 discipline cases between 1788 and 1900, only 410 resulted in acquittals. In a mere 262 cases did clerks record that a defendant pleaded innocent. In cases in which defendants denied their guilt, they secured acquittals 48 percent of the time. Churches evidently attempted to consider pleas of innocence fairly, but members accused of offenses rarely denied their guilt.[12]

When members committed a moral offense, churches imposed conditions for forgiveness. They believed that they had no authority to annul the sinner's debt to divine wrath—only God could do this—but only to declare that the offender's transgression no longer barred fellowship. They could judge only that the offender's submission "appeared to be satisfactory to the church, and the difficulty was gotten over."[13]

The first condition for offenders was to confess. The second was to acknowledge the church's right to discipline them. The third was to demonstrate sorrow and repentance, pledging to refrain from the objectionable behavior and expressing a wish to remain in the fellowship of the saints. Two of these conditions consisted of right thinking. They were a way of "making acknowledgments," recognizing the transgression and the church's rectitude. The third prerequisite consisted of right feeling. If offenders did not exhibit sincerity, the churches refused to accept their repentance. Churches often distinguished this as "penitence," or some similar term, such as "sorrow" or "sincerity." Without a proper feeling, offenders revealed immoral hearts.[14]

In 1859 Mr. and Mrs. Tarwater of Penfield, Georgia, stood accused of having danced; they offered their church an exemplary repentance. Mr. Tarwater "confessed that himself and Sister Tarwater had been engaged in dancing, acknowledged the impropriety of their conduct, and begged the forgiveness of the Church, pledging themselves not again to engage in such amusement." They first made acknowledgments, admitting that they were guilty and that the church was right in judging their conduct improper. Then they demonstrated their penitence, "begging" forgiveness and promising to refrain from the offense.[15]

Churches always assayed the quality of repentance. When one brother Holladay repented for fighting, he did not entirely persuade the church of his true sorrow, for "the Church thoug[h]t proper to lay him Under Suspension a while to try his Sincearity." Although a few churches employed suspension to test sincerity, most southern churches either proceeded to excommunication or continued the trial until they discerned the character of the repentance. This pattern appeared repeatedly. Hopeful Baptist Church agreed to forgive a thief because he expressed penitence and made acknowledgments, "in as much as Bro Rhodes had expressed his sorrow and guilt." In the same way, Ben Battle, a slave member charged with preaching without the permission of the church, "appeared before the church apparently very penitent[,] acknowledged he had done wrong in attempting to preach contrary to the will of the church[,] begged forgiveness and promised to try to obey the church in future." Humble submission to the church was part of the meaning of moral purity.[16]

Church clerks generally did not record details of inadequate repentance, considering it sufficient to record that the offender "made acknowledgements which not being satisfactory" prohibited the church from granting forgiveness. They did record instances in which churches disapproved of a repentance in which an offender did not admit full guilt and responsibility. Offenders who sought to extenuate their guilt suffered the church's displeasure. Churches delighted to forgive transgressors like E. M. Burgess, charged with fighting, who confessed his guilt and "did not justifie himself in the practice." But they could not so easily forgive defendants like Brother Burrows, a student charged with resisting civil and college authority and with "carrying deadly weapons upon his person," because while he "expressed some regrets for the offences," he "made explanations by way of Justifying himself." The churches required offenders to humble themselves, submitting to Christ's court. Repentance without submission the churches found wanting. It manifested a proud refusal to accept the authority of the saints.[17]

When offenders "gave satisfaction," the churches forgave and retained them, unless their sins were too grave. This did not mean that penitents escaped without censure. Not only did churches require the mortification of public repentance and submission, but also they sentenced the penitent to suffer a public rebuke. Like other premodern societies, the South had its shaming rituals. Those who threatened communal values risked public humiliation. In 1730, a group of North Carolina women humiliated a philandering Anglican minister by horsewhipping him. He fled naked and never returned. Men who impeached female purity, traded with slaves, created drunken disturbances, or spoke openly in favor of black freedom faced tar and feathers and a ride on a rail. The church's ritual was less violent but no less effective.[18]

The moderator of the conference, usually the pastor, rendered the rebuke, which was the usual response to lesser transgressions. Ben Battle, who preached without permission, "was forgiven after being reproved." Other offenders were "admonished" by the pastor, "sharply rebuked by his Pastor," or forgiven "with an elaborate admonition from the Pastor." Having only two censures, rebuke and excommunication, churches required the guilty to receive the one or the other.[19]

Excommunication

In treating what they considered grave offenses, churches felt no liberty to forgive and retain transgressors, even when their repentance had all the marks of authenticity. Churches forgave private offenses, but public offenders faced the pruning knife, which the churches called *excommunication*, *exclusion*, or *expulsion*. In the late nineteenth century, *excommunication* lost favor, and *exclusion* achieved almost exclusive usage.

Distaste for the word *excommunication* was probably a harbinger of declining commitment to the authority of the congregation.[20]

Since the days of the apostles, churches had practiced excommunication. In the more inclusive church of the Middle Ages, moral transgressors could often avoid excommunication, although heretics and political foes still faced it and its civil penalties. Protestant churches renewed its use in Geneva, Scotland, and among Anabaptists. English Separatists and Baptists pioneered its use, but it flourished most where churches could exercise it free from government interference, in the American republic.[21]

It was a powerful weapon in the antebellum churches, and its power resided in part in the damage it did to the moral reputation of the excommunicant. It meant mortification and embarrassment. Robert Paine, a presiding elder in the Methodist Church, supervised a case that demanded excommunication, but because the "expulsion and degradation likely involved ruin," he shrank back. The offender, guilty of drunkenness, quailed before the prospect of exclusion, sobbing that he "never was drunk before. Can't help it now; it's over, and I am ruined." Baptist transgressors also feared the shame.[22]

When opposition to discipline emerged, it commonly stemmed from the public mortification. "Mrs. J. H. English, immediately after the exclusion of her son Robert from this church, said in the hearing of several members of this church that the war had commenced." She was incensed that the church had degraded her son, charging that they sought "to drag down her son by excluding him from the church."[23]

Churches sometimes intensified the shame by a practice called "publishing." Presbyterians conducted judicial proceedings in private but announced before the church and world all excommunications and some suspensions. Presbyterian courts believed that this shame fostered repentance, but the censured did not always see it in the same light. So great was the dread of publishing that when Benjamin Morgan Palmer, pastor of New Orleans First Presbyterian Church, intended to publish a member suspended for drunkenness, the offender warned Palmer to desist: "I will arm myself and take a seat in the gallery over the pulpit, and if you attempt to read that paper I shall fire upon you." Palmer, unruffled, read the suspension without incident.[24]

Baptists, with conference meetings open to the public, normally did not publish excommunications before the Sunday church and congregation. When a member once suggested that it would be "proper to have such Excommunications published on the Sabbath day in full congregation, rather than in conference," the church answered that "they deem it improper and unnecessary." In most churches, the pronouncement in church conference satisfactorily publicized an excommunication.[25]

For Baptists, publishing usually meant announcing in print the crime and excommunication, either in secular and religious newspapers or in the printed minutes of association meetings. Churches published excommunicants, especially excommunicated clergy, when they refused to submit to discipline, lest they attempt to escape the stigma that their crimes deserved and to palm themselves off as blameless. In order to "guard the friends of Zion against imposition" and to "bring to condign punishment an offender" for eloping with his wife's sister, the Rehoboth Baptist Church published John Hopkins in the local paper and requested other papers to run the item also.[26]

Members who feared an imminent trial sometimes requested and received a letter of dismission in an attempt to elude discipline. If the church then discovered a transgression, they pronounced excommunication and demanded a return of the letter. In the case of excommunicated preachers, they also demanded the return of their license or ordination papers. In either case, churches generally published refusals. One church sent someone to see Josiah Bulloch to "give him an oportunity [*sic*] of delivering his license to the church, and thus saving himself the mortification of being published." Another excommunicated a member holding a letter of dismission and ordered "the same to be published in the Christian Index." Associations assisted in publishing the excommunicants.[27]

The power of excommunication resided also in its spiritual character, which found expression in ritual formulas. Churches sometimes omitted such formalities, but often they adopted carefully worded resolutions. Penfield Baptist Church excommunicated Benjamin Brantly for slander, contempt of the church, and absence from conferences: "Resolved that in view of the charge established against Bro. Brantly, of suspecting Bro. Northen guilty of the crime of perjury, without sufficient grounds, together with his continued refusal to give Bro. Northen and the church a satisfactory explanation and acknowledgement, and in view of the further fact that Bro. Brantly has absented himself from the church conference without permission and failed to answer the charges brought against him by Bro. Sanders, he be excommunicated." By adopting the resolution, the church pronounced upon Brantly the dreadful decree.[28]

In many churches, pastors pronounced the sentence. When Newnan Baptist Church excluded Jeremiah Mulloy, the clerk's *et cetera*s indicated the use of a formula: "The sentence was immediately pronounced by the Moderator that Jere Mulloy was no more known as brother &c. &c." In a detailed description, William B. Johnson, pastor of Savannah Baptist Church, addressed Elizabeth Jones:

> Our Pastor proceeded to the painful solemn act of declaring to her in the presence of the Church her expulsion from its fellowship & privileges. In doing this he opened to her view the dreadful nature & tendency of the crime she had so habitually committed for a long time. He explained to her the nature of the obligations she had been brought under to abstain

> from all sin. He stated to her the guilt she had contracted in violation of these obligations by the commission of the crime for which she was excommunicated. The nature & design of the awful censure which she had incurred was explained also, and the whole enforced upon her heart & conscience with encouraging words to induce her to turn from the error of her ways to the Lord for mercy & pardon.

Such declarations asserted ecclesiastical authority in churches confident that they possessed the keys of heaven—or, at least, of the church.[29]

The term *restored* usually designated members who regained admission to the church. Because moral offenses broke fellowship, churches at times spoke of forgiveness as a restoration. Part of the gravity of the sentence of excommunication resided in its recognition of the fracturing of fellowship and the remanding of transgressors to the care of the world. Clerks often noted that in voting to exclude a member the church agreed "to excommunicate him from all the privileges of the church." The privileges consisted of the ordinances (baptism and communion), government (election of church officers), and discipline (voting upon admission and expulsion of members). Churches believed that "the government is with the body and is the privilege of each individual member" and that "making profession of their faith, teaching and admonishing one another in psalms and hymns and spiritual songs, admitting and expelling members, and sitting at the Lord's table" were general "duties and privileges." The privileges consisted also in the right of "the poor of the flock" to receive assistance from the church. Church members in "needy circumstances" received aid from collections and committees.[30]

Excommunicated members lost one other privilege: the right to be called "brother" or "sister." It was a badge of membership. One wealthy planter in southeast Georgia refused his wife permission to join because he despised the familiarity this practice engendered in Baptist churches: "You know how it is with these Baptists, it's all sister and brother with them, and as soon as you are one of them, all these poor people who are Baptists will be calling you 'Sister Mary,' and that impertinence I won't stand!" Though patricians found it distasteful, this poignant expression of the boundary between the church and the world was a privilege that ordinary Baptists held dear.[31]

To be excommunicated was to move from being sisters and brothers to being "friend" or even "Mr." or "Ms." Church books distinguished the spiritual kinship of members from the alienation of outsiders: "Brother Buck a servant of friend Wm Daniels had run away"; there was a "difficulty between Bro. Hobbs and Mr. Williams." An excommunicant was "our friend and once a brother" or "our once brother." A young man who confessed drunkenness recommended that the church expel him: "I feel just like I was not worthy to be countenanced by you let alone being called a brother, and I do not wish you to retain me as a brother any longer." He would have to lose his kinship with the saints.[32]

One church in the Washington Association had members who refused to abide by this rule. In an attempt to dissuade the refractory faction from referring to the excluded as brothers and sisters, the church wrote the association for advice: "Does it accord with the directions of our Savior, given in the 18th of Matthew, for us, as his followers, to use the endearing appellation of brother or sister, when we speak to or of those who have been regularly excluded from the fellowship of the church?" The association's response was unequivocal: "No."[33]

Excommunication brought the full force of ecclesiastical authority to bear on offenders. Its significance was not lost on either the sinners or the saints. They had bound themselves to mutual accountability for moral behavior. Though honored as a privilege, the oversight often proved nettlesome, and the churches recognized its gravity. It cast offenders not only outside the pale of society and fellowship but also beyond the pale of discipline.

Restoration

The sinners did not always forsake the company of the saints. They could not participate as members, but they could attend the public ceremonies. One J. Early, excluded from Greensboro Baptist Church, contributed to foreign missions and to the pastor's salary even after his expulsion. By attending faithfully and contributing their money, the chastened gave presumptive evidence of a sincere wish to be restored.[34]

Not all of them sought restoration. Early did not, nor did some 67 percent of excommunicated members. Though the churches expected repentance, they did not always get it. But many of the sinners valued their membership, one out of three seeking restoration, even though it meant submitting again to church authority. Benjamin Brantly enlisted patrons within and without the church in order that his repentance might be accepted. On his third request, the church restored him. Some waited more than three decades to confess and seek restoration. One desired restoration so ardently that when the church requested testimonials of moral rectitude he forged documents purporting to certify his pious deportment. Restored offenders returned from the realm of "friend" to that of "sister" and "brother" by receiving "the right hand of fellowship." Restoration meant peace to a conscience troubled by separation from the fellowship of the saints.[35]

As with forgiving penitents, churches restored excluded members only by unanimous consent, requiring them to convince every member of their true repentance. When the sinners made their request by letter—as often happened with those who had moved away—churches demanded a testimonial from a nearby Baptist church. Generally, however, churches required a personal appearance. They could better test sincerity when the sinner stood before the church's bar.[36]

Satisfying the church meant "making satisfactory acknowledgements and exhibiting . . . signs of a sincere repentance." It meant submission to the judgment of its tribunal, as when "James Mckintire gave in a repentance and Justifies the church in his exclusion," and it required of excommunicants an extraordinary measure of humility. John Jesse sought restoration, "acknowledged that the Church did right in excluding him," and expressed his sorrow and his love for the saints. Then "the record of his exclusion was read," and two members recounted their discussions with him. Jesse promised to submit himself to discipline again, and the church restored him. He had undergone the ordeal of mortification.[37]

Resistance

Attempts to avoid the tribunal, whether by appeal to individual liberty or by rejection of the church's moral jurisdiction, occurred only rarely. When it did occur, it steeled Baptist resolve. Members who fulminated against church courts elicited little sympathy. Their resistance aggravated their crime. It was rebellion against Christ, the church's lawgiver.

The recalcitrant might try to remove themselves from the church's jurisdiction. In 1795, James Hutchinson drew the Powelton Baptist Church's correction when he joined the Masons. The church judged that membership in the secret society was incompatible with church membership. Hutchinson devised a plan by which he might remain a Baptist and a Mason. He "declared himself a member of Bull Run church in Virginia and not accountable to us as a member." The church threw him out. His attempt to elude jurisdiction worsened his crime.[38]

When Sheldon Dunning's church in Savannah charged him with slander and fraud, he denied the charge and rebuked the church: It was "disorderly" because it neglected weekly communion, prohibited voluntary withdrawal, and scheduled its disciplinary conferences on Saturday rather than Sunday. He "excommunicated us from his fellowship," wrote the clerk. In turn, the church excommunicated him.[39]

Two years later, his sister Mary Dunning denied the church any jurisdiction over her. Charged with taking communion with her brother, she also "denied the Church's right and authority to excommunicate her Brother." For herself, she claimed the right of liberty: "She had a right to withdraw from us . . . [and] we had no right to exercise discipline towards her." After drawing out the affair for a year, the church dropped her from the roll (a rare, nondisciplinary act), "no longer to be considered a member with us." Pastor William Johnson and preacher Thomas Williams had persuaded the church that she could go:

> Sister Dunning had said that she had withdrawn from us on Conscientious principles, & that from her known piety & conduct, he was bound to believe her, that the great Doctor Holcombe at Philadelphia, in which City she now was, had borne written Testimony of her Exemplary piety & conduct there, & advised to suffer her to depart in peace, &c, from every consideration he thought it more to the glory of God to suffer her to go from us in peace. . . . To which the Pastor replied, that he thought her in an error in this respect [regarding the injustice of excommunicating her brother], & had told her so, but she nevertheless persisted to declare her belief of her Brother's innocency, & thought him hardly dealt with. But upon the whole he verily believed that this error had originated in her head, rather than in her heart, that he did not believe that she had erred intentionally, and seeing that the Church would sufficiently manifest their displeasure against her by declaring that she was no longer in our Communion, & that her membership shall cease in this Church from this day, so far & no farther he felt willing to say or to do.

Johnson appealed to conscience. Since Mary Dunning erred in good conscience, the church had no right to discipline her.[40]

Within six months, the church changed its mind. Every member but one had voted initially to exclude her. Seeking unanimity, the church now requested the association to advise them whether a member could withdraw "for a difference of sentiment." The association came out for "liberty of conscience." It agreed with Johnson that sometimes liberty preempted disciplinary authority. In 1814, the association reversed itself. It decided that no member had a right to leave a church "without general consent; otherwise, he despises the church, breaks fellowship, and should be dealt with as the gospel directs, in the case of disorderly members." Because a member joined by assuming the covenant of obedience to Christ and his discipline, the attempt to withdraw was an immoral act, a breach of the vow of submission.[41]

The lay leaders of Savannah Baptist Church then tried to persuade the pastor to change his mind, but he refused. Having opened the door to voluntary withdrawal, Johnson walked through it himself. In conference, he rose, declared himself no longer the pastor, and withdrew his membership. Twelve others followed him out of the church, which passed a rule to ensure that this never happened again. Six years later, Johnson recanted, and in 1823 he confessed his errors and obtained reconciliation.[42]

Ironically, Thomas Williams, the preacher who had supported Johnson, tried to withdraw in 1816 on the grounds that the church was not severe enough in its discipline. Williams's slave driver, Aaron Shave, struck and killed one of Williams's slaves, pleading self-defense. The church merely suspended him from communion. Williams viewed the light punishment as "dishonorable." In withdrawing, Williams sought the door through which Mary Dunning and William B. Johnson had passed, lamenting that "he had labored much to bring the Church to a liberal plan, that he was sorry to find her so soon Changing a good & wholesome rule, he conceived that when members were offended at the Church's act they had a right to withdraw their membership." Brooking no further curtailments of primitive ecclesiastical authority, the church concurred with Johnson's successor, Benjamin Screven: "The Church had been too long oppressed under such supposed liberality of Conduct, & that it was high time for them to close their doors against such innovations, where no scripture could justify the practice, but to the contrary directly to the reverse. That members who rent themselves from the Church for a supposed grievance were truce breakers & merited the Censure of the Church." The church revoked Williams's license to preach and suspended him. It eventually expelled him. He had wanted severity toward Shave; he wanted liberality for himself.[43]

For a few, then, the rights of conscience could preempt church authority, but most who resisted the church had no such concern for principle. Some merely walked out of conference when accused. Others ducked the investigating committee. Some would obey the pastor but not the congregation. Others refused to appear when "cited" to do so or sought greener pastures in other folds. Charles Ash told a discipline committee that "he was glad that there were other churches in the city beside the Baptist Church." He was not the only rebel who left the church because of its discipline.[44]

Other members, accepting the church's authority to discipline, complained of its application. They said that it was applied with unequal severity, or that it was too harsh even when impartially imposed. Husbands protested on behalf of wives, and wives on behalf of husbands. A few responded with disdain. W. R. Page of Atlanta told his church that it could "turn him out and be damned." Only a tiny number, it appears, sought remedy in the civil courts. The church responded to threats of civil suits with pronouncements of excommunication.[45]

On occasion, discipline could draw violent responses. Southern men often turned to violence to maintain honor, preserve white rule, and protect community values. From the gentlemen's duels to the yeomen's fistfights, they used force to "patrol their own social and ethical space." Southern courts dealt with crimes of violence at two or three times the rate of northern courts and were more reluctant to punish violent offenders. When Baptist churches shamed their members with convictions, rebukes, and excommunications, censured offenders occasionally resorted to violence to defend their honor.[46]

When Richland Baptist Church excluded William Cooper on charges of stealing a cow, breaking out of jail, and resisting the civil law, Cooper torched the meeting house and threatened "powder and lead" if it should be rebuilt. He also stole the church book and formed a rump congregation, which he declared to be the true Richland Baptist Church. No other threats of violence appeared in more than nine thousand disciplinary cases, however. Southern honor retreated before southern discipline; the demand for self-vindication before the demand for submission.[47]

Submission to the authority of the church was at the heart of the disciplinary apparatus. A particular transgression was secondary. The issue was submission to divine authority mediated by the community of believers. To oppose the church's discipline was to oppose the authority of God. When Fereby West refused to explain her conduct, her church expelled her because she "designed not to be submissive to God and the church." She had flouted the authority of Jesus Christ. Southern Baptist piety required submission to the democratic authority of the saints.[48]

4

Democracy, Race, and Gender

Apologists for the Old South boasted that it was an organic society—every part of the social body in its proper place, contributing to the whole. Like a living organism, it functioned correctly because the highborn and the lowborn fulfilled providential roles determined by race, wealth, and gender. The social distinctions found their way into the churches. No matter how pious, women did not cast off their gender with their cloaks when they entered the church. Masters were masters, and slaves were slaves, whether in the meeting house or out. The churches contained all the strata of southern society, and the exercise of its authority reflected these distinctions.[1]

Yet the Baptists embodied the ideal of an egalitarian church to a degree that could shock other southerners. Despising the leveling tone of Baptist piety, wealthy southerners could appreciate the feelings of the Virginia gentleman who confessed that "if any other people but the baptists professed their religion I would make it my religion before tomorrow." The democratic ecclesiology of the Baptist churches made the Baptists experts in the practice of egalitarian authority.[2]

Baptists had few educated preachers or wealthy members—most members were humble folk. The gentry quickly stereotyped them as ignorant and contemptible. Baptist preachers were objects of ridicule and abuse. In time, Baptist aspirations for social respect resulted in the proliferation of Baptist academies and colleges, from which flowed educated preachers and professionals. As Baptists crossed the threshold "from alienation to influence" after the Civil War, they began to reshape their commitment to democratic authority. In the meantime, they allowed no obstacles of race, class, or gender to hinder their moral discipline.[3]

Democratic Discipline

Believing that ecclesiastical power resided in every member equally, antebellum Baptist churches usually granted female members—and often granted slaves—voting privileges. They distinguished in this context matters of "government" from matters of "discipline." Government related to the election of church officers—deacons, elders, and pastors. Discipline related to matters of fellowship—admitting and dismissing members, forgiving penitent offenders, expelling transgressors, and restoring excluded members. Although some churches restricted women from voting about government, few prohibited their voting about fellowship.[4]

Policies about participation were not uniform. The Dover Baptist Association in Virginia, when asked about qualifications for voting in matters of "government and discipline," apparently advised the churches that neither women nor slaves could vote in either case, rendering their "opinion that none but free male members, can properly exercise authority in the church." Landmark Baptist A. S. Worrell, president of colleges in Louisiana and Missouri, argued likewise against women and slaves voting in the churches. Sylvanus Landrum, who served large churches in Macon, Savannah, and Memphis, argued that scripture prohibited women from voting in church, as did the consideration that women in city churches were vulnerable to manipulation by partisan interests.[5]

In some churches, then, female members lacked the privilege of voting, whether on matters of government or discipline. Jesse Mercer held that discipline constituted a matter of government and that therefore women should not be allowed any vote in disciplinary matters: "Now, then, if women are not permitted to teach and exercise authority in the churches [1 Tim. 2:11–12], how can they vote in matters of discipline which is government?" Mercer expected women to decline the privilege of voting whenever "men should attempt [to offer] it, in view of honoring them." He admitted, however, that he was pleading the minority position. "We suspect," Mercer wrote, "it is the general practice of the churches of our order, to allow women this use [voting on matters of discipline]."[6]

Mercer's suspicions were well founded. Commenting on "the duties and privileges of Female members in a Gospel Church," Henry Holcombe, pastor of Savannah First Baptist Church, wrote that "the sexes, as believers, are one in Christ, and in all that regards christian fellowship, . . . admitting and expelling members. . . . On all these duties and privileges, the Apostolic addresses to a church appear to us to be indiscriminate." Several readers of the *Christian Index* wrote defending the right of women to vote on discipline, suggesting that no scriptural doctrine stood in the way. The Atlanta Baptist Ministers' Conference, discussing Marietta pastor J. A. Wynne's talk on women in the church, concluded that women could not hold "official authority" as a deacon or elder, but "could teach in Sunday-school or pray and vote in the church."[7]

Though differing on whether women should vote in church government, Baptist associations advised the churches that women should vote on discipline. When asked whether "it is consistent with gospel discipline, for a female member to speak in conference or not," the Hephzibah Association counseled that "we conceive a woman's privilege in conference, to be the same with the man's, in all points except matters of the ministry and government." The Sarepta Association, responding to a query asking whether women were "equally privileged with the Males, to vote in all matters in the church, relating to government & discipline," answered that "we think they are equally priviledged with the male members." The Western Association took it for granted that females should vote on fellowship and at the same time admitted that churches differed about their right to vote on government. The association advised that "the right of sisters to vote in the government of the Churches is a question which each Church should decide for itself, and a disagreement, on this subject, should not affect the fellowship of the Churches."[8]

Baptist churches generally followed this advice. The Powelton Baptist Church gave women the right to vote only on "cases respecting fellowship." Another church made drinking distilled liquor a transgression "by a unanimous vote, both of males and females." Although church clerks rarely recorded details of church balloting, occasional glimpses confirm that women frequently voted. One clerk wrote that the church determined a discipline case "by a vote of seventeen (17) members male and female." Another recorded the names of fourteen members—ten of them women—who voted against excommunicating an offender. The clerk of Savannah Baptist Church recorded that one "Sister Hill, the only dissentient," had succeeded, by her vote, in impeding the will of the majority.[9]

The divergent opinions collided in an 1855 effort to unite the First and Second Baptist Churches of Savannah. Whether or not the women of Savannah First Baptist Church voted on government, they clearly voted on fellowship. Since Savannah Second Baptist Church prohibited women from voting at all, it insisted on terms of union that gave the vote to the men only. First Baptist Church balked, but finally made the sacrifice: Ninety-seven women of the church wrote a document agreeing to "transfer to our Brethren all the Spiritual & Temporal business of the church to their charge, having perfect confidence in their ability and judgement to manage the business of the church, and furthermore we strongly recommend a union of the two Baptist churches of this city, believing it will result in much good."[10]

Many churches allowed slaves to vote on discipline. A member charged with drunkenness and trading on the Sabbath at a camp meeting failed to obtain forgiveness because two black members were not satisfied with his repentance. One church refused a slave applicant because they feared that some of the slave members "might not be willing to her reception." Greensboro Baptist Church appointed an investigating committee after "Charles Servant of Mr. Terrell . . . made repeated applications for admission into the church, [and] Phillis a Coloured Sister . . . as repeatedly made objections." Although Phillis evidently stood alone, the church decided to sustain her objection. The church books provide only glimpses, but they reveal at least a measure of black participation in the disposition of "matters of fellowship."[11]

Although in theory slave votes could have opposed white votes, there is no evidence that they could do so decisively. Black delegates to the Sunbury Association, wrote one black Georgia preacher, thought it imprudent to oppose the will of the "white brethren of power in the land," even when they knew they were in the right. Although they had a vote, it was "at most times timidly used." In the churches, slaves cast votes that dissented from whites only when it involved a black.[12]

White Baptists assumed that black members would administer discipline in familiar ways. After all, they had accepted the same gospel, embraced the same doctrines, and avowed the same principles of church government. Any worries about black suffrage in the church came from concern that blacks lacked the education and experience to administer church government wisely.[13]

The constraints of slavery reassured whites. Because churches conducted business and discipline on a Saturday, when slaves could rarely attend, black attendance probably remained low. Some churches established a church within the church by organizing a monthly Sunday conference for blacks. In any case, black members demonstrated no disposition to oppose white members. Although they embraced similar theological and ecclesiological principles to the whites, their social subordination precluded any determined opposition to white wishes. Even when blacks outnumbered them, whites did not fear that blacks would hinder their government of the church, much less overthrow it. White confidence overcame the occasional white anxiety that cropped up under the strain of sectional tensions over slavery. In 1860, a church in Georgia's black belt discussed a motion "to debar the blacks from Voting in cases touching fellowship." The clerk recorded no details of the debate—if there was one—but scribbled the conclusion that it "was decided that they should continue to Vote."[14]

Both women and blacks supported the discipline in other ways. White men usually manned investigating committees, but women sometimes served when the defendant was a woman. Little Ogeechee Baptist Church in eastern Georgia accused Martha Hodges with disorderly conduct and "agreed that there be a committy appointed to visit her and advise with her & report to the next conference, agreed that Sisters Jane[,] Hodges[,] Conner[,] & Lundy be that Committy." The clerk of Bethesda Baptist Church recorded that "sister mays has used spiritous Liquors to intemperance; Ordered that Sister Nancy Bethoon & Sister Phebe Greene Visit on that occasion & Report at the next conference." Occasionally, churches appointed men and women to the same committee, as when LaGrange First Baptist Church added four women to a committee of four men who had been dragging their feet in investigating some women accused of dancing.[15]

In the same way, churches sometimes appointed blacks to investigate other blacks or asked black and white members to serve together. Black members often constituted the entire committee. They also were appointed to permanent discipline committees charged with handling the discipline of the black portion of the church. Kiokee Baptist Church appointed "the Black Breat[hren] Billy[,] tom and Abram a committy to watch over the black breathren." Little Ogeechee Baptist Church "appointed Brother Tom of couler belonging to Mrs Lipsey and Jeffery of couler belong[ing] to Mrs. Hage, as watches of the Coloured members of this Church and notice the disorderly conduct that may take place among them and report accordingly." Churches adopted this expedient whether or not they held a regular Sunday conference for black members. Across the South, Baptist democracies were remarkably egalitarian.[16]

Women and Democratic Religion

Southern churches were female preserves, and throughout the nineteenth century women made up between 60 and 65 percent of the membership of Georgia Baptist churches. Yet it was the waywardness of the male minority that kept Baptist church discipline in business. Churches hauled their male members before the bar on a scale out of all proportion to their numbers. Every year 8 percent of white male Baptists passed under the church's rod of discipline. But white men also enjoyed the most leniency. Churches were reluctant to excommunicate them. In the antebellum period, they excommunicated male defendants in 47 percent of the cases and female defendants in 66 percent. Despite the leniency, they excommunicated far more men than women, ejecting twice as many between 1785 and 1860.[17]

It is tempting to see them as unjust, but they would have been puzzled by such a judgment. The egalitarian values unleashed in the Revolutionary War period were still battling more ancient traditions. Southern Baptists, egalitarians in the church, resisted social egalitarianism; they honored the social hierarchy, and they read scripture in accord with it.

They divided society into its constituent institutions—family, voluntary societies (such as churches, fraternal organizations, schools), and civil government. Understanding one's location in the order was essential to virtue, for it revealed one's duties. Georgia Baptist preacher A. T. Holmes saw in the creation of Adam and Eve the foundation of this "social principle," which also governed the duties of masters and slaves: "Founded upon the union thus originally instituted, certain relations are discovered to exist, in which are involved certain duties, each relation urging its claim respectively. Thus, the husband sustains a relation to his wife, the parent to his child, the citizen to his country, in each of which distinctive duties are to be discharged, growing out of the particular relation sustained." Methodist apologist H. N. McTyeire, editor of the *Nashville Christian Advocate*, agreed that "different relations . . . imply distinct obligations."[18]

For Baptist Professor S. G. Hillyer, the duties of "domestic government" derived from the nature of the family. The fifth commandment, he argued, "places the parent virtually upon a throne, with a sceptre in the right hand and a crown upon the head. . . . Parents are sovereigns, of whom it can be truly said, that they reign as kings and queens 'by the grace of God'; for their rank and authority rest upon the constitution of the family, of which God is the original and efficient founder." Because God created the institutions of society, the duties derived from social position constituted divine commands. Human happiness resided largely, according to this theory, "in fulfilling the duties of the station in which Providence has placed us."[19]

The moral obligations of husbands and wives, parents and children, and masters and slaves affected the way churches viewed offenses, and members who transgressed could expect the church to treat them differently according to their position. Some misdeeds—drunkenness or adultery, for example—brought swift censure regardless of social position, but social position usually made a difference.

Women encountered greater severity than men. They were almost one and a half times more likely to suffer excommunication than males. Even for similar offenses, the churches treated them more severely. Georgia Baptists between 1785 and 1860 excommunicated, for offenses against the church, 69 percent of male defendants and 84 percent of female; for alcohol-related offenses, 48 percent of male defendants and

65 percent of female; for sexual offenses, 81 percent of male defendants and 88 percent of female; and for violence, 41 percent of male defendants and 52 percent of female. Only for offenses involving property did the churches exclude male and female defendants at approximately the same rate, 65 and 67 percent, respectively. Churches judged men more harshly for worldly amusements, dancing being the chief offense, expelling 58 percent of male dancers and only 39 percent of female. With minor exceptions, discipline varied consistently by gender.

Woman, after all, was the protector of morality. She was "the top-piece of Creation—the beauty of the whole earth—and the glory of the man!" By virtue of the divine creation, woman had the duty of preserving the home and its school of virtue. "By inflexible necessity," wrote editor Henry Holcombe Tucker, "womanhood and manhood involve different duties." Women exercised their moral influence as mothers and wives. The Macedonia Temperance Society in Meriwether County encouraged women to join because "the influence which they very justly possess over the morals and taste of the community is very great. . . . They are most commonly the warmest advocates of benevolent and good works." Jesse Mercer, pleading for female education, concurred: "In the formation of the social frame, what constituent so important as the influence,—the mind of woman! She gives to the life of man its moral tone. . . . Her education, therefore, should look to the great duties to which she is destined,—to the all-important situations which she is to occupy in society. She is to be educated as one, who is hereafter to sustain the relation of a mother;—one who is to educate future sons of the republic." Baptists designed women's education to nurture piety.[20]

Southern evangelicals established an array of female seminaries to give impulse to the divine social order. By 1852, Southern Baptists operated at least forty-three female academies and colleges. Georgia topped the list with two female colleges and eight female seminaries. Before the war, southern Presbyterians established dozens of parish-based coeducational primary schools and at least eleven female academies. Southern Methodists may have had as many as thirty or forty female academies. Evangelicals actively promoted female education, as long as it schooled women to be women. The prosperity of church and society depended on its success.[21]

The task for women was always to refine purity and piety. The demands of purity required them to avoid everything from familiarity with men to novel reading and tobacco. It meant embracing "true delicacy"—"a refined and practical modesty, which shrinks from everything which is offensive to decency or injurious to morality." The demands of piety were many, but they especially included worship, prayer, and the devotional reading of scripture. Religious reading stood at the center of the family circle and family prayer at the center of devotion. Robert Fleming, principal of the Female Seminary in Newnan, upbraided frivolous women: "For the toilet-table of her apartment, or the centre-table of her parlor, to be loaded with the books of fiction, or the pamphlets of fashion, and be destitute of the Bible and religious periodicals, is a reproach to her head and her heart." It would be far better, he said, for women to persuade their husbands to establish the "family altar."[22]

Evangelicals looked to women to sustain the church. Though God prohibited them from assuming official authority, he bestowed on them "the high privilege of moulding and shaping the character of those who are to fill the places of responsibility in the church." Ministers looked to women as their supporters, sometimes confiding that their female parishioners understood them best. J. B. Hawthorne of Atlanta First Baptist Church, postwar crusader against social vice, felt that women alone valued his opposition to "error and ungodliness." When the whiskey rings tried to destroy him, he said, Christian women stood by him with "dauntless devotion."[23]

Women were active in southern "benevolent societies." Missionary societies and charitable organizations proliferated widely. As early as 1829, the Georgia Baptist Association—one of seventeen associations in the state—reported "28 Sabbath Schools, containing more than 1,000 Pupils; 10 Tract Societies; 9 Temperance Societies; besides Bible, Singing, Ladies Working, and other benevolent institutions." The support of women was essential to their success.[24]

Women also organized independent societies. In Georgia, Baptist women acted jointly in at least twenty-three women's groups before 1860. Rural women joined them, but they prospered most in towns. In 1856, the Macon Ladies' Charitable Association disbursed $544 toward the relief of fifty-three families. The Macon Female Tract Society distributed the same year eleven Bibles and 3,398 tracts. Female sewing societies raised money for church lamps, organs, and debt payments. The first benevolent societies in America arose in the eighteenth century to support missionary activity to Native American, frontier, and overseas heathen. In the 1790s, mission societies began to multiply at a rapid rate, spurred by interest in William Carey's mission to India in 1792. Throughout the nineteenth century, societies proliferated across the country to raise funds for every kind of benevolent work.[25]

Missionary activity shaped Baptist identity. When Congregationalist missionaries Adoniram Judson and Luther Rice became Baptists in 1812, Rice returned to organize Baptist support of Judson's Burma mission. In 1814, delegates from Baptist mission societies gathered to form the Baptist General Convention for Foreign Missions, known as the Triennial Convention. Baptists in the South organized in support of the convention's efforts. Georgia's Jesse Mercer was president of the Board of Foreign Missions from 1830 to 1841. Southerners William T. Brantly, John L. Dagg, Basil Manly Sr., William C. Crane, and Thomas Stocks served as officers of the convention's boards, and other southerners served as board members. When southerners withdrew from the northern-controlled boards in 1845, they formed their own convention as an outlet for missionary zeal.[26]

No activity drew the talents of women more than missions. In 1800, fourteen Congregational and Baptist women organized the first female society, the Boston Female Society for Missionary Purposes. By 1818, ninety-seven female societies corresponded with the Boston society. Female cent societies spread by the hundreds. By 1839, Congregational missions had the support of 923 men's associations and 680 ladies' associations. The 1817 Baptist Triennial Convention reported that 110 of its 187 member societies were "Female Societies." The Monroe Missionary Society, comprising women of Walton County, Georgia, felt the power of the call to missions:

> A portion of the Females of Monroe, Walton county, feeling it to be their duty to engage in works of Benevolence, . . . and having heard the pathetic appeals from Burmah's heathen shores, to send them the word of God translated into their own native tongue, and being touched with sympathy in view of the deplorable condition of their own sex in that benighted land, have united themselves into a Society, the principal object of which is to raise a fund to aid in publishing the Bible in the Burman language. They have employed a small portion of their time in manufacturing such articles as they supposed might be sold to an advantage. . . . Some of them are Baptists, some are Methodists, and other are not members of any church.

Women contributed large sums toward missionary endeavors, often outdoing the male part of the church. By 1889, Baptist women had organized 216 women's missionary societies in Georgia.[27]

Women sustained southern piety also at conference meetings, which they were expected to attend. A model decorum that stated in typical fashion the duty of men to attend church conference added that "female members are expected to attend promptly when possible to do so." Some churches required it. Required or not, however, women showed up in force and frequently voted, even on matters of government, such as the election of deacons and pastors. They probably outnumbered the men. At one conference of the Savannah Baptist Church, called to elect a new pastor, women outnumbered men twenty-one to five; at a regular conference they prevailed twenty-seven to four. Jesse Mercer cited such attendance figures as an argument against women's right to vote on discipline, since to give them this privilege would make them the moral governors of the church. Women, in fact, had the larger part in discipline.[28]

Because the scriptures assigned different duties to women and men, Baptists treated their offenses differently, and women did not chafe at the double standard. They often felt that the men, left to themselves, would have allowed moral standards to fall. A female reader of the

Christian Index, conceding that "woman is put in subjection to man," objected to Mercer's views by insisting that men could not be trusted to protect either doctrinal or moral purity: "Because the male members of the church wink at drunkenness in the preacher, or prefer an Arminian, must I, knowing the sin to be indulged, and a Calvinist too, be silent, with all subjection? My Dear Sir, I feel that such is not the tyranny of the gospel dispensation."[29]

As evangelicals saw it, God had sentenced man to a more vicious corruption than woman. Both sexes were wicked, but pastors like Atlanta's Hawthorne could chastise women for "natural infirmities" while describing "the infirmities of your brothers" as "much more serious." He could even describe women as "naturally so much better than men, so much gentler and sweeter." Women were innately "more pious and warm-hearted in the service of God than men."[30]

The encomiums to female virtue had a price, exacted in the ecclesiastical courtroom. In this scheme, drunkenness was wicked in a man, but an outrage in a woman. A female drunk assaulted every sensibility of goodness and virtue; her sin threatened the divine order. For men, tobacco was a pernicious habit; in women, it was a depraved appetite. Infidelity by men was abhorrent; by women, worse than abhorrent.[31]

Men seemed determined to prove that they were by nature morally inferior. Throughout the century, they outpaced their sisters in rates of offenses. In the antebellum period, churches prosecuted white men for drunkenness at a rate forty-five times higher than the rate for white women, seven times higher for worldly amusements, five times higher for offenses against the church, and ten times higher for offenses involving property, violence, or speech. Only with sexual offenses did the sexes achieve parity, churches prosecuting both at virtually the same rate.[32]

But churches found male wickedness less shocking, less dangerous. Male transgressors suffered excommunication at a rate one-third lower than the rate for women. Churches could sentence them more leniently because they deemed their offenses less subversive of good order. In accord with the prevailing philosophical ethics, evangelicals evaluated morality not only by the nature of the act but also by its consequences. Mercer quoted philosopher William Paley to prove that any act resulting in evil was itself evil. Women's sins were worse than men's, by this logic, because they had more evil consequences; they damaged the home-centered piety of the divinely mandated social order.[33]

Blacks and Democratic Religion

In the antebellum South, Baptist churches became spiritual havens for an increasing number of African Americans. Baptists boasted about the converted slaves, whose religion refuted abolitionist beliefs that southerners neglected the souls of slaves. Like women, however, blacks had to bear the double standard. Churches disciplined blacks less frequently than whites, but when they cited them they more frequently excommunicated them. The similarities with women were striking. Black defendants were expelled at the same rate as women defendants: 66 percent. Churches excluded white defendants in only 46 percent of the cases, a rate merely one point below that of cases with male defendants.

Blacks had a unique place in the social order. Their status as servants determined their moral duties, but the link between servility and race meant that emancipated blacks found themselves after the war still assigned to the inferior position they had as slaves. The moral obligations of slaves remained binding on them. As slaves, their divine duties consisted mainly of obedience and veracity, virtues of loyalty to earthly masters. Protestant ministers from New England to Georgia had been interested in the conversion of slaves since the seventeenth century and evangelized and baptized them, though they had little success until late in the eighteenth century. Organized efforts to convert the slaves escalated in the 1830s and 1840s as denominations formed societies and sent missionaries to the plantations. Evangelical clergy gained the trust of masters by teaching converts that Christ commanded slaves to be faithful, obedient, and honest.[34]

Such virtues appeared in memorials for pious slaves: "This day about one O'c[loc]k departed this life Major a coloured man about fifty years of age belonging at the time of his death to P. H. Greene who owned him about forty years, never having an occasion of laying the weight of his hand on said man in anger, he was always submissive, gentle, honest to his master in all things, and truthful. The last word he spoke just before he died when he was asked by his master Do you think you will soon see your Savior he said I hope So." Major's piety was exemplary because he remained submissive and honest to his master.[35]

White Baptist writers assumed that God gave blacks a nature suited to the duty of submission—a nature formed by both biology and culture. They described black character as combining features of women and children. Slaves were like women in their natural bent toward piety, like children in lacking the moral and intellectual training for a self-discipline in which reason ruled the passions. Nothing was more self-evident to whites than that African Americans were "eminently a religious people." C. F. Sturgis, who succeeded Mercer as pastor of Washington Baptist Church, scorned debate on this point: "The next great characteristic of this people, and that which, more than any other, lays the foundation for their moral elevation, is the religious element that so strongly distinguishes them. There is no need of reasoning to prove the existence of this sentiment. The man who doubts or denies on this point, avows his entire unacquaintance with the psychological character of this people." African Americans would "receive the gospel with more readiness than the whites."[36]

Apologists for slave religion distinguished the religious bent of African Americans from the female bent toward virtue. In women, piety unfolded into virtuous character. In slaves, some whites seemed to think, piety flourished irrespective of virtue. Blacks were like children. They lacked the self-restraint formed by the love of virtue, Josiah Law explained, because "all are strangers to intellectual, and a large portion of them to moral culture." Blacks were more wicked than whites, in this view, because passion ruled them.[37]

Because slaves achieved virtue in this scheme as children, without cultivation of their rational and moral faculties, whites pointed to slave virtue to shame lesser moral attainments among whites. If slaves eschewed liquor, it was so much the worse for the reputation of liquor-consuming whites. In 1830, the Sunbury Baptist Church, near the Georgia coast, reported that "we have a Temperance Society, of colored people, many of whom are non-professors [non-Christians]; this is a severe reflection on rum drinking christians."[38]

But in the three decades before the Civil War, some white Baptists tried to provide slaves with the moral and intellectual instruction requisite for virtue. Washington Baptist Church appointed preacher W. H. Pope as a missionary to the slaves in 1856 and paid him a $500 salary. Baptists and Congregationalists in coastal Georgia formed a slave-mission society in 1831 and hired Presbyterian minister Charles Colcock Jones as their missionary. The Sunbury Association resolved to employ two missionaries to "our colored population" in 1841. The Southern Baptist Convention's Board of Domestic Missions appointed missionaries to the slaves and entered joint efforts with local and state agencies. They paid missionaries to do this; they urged their pastors to attend to it, but they cast the burden mainly on the masters. Josiah Law explained their duty: "We should regard them as children, for they are children in intellect, and we should endeavor to make our government of them as much parental as the circumstances of the case will admit. Their moral characters should engage our constant and particular attention. To elevate the standard of morals among them, we must acquaint them more fully with the principles of right and wrong, we must give them more light." The Greensboro Baptist Church made the duty to convert slaves a part of its constitution: It was the duty of "the heads of Families to pray in their families and give their children and servants religious instruction." But crusades for African-American virtue foundered on the contradictions of southern slaveholding ideology.[39]

According to the laws of southern states, slaves were alternately human beings with inalienable rights and human property with rights alienated to their owners. Southern churches entertained similar contradictions. They welcomed slaves who professed faith; they accepted the social inferiority of the slaves—an inequality so radical that it overwhelmed the ideal of spiritual equality. White church members could not deny that slaves were as much "moral and accountable beings" as they. Apologists for slave religion therefore appealed to masters to recognize their slaves as members of the household, entitled to the same spiritual nurture as biological children. Attention to spiritual needs would link the affections of "the entire family, black and white." Slaves should "have their share in the Home-Altar, . . . not by invitation only, but as a fixed rule, a duty."[40]

Having fixed the moral duties of the slave's social position, Baptist churches could allow a measure of spiritual equality. Black members frequently voted in cases of fellowship. The rituals of admission to the church suggested spiritual equality. A slave convert no less than a white "related his experience" in church conference. Black and white converts marched together to the creek or spring for baptism. S. G. Hillyer recounted how his mother embraced Christ after witnessing a white church receive a slave applicant:

> When the door of the Church was opened only one came forward, and he was a middle-aged negro. The young lady [Hillyer's mother] said to herself: 'Surely the Church is not going to receive such a creature as that, he can not tell an experience.' Perhaps she scarcely deigned to listen to the poor darkey's words, preferring probably to indulge in her own thoughts. But presently, very much to her surprise, the members rose to their feet and, with a sweet song of welcome, began to give the humble candidate the right hand of fellowship. He had told an experience that was responded to by every pious heart in that house.

Converts, whatever their color, shared a religious experience—a conviction of sin and a movement from the despair of condemnation to the joy of divine deliverance.[41]

White Baptists recognized that their rituals implied spiritual equality. They believed that social distinctions toppled under the leveling power of the gospel. Adiel Sherwood, a Baptist preacher who at twenty-seven left the Northeast to settle in Georgia, marveled at the egalitarianism of faith. He once recalled the constitution of a new Baptist church:

> Two aged black slaves, who belonged to the church with their master and mistress, on account of their age and infirmities, had been overlooked when the constitution of the church was read, and the right hand of fellowship was given to all the others. The mistress mentioned the circumstance with much feeling, and then sprang forward and gave them her right hand, followed by her husband and all the other church members. In the evening of that same day, a meeting was held in the house of the master, and, when they entered, the mistress called them, resigned her seat to them, and sat herself upon the stairsteps during the meeting. . . . And thus it is seen that the gospel levels all distinctions.

Predominantly white churches could sustain the innocence of black members even when the accuser was a leading white member. Aged, indigent blacks could receive the same financial assistance as poor whites. In this gospel egalitarianism, white Baptists saw not only evidence of the power of the gospel but also a refutation of abolitionist accusations that southerners neglected the spiritual needs of the blacks.[42]

Yet white Baptists found it impossible to overcome the ideology and the reality of social inequality. The churches expressed the social inferiority of African Americans most visibly in the seating of their meeting houses. Church seating had traditionally reflected social divisions. New England Puritans seated Africans and Indians in galleries or rear seats. Whether Congregationalist or Anglican, churches seated persons of highest social status in the best seats. Advocating a common worship for both races, Baptists assigned the blacks to the worst seats.[43]

There were limits to this partiality. A white member once complained that "his feelings were hurt in that of Turning the black Brethren and Sisters out from amonts [amongst] us in that Shelters [were] built at the end of the meeting house." One church attempted to split the hair by requesting the deacons to see that "the negroes be not deprived of the seats assigned them; unless there be not otherwise room for the Whites." Yet the seating of the saints revealed the force of inegalitarian social ideology.[44]

White Baptists felt similar ambivalence about independent black churches. When black Baptists formed First African Church in Savannah in 1777, three other such churches had already formed in the South. From Maryland to Mississippi, slaves formed independent congregations. By 1864, two of three independent black Baptist churches were in the South, and Georgia had 24 percent of them. Savannah First African was formed by freed slave Georgia Liele, who transplanted a part of the congregation to Jamaica in 1782. In 1788, Andrew Bryan became pastor and expanded the church from 80 members to 1,400 by the time of his death in 1812, making it the largest church in the state. His nephew Andrew Marshall succeeded him and saw the church grow to 2,800 in 1832. Augusta's Springfield African Church underwent similar growth. Begun in 1791, by 1832 it had 1,300 members. Georgia's coastal region had a long tradition of independent black congregations.[45]

Blacks often requested permission to have their own worship meetings. Whites generally consented, though not without misgivings. The question of control was a minor issue, for when whites decided that blacks had disorderly meetings, they abolished them. Whites even showed some irritation at state laws requiring their presence at black religious meetings, and they frequently neglected them. Some whites favored white oversight simply to preclude the criticism that all-black meetings encouraged rebellion.[46]

White Baptists had misgivings about independent black services mainly because they doubted that blacks could conduct them profitably. They wondered where blacks would find patriarchs to shepherd their flocks. Since the slaves were their spiritual children, moreover, they were accountable to God for black spiritual welfare. It was "unquestionably better for them to stand connected with white congregations, where they can be under the supervision and tuition of those better informed than themselves." In the end, whites relented. They justified their course by appealing again to spiritual welfare: Blacks could not attain maturity without independent services. They could not profit from reasoned discourses designed for the more literate whites. They needed simple messages.[47]

To a certain extent, the unequal condition of slaves forced the churches to establish separate services. Slaves could not often attend conferences on Saturday, so whites established a Sunday semiautonomous church conference for blacks, preparing the way for independent worship services. As early as 1804, one Georgia church "agreed to hold conferance at this place on the last Sunday in this month for the accomodation of the Black Brethren." By 1808, the same church was taking measures to regulate apparently informal services led by black church members, probably on the plantations. In 1821, the church "granted the black brethren the use of the meeting house one sabbath in the month for divine services." Another church established black conferences in 1791, reinstituted them in 1800, and permitted black worship services in the meeting house in 1823.[48]

Black Baptists required opportunities to relate their conversion experiences and to accuse, confess, forgive, and excommunicate. Whites described Sunday conferences variously as "for the benefit of the black Brethren," for "transacting business for the Black Brethren," "for the Convenincey of the black people, to hear Experiences from them," and "to Keep order among the black Brethren." The conferences usually had a white moderator and clerk, but they appointed their own discipline committees, elected their own deacons, and managed their own ecclesiastical affairs, with the white congregation giving advice and consent.[49]

Yet white Baptists were content to leave their black fellow members in spiritual childhood. White leaders acquiesced in state laws against teaching slaves to read. Fearful of claims that religion undermined slavery, they assured suspicious southerners that black Baptists "are not taught to read. . . . We know of no one in our State who advocates teaching them to read, under existing circumstances." During the Civil War, as white Baptists began to suspect that God was punishing the South, not for slavery but for abuses of it—"God, our Heavenly Father, often chastises most promptly those whom he most loves"—Baptist leaders joined others in an assault on state laws that abridged the rights of slaves to read, to marry, and to preach and teach the gospel. But only after emancipation did white Baptists show any determination to train black leaders for pastoral ministry.[50]

Whites also struggled to maintain the balance between spiritual equality and social inequality in the association meetings. In 1849, the

Franklin Covenant Baptist Church, composed of black members, sought admission to the Hephzibah Baptist Association. Delegates voted twice but finally agreed by a small majority to accept the church and its representatives. The Sunbury Baptist Association, whose churches on Georgia's coastal plain had mainly African-American members, accepted black delegates and accorded them voting privileges, and black delegates voted on occasion against resolutions supported by white delegates. In 1849, the association met with fifteen white and eleven black delegates; in 1856 with fourteen white and fourteen black. The Georgia Baptist Association also received black delegates.[51]

This practice was not popular with many white Baptists. Some associations refused to recognize black delegates and required black churches to elect white delegates. One advocate of black representation excoriated associations that refused to seat black messengers:

> It is known . . . that in some of these bodies, colored delegates are received and allowed to exercise all the rights granted to the white representatives. From the fact, however, that they are generally ignorant of the Bible, of church government, and of the state of religion in their immediate bounds, doubts have been entertained and expressed as to the expediency and divine right of their granted prerogatives. . . . Some of our Associations not only deny them this privilege, but maintain that it should in no case be granted, and, if I am not mistaken, this sentiment prevails more generally than most persons imagine. . . . It seems to me that if the Bible has anything to do with it, and I presume that it has, that they ought to be represented. . . . Revelation teaches that God is no respecter of persons, . . . that there is neither . . . *bond* nor *free*, but that we are all one in Christ. . . . It is not a question of ignorance or knowledge . . . nor of piety and impiety. The most ignorant white representatives may be received, whether they are very pious or not, but a colored delegate must not be received, however intelligent or pious he may be.

John F. Dagg, editor of the *Christian Index*, approved of receiving black representatives but considered it a question of policy, to be determined by each association. Even the Sunbury Association had a change of heart and in 1857 voted first to reduce the representation of black churches and then to deny black delegates the right of suffrage.[52]

Churches exercised moral discipline over blacks in a manner consistent with their status as children. Because they surrendered their reason to their passions, they required more severe punishment to arouse feelings of shame and fear. But for like reasons, churches were quicker to restore blacks to membership. Blacks applied for restoration at a rate 50 percent higher than whites. The churches denied only 6 percent of their requests, compared to 10 percent of requests from whites. They also granted blacks acquittals at a slightly higher rate than whites.[53]

Churches accused blacks of offenses less frequently than whites, both absolutely and relatively. Although gender rather than race was the best predictor of liability to prosecution—men being five times as likely as women to be accused of crimes, and three times as likely to be excommunicated—race rendered significant predictability. Churches were almost twice as likely to accuse whites as blacks.[54]

In many cases, churches excommunicated white and black defendants with approximate parity. For offenses involving alcohol, speech, or amusements, black defendants suffered excommunication only slightly more often than whites. For sexual offenses and offenses against the church, they received excommunication less frequently than whites. But for two offenses, churches were more severe to black defendants: For violent offenses and offenses against property, black defendants suffered exclusion one and a half times more often. Churches may have viewed theft by slaves as intractable; perhaps they viewed it as a betrayal of the master's trust and paternal care. Slave violence probably brought more frequent excommunication because whites could not avoid seeing in it the specter of slave rebellion and the loss of their divinely ordained social order.[55]

Baptist churches gave themselves little room to maneuver. Adultery was a grave sin regardless of who committed it, and adulterers rarely escaped excommunication. To the extent that churches could take into account mitigating and aggravating circumstances, however, they treated blacks and whites differently, as they did women and men. They saw in each group different natures and different duties—differences that affected the moral texture of unrighteous acts. Caught between their hope for ecclesiastical equality and southern society's commitment to an unequal social order, Baptists felt the pull of both ideals, but they did not permit their ambivalence to impede the exercise of democratic authority.

5

African-American Democracies

Although most Georgia church members in 1860 were white, black Georgians had entered the churches in large numbers in the preceding three decades, by that time constituting between 35 and 40 percent of Baptist church members and 32 percent of Methodist church members. They flowed into the churches at even higher rates in the postwar era. By 1890, Georgia claimed 341,000 black communicants in all its denominations, more than any other state.[1]

In 1870, Georgia Baptists numbered 115,000 in a state population of 1.2 million, with blacks having a 44 percent share among Baptists. In the following decades, Baptist churches proliferated, especially African-American churches. By 1883, black Baptists outnumbered whites 131,216 to 123,851. In 1906, Georgia had 334,000 black Baptists, far more than any other state. By this date, they constituted 59 percent of Georgia's Baptists, and almost one in three African Americans in the state belonged to a Baptist church. Throughout the South, African Americans pitched the largest tent in the Baptist camp.[2]

The popular success did not alter the ideal of democratic religion. The African-American churches claimed a prerogative of command over a wide expanse of individual freedom, and members pledged submission as a condition of membership. They endeavored to prove themselves good Baptists, and this meant attending democratic discipline.

African-American Baptists and Religious Authority

Black Baptist church records are difficult to find. This portrait of African-American religion derives in part from the records of dozens of black Baptist associations throughout the South and from the church books of four African-American churches: Springfield African Baptist Church in Augusta, Georgia; Gillfield African Church in Petersburg, Virginia; and Green Street Baptist Church and Fifth Street Baptist Church, both in Louisville, Kentucky. All four churches were large urban congregations and practiced discipline in similar ways. They were less strict than rural black congregations but stricter than white congregations.[3]

The picture that emerged is clear: African-American Baptists filled the dockets of their ecclesiastical tribunals well into the twentieth century. In the antebellum period, the sample churches prosecuted 4 percent of their members annually, a rate 39 percent higher than the white-controlled churches attained. They excommunicated members at a rate 65 percent higher than the whites, nearly 2.5 percent of members each year. Between 1861 and 1900, when the white churches were relaxing their discipline, the African-American churches maintained most of their rigor. They still prosecuted 3.5 percent and excluded 2.3 percent of their membership annually. Defendants in the black churches received excommunication more frequently than in the white churches. Both before and after the Civil War, black churches excluded more than 60 percent of those accused.

But the independent churches in the sample lagged behind other black Baptist churches in disciplinary zeal. Black Baptists in the South reported to their associations that they excommunicated 3 percent of their members each year between 1861 and 1900, a rate 32 percent higher than the sample churches. Many churches must have prosecuted more than 5 percent of their members annually.[4]

These rates are higher than the rate for black Baptists in the antebellum white churches. The antebellum churches prosecuted just under 2 percent of their black members annually and excluded a little over 1 percent. They were slightly more likely to exclude black defendants than were the African-American churches. Before and after emancipation, black Baptists exercised a discipline fully as rigorous as the discipline of antebellum white Baptists.[5]

Black Baptists, like prewar white Baptists, rejected much of the emerging American individualism. The two groups cherished both the democracy and the disciplinary authority of the community of saints. Both agreed that society should leave individuals free to unite with the church of their choice, but both also agreed that churches had to be free to enforce moral discipline. For both groups, individual freedom encountered harsh limits when it collided with the divinely revealed moral restrictions. They likewise rejected subjectivism in the interpretation of the Bible in that the congregation, not the individual, was the interpretive authority. When individualism and ecclesiastical authority came into conflict, the African-American Baptists, like the white, subordinated individual rights to church authority.

Social Equality and Baptist Segregation

African-American religion took many forms. Historians have sometimes paid insufficient attention to the differences. Black Baptists felt keenly the differences that separated them from black Methodists and Presbyterians. They felt that their spirituality had more in common with the white Baptists than with the black pedobaptist denominations. They shared the white Baptists' vision of democratic religion. But they shared with other black evangelicals the conviction that Christianity entailed the social equality of the races, a conviction that most white evangelicals rejected.

African-American Baptists differed about the relative merits of cooperation or separation from white Baptists, but the contention centered on such joint benevolent endeavors as education, denominational publishing, and missions. Some argued that only independent effort and self-reliance would bring moral advance. Others answered that without white benevolence the efforts would come to nothing. They agreed widely that they must have separate churches.

When white Baptists repudiated the social equality of blacks, they ensured that black Baptists could not share in the governance of their churches. Whites claimed to rejoice in the civil equality granted to former slaves—"we are all free alike, and are all fellow-citizens of the great American Republic, whose constitution guarantees to us all, without distinction, equal rights and equal privileges forever." But the mixing of blacks with whites as social peers, long rejected as poor policy, now became a moral evil.[6]

When southern whites elected Democrats and installed Redeemer governments in place of their Reconstruction oppressors in the 1870s, it was still some time before they enforced segregation of the races. Although informal separation was already in place in churches, hotels, and schools, other areas of life were more integrated. Segregation laws in the South gained impulse from the segregation of public transportation: Nine southern states passed railroad segregation laws between 1887 and 1891. At the same time, southern states began to pass laws designed to prevent blacks from voting. During these years, the specter of interracial violence haunted the South. Southern prisons were filled with black men convicted of property crimes. Newspapers sensationalized black crime and warned blacks to keep their place. Homicide rates among both races were the highest in the world. Violence was part of southern culture, and interracial tension precipitated racial violence.

Lynching symbolized powerfully southern culture's commitment to violence, white supremacy, and racial segregation.[7]

In 1889, E. K. Love, pastor of Savannah First African Baptist Church and president of the national Baptist Foreign Mission Convention, set out with other black Baptists for the convention in Indianapolis as first-class guests of the East Tennessee, Virginia, and Georgia Railroad. Love and his party made it only to Baxley, Georgia, where fifty whites armed with clubs and pistols boarded the train and beat the "well-dressed" delegates and drove them from the train. Black Baptists felt it keenly when white Baptists also kept them at arm's length.[8]

H. H. Tucker, editor of the *Christian Index*, explained the white Baptists' justification for insisting on the social inequality of the races: "It is true that the creation of God made us one, but it is also true that the providence of God has made us two; and what God has put asunder let not man join together. As God has made two races of us, there ought to be two; he would not have made two if one had sufficed. If infinite wisdom has thus decided on plurality, it is our highest wisdom to acquiesce in it. If God himself has drawn the color line, it is vain as well as wicked for us to try to efface it." Whites like Baptist pastor E. B. Teague believed that the tenet of perpetual social inferiority should form no obstacle to good relations between black and white Baptists. The black portion of Teague's Selma, Alabama, church had constituted their own congregation, which met in the church basement. Speaking by invitation to the black church, Teague told them that he had not changed his opinions that they would be "servants in fact to the end of time." Teague boasted that they had later invited him to teach ministerial candidates and assist them in other ways.[9]

White Baptists praised African-American preachers who refused to agitate the question of social equality. They did not trust the piety of preachers who would not accept the "proper place" of blacks. Whites appreciated it when blacks sought out their aid and counsel, in part because they saw the requests as admissions of white superiority. On rare occasions, white churches invited trusted blacks to preach.[10]

Political polarization strengthened the barrier to fellowship. Although the Republican party in the South had some success among upcountry whites, its main strength was among the newly enfranchised blacks. In the 1867 elections, 70 to 90 percent of eligible black voters turned out, and the Republican agenda triumphed in every southern state. Most white southerners found Republican rule galling, for it meant rule by Yankees and blacks. Baptist professor Basil Manly Jr. grieved at leaving his beloved South Carolina for Kentucky, but he said that he longed to exchange "the degradation of this negro government" for white rule.[11]

Postwar blacks became ardent students of civil democracy by forming political organizations and becoming party workers and candidates. Along with free blacks, artisans, and soldiers, ministers assumed a leading role. In 1867, a black Baptist minister named J. W. Toer toured Georgia with his magic lantern slide show depicting the benefits of Republican rule. Baptist preacher Thomas Allen won election to the Georgia legislature, as did numbers of black clergy across the South. When Redeemer Democrats gained control of southern states, the black clergy turned their influence against emerging Jim Crow laws and in support of local prohibition ordinances. With the exception of their agreement about prohibition, black and white Baptists were at odds in the impassioned political struggles of the period.[12]

When the Democratic party triumphed in the 1874 elections, David Butler, editor of the *Christian Index*, clothed the event in religious garb: "The social elevation of the negro by legal enactments could find no argument in his natural inferiority to the white race, but its positive condemnation. It is unnatural, and, therefore, morally wrong. . . . The political victory of this month is a Christian triumph." Such social views made separate church organizations inevitable. The black Baptist minister Garrison Frazier conceded this in 1865 in an interview with Secretary of War Edwin M. Stanton and General William T. Sherman. When asked whether they would prefer to live "scattered among the whites, or in colonies by yourselves," Frazier, with the assent of others, answered that white social opinion necessitated separation: "I would prefer to live by ourselves, for there is a prejudice against us in the South that will take years to get over."[13]

Nor could African-American Baptists accept white pastors. They reckoned that white Christians, especially white preachers, had practiced their religion in hypocrisy. Though they preached against stealing, they upheld a system founded on the theft of human beings. Preachers and church leaders had brutalized slaves often enough to attract notice. Black Baptists preferred to entrust the intimacy of church fellowship, the freedom of worship, the integrity of discipline, and the orthodoxy of preaching to their own race. A. T. Holmes complained that black Baptists "are not willing, as a general thing, that white men shall labor among them as preachers. . . . Even while they were slaves, a negro preacher would gather crowds to hear him, when such men as Drs. Fuller, Poindexter and Winkler, would command, comparatively, small congregations."[14]

Great preachers emerged to lead Georgia's black Baptists. William J. White was pastor of Augusta's Harmony Baptist Church. He was an agent for the Freedman's Bureau and a delegate to the Republican National Convention. He edited the *Georgia Baptist*, which became the state convention's official paper, from 1880 to 1913 and was vice president of Spelman Seminary. E. R. Carter served Atlanta's large Friendship Baptist Church. He stumped for prohibition around the South and helped get Atlanta's 1885 antiliquor law passed. E. K. Love served the "largest church in the United States," Savannah's five-thousand-member First African Baptist Church. He also served as assistant professor, associate editor, and missionary for the American Baptist Home Mission Board and for the American Baptist Publication Society.[15]

Black preachers had staked a claim to authority in black churches that no living white preacher could match: Many had endured suffering at the hands of whites for preaching the gospel. In colonial Savannah, black Baptist Andrew Bryan refused to stop preaching and suffered a public flogging; he said that he rejoiced to be whipped and was willing to die for the cause of Christ. When Bryan's successor, Andrew Marshall, lost favor with white Baptists around 1820 because they suspected him of following Alexander Campbell's teachings, he was publicly whipped under selectively enforced laws. This title to moral authority impressed some white preachers: One white minister praised Willis Warren, a black pastor in the vicinity of Albany, Georgia, saying that "he would go farther to see Willis Warren and hear him preach, than he would to see Spurgeon or any other distinguished preacher . . . because he can say what no Baptist preacher now living can say, that he has been repeatedly whipped for preaching the Gospel and yet held out."[16]

Robert Ryland, white pastor of Richmond's First African Baptist Church for twenty-five years, recognized that although his learning and piety evoked esteem from white Baptists, his two thousand black parishioners preferred a preacher of their own race. Ryland recorded that black preacher Joseph Abrams "was heard with far more interest than I was, and on this account, I should have often requested him to speak, but for fear of involving him and the church in legal trouble. On one occasion he was describing the trials to which early christians were subject, when he said, 'These troubles were not confined to the apostolic age. Even I can say with Paul, "I bear in my body the marks of the Lord Jesus,'"—alluding to a whipping that some wicked men had given him in his early days for preaching the gospel. The effect was thrilling." Under such circumstances, black Baptists rarely sought out white pastors or their preaching.[17]

Whites nevertheless expressed surprise and dismay that blacks so quickly sought independence from the white churches. They still believed that God had given them responsibility for the moral and intellectual development of southern blacks. Emancipation merely imposed new duties: "Has the time come for us to approve and advocate the education of the colored people in our midst?" Several associations answered: "It has." Whites had the "solemn duty" to educate the former slaves "up to a point of intelligence where they can stand alone, and take care of themselves."[18]

After the war, northern denominations spent millions of dollars to provide schools and teachers for southern blacks. Southern denominations later joined this effort but directed most of their educational efforts at restoring the lost endowments of their academies, colleges, and theological schools. The northern Home Mission Board established Atlanta

Baptist Seminary (now Morehouse College) as the Augusta Theological Institute in 1867. The school closed in 1870 because the northern teacher faced local resistance to his egalitarian agenda. White Georgia Baptists revived the school by persuading the northern board to appoint Georgia native Joseph T. Robert as its head. As a southerner, Robert could safely promote black education because he did not advocate black social equality. Individual Georgia Baptists and the Southern Baptist Convention supplied scholarships for students.[19]

The Southern Baptist Convention heard annual reports on the condition of the black population, sought help from northern Baptists, and appointed a number of missionaries, some of them black, to preach among them, build churches, provide basic education, and establish Sunday schools. The Home Mission Board resolved to establish a theological school for black ministers. White and black Georgia Baptists cooperated with the northern board to support four freedmen as missionaries to Georgia blacks.[20]

Georgia Baptists conducted their own institutes for training black ministers. E. W. Warren of Macon First Baptist Church enlisted the aid of other white Baptist leaders in 1869 to conduct a month-long course for black clergy, whose travel expenses and board were paid. The institute continued annually for many years, and the state convention appointed a missionary to conduct similar institutes throughout the state.[21]

Unable to dispel the sense that God had made southern whites the guardians and pedagogues of black southerners, the whites expressed pain and confusion as their spiritual children struck out on their own. One church could not elude feelings of responsibility even after the African-American members had formed a new church. Although the former slaves "are almost entirely unacquainted with the management of Church affairs, they have evinced no disposition to receive enlightened instruction; but on the contrary have seemed disposed to keep themselves in the dark, by shutting off from them those who might lead them aright. . . . Our church hereby advise most affectionately the brethren of our sister Church to whom we feel that we should speak rather as a parent to a child, that if they wish to prosper as a church of Christ, they should seek every means of obtaining light as possible." The churches were unwilling to perform this God-given duty before the war and unable after it.[22]

Some whites made the attempt. They insisted that their African-American spiritual progeny loved them and appreciated their assistance. White pastor J. J. D. Renfroe boasted that the black members of his Alabama church had declined to form their own church and "always crowd the house to hear me preach. . . . Our church, in this place, has attempted to get along with them just as we did before the war, and we have succeeded." P. F. Burgess, for four years the white pastor of Goshen

Colored Baptist Church, praised the good sense of this church to "have always chosen their own preacher, and have never had anyone but a white minister to preach to them." Black Baptists sometimes requested white preachers. White Baptists took such exceptions as vindication.[23]

Former slaves who remained in white churches were proof to whites of the superiority of their religion. When Anderson Battle, an African-American member of a white Baptist church, died in 1897, the church inscribed a memorial in the church book: "Soon after his conversion . . . it appeared to him that there was a difference in the religion of the races and after much prayer and inquiry, being Satisfied his White brethren [had] both the piety and intelligence, he applied to the Bethesda Church for membership and was baptized into her fellowship by Bro J. S. Callaway Oct the 6th 1877. . . . He loved to talk about God and the bible. . . . Brethren let us imitate his example and live for the glory of God. . . . He was often importuned to take his letter and Join the Colored people's Church of his own race, and upbraided much for leaving them, yet he remained faithful to his White brethren." Battle's choice showed that whites were the true friends of black Baptists.[24]

Faced with evidence that African Americans were less than grateful to their former caretakers, southern whites blamed it on northern philanthropists, educators, and missionaries who had filled the minds of former slaves with notions of social equality. The Freedmen's Bureau and northern benevolent societies sent hundreds of agents and missionaries to the South. Many missionaries agreed with the bureau's intention to give the freedmen land in addition to protection and schools. The bureau confiscated 850,000 acres and set out to provide black households with forty-acre tracts. Although President Johnson ended the bureau's land redistribution program—most of the bureau's land went back to its former owners—northern-sponsored social reform made southern whites nervous.[25]

The meddling northerners had made it impossible for blacks to receive assistance from southern whites, who understood them better. Whites were being frustrated in fulfilling their divine duty to enlighten black Christians because

> there has been a labored effort, since the war, to alienate the negro from his former owner. An influence has been at work to array them in opposition to each other, and strong inducements have been presented, urging the negro to persist in his opposition, in the form of mules and forty acre farms. Songs and sermons, lectures and lessons have all been used to convince the negro that the Southern white man is his enemy. . . . Wherever this influence has been exerted most successfully, there have been manifested, most signally, the jealousy, suspicion and hostility of the negro, and there have we witnessed his boldest attempts to assume the position of equality with the white man.

The southern whites believed that "providence has schooled us for two centuries that we may be the better qualified to teach and elevate" the black race. White preachers filled news items with accounts of how they were welcomed into the meetings of black associations and black churches and how the African-American preachers "constantly asked advice and expressed gratitude for assistance rendered."[26]

When requested, white Baptist churches dismissed their black members without objection and assisted them in setting up new churches, but they did not welcome the independent churches. When black members of Athens First Baptist wanted to separate, white pastor F. H. Ivey and a white deacon unsuccessfully tried to persuade them to remain. "The question was discussed in the kindest manner on both sides." The black members voted in favor of separation anyway.[27]

White associations likewise counseled against separation. When churches asked the associations whether it was "advisable for the colored members of our Churches to take letters of dismission and form Churches of their own," the associations answered that "it is lawful, but we do not think it expedient at present in the country." It was not expedient, white Baptists felt, because they had not yet given their black members sufficient training to govern churches according to gospel order. Therefore, Baptist preachers urged that "it would not be best to separate from them in our church relations. At present they are not prepared to set up churches for themselves, and to direct the affairs of the Kingdom."[28]

By 1880, the exodus of African Americans from white churches was largely complete. Black churches formed their own associations and state conventions. Black Baptists in Georgia joined the formation of the National Baptist Convention in Atlanta in 1895. Savannah's E. K. Love was elected president of the national Foreign Mission Baptist Convention, one of the precursors of the National Baptist Convention. But blacks did not seek to alienate themselves from white Baptists. On the contrary, they considered themselves members of the same denominational family as the white Baptists, despite their separate organizations. The question of social equality and the depth of emotion that attended it kept them separate, but separation did not diminish their commitment to the Baptist tradition of democratic religion.[29]

Black Baptists and the Baptist Heritage

African-American Baptists embraced democratic authority in part because they claimed Baptist identity. "Our church has come through trials and persecution in all ages, from the days of Christ till now. For there never was a time since our blessed Lord . . . but that there were men and women practicing and believing just what Baptists are practicing and believing to-day." They hoped to give impulse to "the Baptist chariot, conquering and to conquer, until we shall plant the Baptist church upon every mountain, hill-top and valley, from shore to shore, from pole to pole."[30]

The traditional doctrine of Baptist succession found clear expression in statements of black Baptist leaders. W. H. Tilman, who in 1874 became a missionary of the black Missionary Baptist Convention of Georgia, traced African-American Baptist history through the trail of blood back to John the Baptist: "The Baptist church history, we claim, is written in blood. During all the world's dark ages they were preserved among all the nations and called by all manner of names—heretics in the first two centuries. They mingled with the Messalians, Euchites, Montanists; in the third, fourth and fifth centuries with the Novatians, and Donatists; in the seventh with the Paulicians; in the tenth, the Paterines; in the eleventh century, the Waldenses, Albigensis [*sic*], Henicians [*sic*], and Christians." African Americans now stood in this bloodline, proving that they were worthy of the Baptist name by recounting their own suffering. "All through the winding ages the Baptists have been called to endure keen sacrifice and terrible suffering." Andrew Bryan and Andrew Marshall both suffered for establishing the first African-American Baptist church in Georgia, the first being "whipped until he bled profusely." William J. White, longtime editor of an African-American Baptist weekly, connected black Baptists to this tradition while advising them not to celebrate Easter. "The Baptists are a peculiar and distinct band of God's believing children. They have fought for nearly two thousand years in defense of the teachings of the new testament. . . . The Baptists did not spring from the Catholic [church], and consequently have no part nor lot with Catholic feasts and festivals."[31]

While they identified themselves as heirs to the same Baptist heritage that white Baptists claimed, they put a polite construction on their separation. "Our white brethren do not deny our relation through the blood of our Lord Jesus Christ, but popular sentiment is so much against social equality that our brethren are afraid to allow us religious affiliation for fear that it might be termed social equality." Black Baptists were wounded by the aloof posture of most white clergy. One black pastor gently rebuked his white comrades and insisted upon their unity: "We are sorry to say that while we have been brethren for the last century, the world hasn't been able to discern that brotherly affection which characterizes brethren. . . . Oh, brethren, for 100 years we have been trying to catch you. We really thought sometimes that you were running from us instead of running toward us. . . . You were our brethren in *ante bellum* times, you are our brethren now, and you will be our brethren to-morrow." Many black Baptists sought the advice, assistance, and endorsement of whites because they saw themselves as heirs to the same tradition.[32]

Before emancipation, they embraced the Baptist heritage of Calvinism. Although some historians have posited that black Christians discarded original sin, predestination, and orthodox Calvinism, many black Baptist preachers taught it in their churches. Harry Toulmin, an English

Unitarian minister, praised in 1793 the sermon of a Virginia slave, even "though he introduced the Calvinistical doctrine." George Liele, an African-American Baptist preacher first in Savannah and then in Jamaica, told the English Baptist John Rippon in 1791 that he believed in "election, redemption, the fall of Adam, regeneration, and perseverance." Andrew Marshall, from 1812 to 1856 pastor of the oldest independent black Baptist church, Savannah First African, deemed that his favorite books were the strictly Calvinist commentaries of the English Baptist preacher John Gill. Marshall's preaching pushed Calvinism to the edge of antinomianism. His doctrinal preaching made him all the more popular with his burgeoning Savannah congregation. His preaching impressed geologist Charles Lyell, as it did Presbyterian leader J. L. Kirkpatrick, who was delighted to hear Marshall present "so clear and decided a testimony to the precious though unpopular [Calvinistic] doctrines of Grace."[33]

John E. Dawson, white pastor of the Baptist church in LaGrange, Georgia, attracted the criticism of a slave preacher during the 1840s for not preaching predestination more often. Dawson's sister, bemused that an uneducated slave would criticize her brother's theology, described the encounter between the two men: "He was accosted on the street by a colored brother, who enjoyed some popularity as a preacher. Though altogether illiterate, he thought well of himself. . . . Said he, 'Bro. Dawson, why don't you preach more about Election?' 'Because, Bro. Giles,' replied my brother, 'I know so little about it.' 'O, Brother Dawson, I'm astonished to hear a smart man like you talk so; why I understands it just as well, and I have great freedom in preaching it to my people.' Introducing a companion who had accompanied him, he said: 'Why, I have brought this Methodist brother along to get you to convince him.'" Rebutting the charge of Arminianism, Dawson professed firm belief in the "sovereign, electing, love of God," claiming, "I have never discussed these high themes much, because I have not understood them, and I do not like to meddle with questions too high for me."[34]

After emancipation, the African-American churches retained much of the heritage. Charles O. Boothe, pastor of Dexter Avenue Baptist Church in Montgomery, Alabama, promoted Calvinism in the only black Baptist theology text published during this period. His 1890 *Plain Theology for Plain People* asserted that "before the foundation of this world" God unalterably "chose certain persons." He counseled reverence before the mystery of predestination and reprobation: "If we ask why they were chosen and others left, we find that no answer has been given by him who alone can explain his reasons."[35]

The African-American associations enshrined Baptist Calvinism in their creeds. In Georgia alone, at least fourteen hyper-Calvinist Primitive Baptist associations arose. However, the black missionary associations were just as committed to the doctrines of limited atonement and unconditional election as the black Primitives. When black Baptists in Mississippi met at their Baptist Missionary Convention in 1870, they adopted a confession asserting that "all who share in the saving benefits of his atonement were chosen in Christ before the foundation of the world."[36]

In many instances, the black churches and associations adopted the same Calvinist "Articles of Faith" that the white churches had adopted. Black Baptists demonstrated their sense of identity as Baptists when they invited white ministers to help them form new churches or associations. Whites joined them in examining letters of dismission, articles of faith, and views on church government, and blacks and whites together extended "the right hand of fellowship" to the new churches. Black Baptist associations received the new churches only after they were "examined by us and found orthodox."[37]

Confessions of faith in black associations were Calvinist. Among the African-American Baptist associations in Georgia, the confession adopted most commonly gave full expression to the doctrines of grace.

> ART. III We believe in the fall of Adam and the imputation of his sin to posterity, in the corruption of human nature, and in the impotency of man to recover himself from his lost estate. . . .
>
> ART. IV We believe in the everlasting love of God to his people in eternal and particular election of a definite number of the human race to grace and glory and that before the world began there was a covenant made between the Father and the Son in which the salvation of the redeemed is made secure.

The second most common pattern of confession was more concise but just as Calvinist, asserting original sin, "the impotency of man to recover himself of his own free will and ability," and election, that "those who were chosen in Christ will be effectually called, regenerated, . . . so that not one of them will be finally lost." Even the most elliptical confessions, such as that of the Zion Baptist Association, confessed "the doctrine of human depravity" and "election to eternal life."[38]

Black Baptist preachers had to show their orthodoxy to be ordained. White ministers, whom black churches frequently invited to ordain black ministers, rejected candidates who rejected Calvinism. They never hesitated to reject unworthy candidates, white or black, and Arminianism was grounds not only for rejection but also for disfellowshiping. Baptist associations refused to ordain any candidates who did not "believe it to be expedient to preach and contend for the doctrine of predestination and election."[39]

Prerequisite to ordination was a public two-hour examination on candidates' conversion, call to the ministry, theology, and views on church government. As late as 1892, a white presbytery (as they called such a group of Baptist ministers) might require an ordination candidate to elucidate "his doctrinal views on Inspiration, the Trinity, Total Depravity, Divinity and humanity of Christ, the work of the Holy Spirit in Regeneration, the Atonement, Salvation by Grace, Justification through Faith, Foreknowledge and purpose of God, Predestination, Final Perseverance of the Saints, Baptism, . . . the Lord's Supper, . . . the Church, . . . and Associations, Conventions, Societies, etc."[40]

They did not relax their standards for black candidates. Both before and after the war, black candidates underwent careful scrutiny. A white presbytery omitted nothing when examining "Bro Milton the Colored Preacher" in 1855: "The Presbytery being perfectly Satisfied as to his call and to his knowledge of all the doctrinal points believed and practised by the Baptist denomination it was unanimously agreed that Milton should be Ordained." When a white presbytery ordained a former slave in 1868, one member commented that "Brother Bell stood his examination well, and was considered unusually sound in the faith."[41]

African-American Baptists demonstrated a similar rigor in their ordination examinations. They showed no hesitation to reject candidates, and their councils required evidence of sound doctrine and morals. One ordination council reported that they had "Examined Bro. A. Cooper and have not found him the proper Subject for ordination." The church requested an explanation. The council replied that "they found Bro. Cooper Deficiant interlectualy and moraly."[42]

To secure ordination, candidates appearing before African-American presbyteries had to give "perfect satisfaction to both council and church as regards his Christian experience, call to the ministry and soundness in doctrine." A presbytery of four black ministers examined one candidate on his conversion, his call to the ministry, and his doctrine:

> The Rev. E. P. Johnson and the pastor, D. C. Bracy, were called on to examine the applicant on christian doctrine. As everybody knows that the Rev. E. P. Johnson is one of the deep thinking men of the race, when he and his partner Bracy got through with the applicant, he (F. B. Jordan) was found with a straw in his mouth chewing on it as if he was mad with it; the Chairman told him to take the straw out of his mouth, so he did but it was not long before the Chairman had to give him another straw for the straw was helping him, so he said. This Bro. Jordan was glad when Rev. Johnson turned him back over to the Chairman. Then Rev. D. S. Klugh of your city [Augusta] examined him on church government. All who know Rev. Klugh know that he is quite a deep thinker and when he got through with him the straw was lost and the applicant almost speechless with eyes leaking tears and deep sorrow on his face.

Jordan managed to satisfy the council, which recommended his ordination. Such councils—often consisting of black and white ministers—maintained both Baptist identity and Calvinist orthodoxy.[43]

The African-American churches did not nurture the Calvinist heritage; it weakened from the neglect. Black Baptists did not reject the concepts of total depravity and election to grace but occupied themselves with a more pressing concern: the race issue. Baptist piety entailed ameliorating the social distress. Their sermons, newspapers, and association meetings addressed the question of how to accomplish both Baptist advance and racial uplift. Associations purposed "the better advancement of the cause of Christ, and unwavering fidelity to the colored race." They sought to educate their children for "the advancement of the Baptist cause and the betterment of our people generally."[44]

Looking to the past, T. J. Hornsby averred that white Baptists before the war "believed and preached the same doctrine that they embrace, believe and preach to-day" and that "the colored Baptists embraced, believed and preached the same, yea, the very same." Blacks sometimes claimed to be even more orthodox than whites: "There is one thing you'll not find among the negro Baptists that is found among the white Baptists. Among the negroes there are very few Free Will Baptists and open communionists." African Americans were true Baptists who maintained the exclusivist vision of the church. The question was whether white Baptists would own the fact. Black Baptists were grieved that, although the whites recognized them "as brethren, for we are one in doctrine and church ordinances," they did not treat them as brethren. When they visited white associations, they received "back seats as usual." They could conclude only that what separated them was the insistence of whites on social inequality, for they had not wavered from orthodoxy.[45]

Democratic Authority and Voluntary Submission

They remained firm also in their exercise of discipline. Black Baptists continued to support a democratic church in which the members subordinated their individual rights to the moral authority of the saints. They constituted themselves churches in traditional fashion with church covenants and articles of faith. Augusta's Springfield Baptist Church periodically read publicly its church covenant, which so clearly expressed the duty of members to submit that clerks sometimes called it "the discipline." The pastor at Springfield made known to new members "the Rules of the church." When converts joined, they entered a covenant of authority.[46]

Black associations adopted statements of "Gospel Order" that described the desired submission: The church was "a congregation of faithful persons who gained christian fellowship with each other and have agreed to keep up a godly discipline agreeable to the rules of the gospel." The discipline was necessary for "the purity of the church and for the reclaiming of those members who may be disorderly, either in principle or practice, and should be kept up for the glory of God."[47]

Before the Civil War, black churches and the semiautonomous black congregations within white churches appointed a few men, often the deacons, to oversee the flock. Their function was moral oversight. They had responsibility for all phases of discipline: making accusations, investigating charges, and laboring with offenders. After the war, they continued the same practice.[48]

The churches continued to require straying members to confess sin and express submission. Even when the church forgave, it asserted its authority by condemning the sin and rebuking the offender. When Springfield Baptist Church charged sister A. L. Butts with dancing, "she came forward and acknoledge her Guilt and ask the forgiveness of the church. She was Received With a charge from the chair to go and Do So no Moore." When Randall Culbreth confessed to fighting and sought pardon of the church, "his act was condemned and he was Rebuked by the Pastor and told to go and do so no Moore." Expelled members seeking readmission had to vindicate the church, as when William Jones, excluded for blasphemy, "came forward [and] acknoledge that the church did him Right by Excluding him."[49]

Members who refused to accept this authority had to leave. William Anderson confessed to drunkenness, but before his case could be decided he "vacated his Seet" and left the church conference. The conference charged him "with contempt to the church" and excluded him. Later restored to membership, he almost repeated his mistake when he voted against excluding a member charged with blasphemy. "Bro. William Anderson refusing to vote with the church was called forward to know his objections for so doing. After hearing from and Showing him his rongness for So doing, he ask the pardon of the church."[50]

In the winter of 1898, one deacon at Springfield Baptist Church tired of the distasteful diaconal duty of managing discipline. "Dea. John Hughs was reported to the church for refusing to report or look after the case of Bro. S. Harris who was reported to him." When Hughs appeared before the church the next month, he defended his course, saying that "he was not going to hunt up Sin." The church argued at some length to show Hughs the error of his position. Failing to persuade him, they removed him from the office of deacon. In the end, however, he begged the church to forgive him for not discharging his duty, and the church restored him.[51]

Black discipline did not vary much from white discipline. Blacks adopted the same standard of sexual morality: fornication was as bad as adultery. The antebellum white-controlled churches tried black members for sexual offenses at an annual rate of sixty trials per ten thousand black members. The antebellum independent black churches prosecuted sexual offenses at the higher rate of eighty trials per ten thousand members. They also excommunicated 95 percent of their members accused of sexual offenses, compared with the 83 percent rate at which antebellum white-controlled churches excluded blacks accused of the same offenses. As a result, they excluded their members for sexual immorality at an annual rate of seventy-six per ten thousand members and surpassed the rate at which the antebellum white-controlled churches excluded black members for the same sins by 50 percent. The black churches maintained virtually identical rates from 1861 to 1900.[52]

African-American Baptist churches also did not tolerate such offenses against the church as absence, contempt, heresy, or joining other denominations. Members who took letters of dismission but did not join another Baptist church risked excommunication if they did not repent, for joining other denominations was a betrayal of sound doctrine. Springfield Baptist Church disapproved, for example, of the holiness doctrine that believers could attain perfection, or entire sanctification, in this world. Deacon Scott raised the question "if it was Right for our members to unite with a party of people who clame to be Sanctyfide, and it was decided it was not Right. . . . Any of our members who unite with them or any other church without the knoledge of this church be Reported for Such and be Dealt with by the church." Springfield surpassed antebellum white-controlled churches in the trial rate of members for offenses against the church.[53]

Although the African-American churches were milder than the antebellum white-controlled churches in cases of crimes against property, they refused to countenance such offenses. The white churches often charged slave members with stealing the produce of the field or barn. The antebellum independent black churches accused members of crimes against property at less than half the rate of the white churches. After emancipation, the rate fell even more. In the antebellum period, the independent black churches expelled the accused as often as the white-controlled churches; after emancipation, they treated the guilty with more sympathy, excommunicating accused thieves half the time, whereas the prewar white-controlled churches excluded blacks accused of theft three-fourths of the time.[54]

African-American Baptists did not make peace with "worldly amusements." They accounted as offenders members who danced, fiddled, played cards, cast dice, or played billiards, as well as those who attended the circus, theater, or opera. It was as true after the Civil War as it had been before: "When I jined de church, I quit dancin'." In cases involving amusements, the antebellum independent black churches prosecuted their members at a rate two and a half times greater than the rate at which the antebellum white-controlled churches prosecuted black members. After emancipation, the white churches grew more tolerant of dancers, but the black churches tightened the reins. They tripled the rate at which they brought dancers to trial and excluded the accused twice as often. In 1887, the Springfield church passed a resolution to treat dancing and attendance at balls as grave or "speedy offenses," which, like adultery, required excommunication. Some members felt that amusements did not merit the same penalty as adultery, and they presented in 1901 a resolution to remove from the list of speedy offenses such amusements as attending the circus and the opera. Although the resolution eventually passed—after prolonged debate—the church continued to exclude circusgoers and opera patrons in the same speedy fashion as adulterers.[55]

After emancipation, black Baptists expressed ideas and practices strikingly similar to those of antebellum white Baptists. Slave religion was far more than a form of social resistance. Black Baptists rejected slavery and the doctrine of racial inferiority, but in ecclesiology and theology they shared a broad consensus with white Baptists. They ordered their churches according to the Baptist ideal of democratic religion.

6

Freedom, Authority, and Doctrine

Baptist discipline manifested fidelity to the evangelical exclusivist temperament, especially to its insistence on a church separate from the world and established in purity. Manifesting the same commitment to exclusivism in their approach to theological truth, Baptists turned to ecclesiastical authority to ensure pure belief as well as pure deportment. They strove to repel the onslaught of modern ideas by means of church discipline. Erroneous beliefs merited exclusion from the church, and Baptist covenants linked church discipline to sound belief. They pledged to exert "a Godly Discipline" against any departure from "the Faith, once delivered to the Saints."[1]

Popular Theology

God required churches to maintain orthodox dogma, southern Baptists believed. The church's duty was to proclaim the gospel of Jesus Christ in the expectation of the supernatural regeneration and salvation of lost souls, and this evangelistic purpose required doctrinal purity. Without orthodoxy, churches could neither sustain their evangelistic mission nor properly retain the name "church of Christ." Baptists saw orthodoxy as the foundation of morality in that right belief results in right behavior. They were to be patient with people, but not with error, which led to immorality and damnation: "No error is small; all error is great. No truth is insignificant; all truth is important. The antagonism between truth and error is eternal; to take sides is both a duty and a necessity. To side with right is peace, joy, and triumph; while the opposite is wretchedness, disgrace and everlasting defeat."[2]

Error had such dire consequences, said Alabama Baptist editor Samuel Henderson, because "character is the outgrowth of principle." Comparing them to New York's liberal Henry Ward Beecher, Henderson castigated preachers who sought "to Beecherize the pulpit" and who denigrated "those old doctrines of grace" because people might be repelled by Calvinism's harshness. Such an approach, Henderson concluded, might attract crowds but could not produce moral lives. "What good will numbers do us without piety? Is that progress that multiplies our membership and dwarfs our godliness?" At bottom, argued one preacher, it was sound doctrine that preserved virtue. "Loose doctrine leads to loose discipline, and loose discipline invariably results in loose practice." A variety of false doctrines, wrote Samuel S. Law, "would overturn the very foundations of our hope, or destroy all practical godliness." Jesse Mercer viewed "a right apprehension" of fundamental doctrines as "essential to Christian character." Orthodoxy, southern Baptists widely believed, was the foundation of morality.[3]

Baptist leaders claimed that salvation itself depended upon correct theology. When he read the claim that "the best preaching has nothing to do with doctrines, for doctrines, after all, are of no importance," David E. Butler, editor of the *Christian Index*, replied that "doctrinal sermons are usually good. The best preaching has most to do with doctrines, for doctrines, after all, are the grand essentials to the soul's salvation." There is "nothing," wrote J. H. Harris, "better than orthodoxy."[4]

Jesse Mercer once sought to persuade subscribers that his *Christian Index* was worth the subscription price by reassuring them that its editor "is rather of the Old, than of the new school; and inclines to the old fashioned doctrine of free grace, as preached among the Baptists, near half a century ago." He endorsed the "calvinistic writers" of the former generation, "Gill, Owen, Brown, Toplady, and Hervy," who taught that "the Atonement is special, both in its provisions and applications." Mercer's list conveyed immovable orthodoxy. Puritan Congregationalist John Owen (1616–1683) wrote extensively on the main themes of high Calvinism. Separatist Congregationalist Robert Browne (d. 1633) taught the duty of establishing true Reformed churches apart from the Church of England. Episcopal priest and hymn writer Augustus Toplady (1740–1778) was a great admirer of John Gill's exposition of Calvinism. Gill, pastor of Horsley Down Baptist Church in London from 1720 until his death in 1771, elaborated a stiff version of Calvinism in his commentaries and *Body of Divinity*. Gill's works had wide influence among Baptists, though his reputation suffered when antimissionary

Baptists claimed him as their inspiration. Georgia Baptists studied his writings, and Mercer sold sets of Gill's commentaries to all who could afford the $35 price. Although Mercer pledged to avoid quibbling controversies, he also pledged to uphold doctrine.[5]

Not only ministerial candidates but also deacons submitted to a test of orthodoxy. After Bethesda Baptist Church members elected their choice for deacon, minister Enoch Callaway "examined brother Watts on the principles of his faith." Countless other ministers examined countless other deacons. Well into the nineteenth century, candidates for the office of deacon "were brought before the presbytery, . . . gave satisfactory answers to all questions asked, . . . being found orthodox in all points." Only then were they installed.[6]

Baptists tended to equate preaching with proclaiming orthodox dogma. When anyone sought permission from the church to exercise spiritual gifts in public ministry, churches "liberated" or "licensed" all who satisfied the church that their gifts were genuine. But they distinguished preaching from other offices: Some could lead prayer and singing, others exhort, but only a few could preach. When someone in the church charged slave member Ben Bugg with "preaching contrary to the Laws of the State & without permission from the church," the church accepted his plea that he had "never exercised further than prayer meeting & exhortation." Preaching was something else. It was not merely "exhortation"; it was "exercise in . . . Doctrine."[7]

Preaching was subject to the theological judgment of the church. Two slave members asked Phillips Mill Baptist Church for permission to "exercise their gift in Doctrin," but when the church heard them teach, "it was thought best only to liberate them to Sing and pray in public." The laity had a high interest in doctrinal questions. Most churches read their church covenants, including their confessions of faith, four times a year. The ceremonies familiarized members with the doctrines and occasionally created debate. After the covenant was read in Powelton Baptist Church, "an objection was started [stated?] by some of the Brethren, to that part that denies the ability of natural men to perform actions that are morally Good." The church discussed the matter at two conferences before dismissing the objection as "groundless." On similar occasions, the men and women of Powelton Baptist Church "spent sometime in discussing a portion of the covenant" or "freely discussed" their church covenant.[8]

Differences over doctrine led to schisms. Powelton Baptist Church divided when four members walked out and formed their own church in 1791. They were disgruntled that the church had not charged other members with heresy for believing Andrew Fuller's general provision approach to the doctrine of the atonement. An English Baptist, Fuller (1754–1815) admired the evangelical Calvinism of Jonathan Edwards and deeply influenced Baptist missionary William Carey. His *Gospel*

Worthy of All Acceptation urged the obligation to evangelize the lost. Hyper-Calvinists thought him an Arminian because he argued that Christ's death was for all in its provision, but for the elect only in its intention and application. He was popular among southern Baptists because, in addition to upholding the doctrine of particular election, he insisted on church discipline and evangelistic preaching.

The four Calvinist stalwarts at Powelton were angry that the church tolerated this modification of Calvinist particular redemption. The church saw the matter differently. Pastor Silas Mercer asked whether the church should "excommunicate a member, for holding what is called a general provision?" The majority thought not. The church expelled the four separated members for creating a schism.[9]

The disagreement revealed the extent to which ordinary church members were interested in intricate points of doctrine. It also revealed the extent to which Baptist laypeople were willing to break fellowship over doctrine. They were willing to divide not merely over doctrine but also over a disagreement about whether certain doctrines were heretical. Most members of Powelton probably were not general provisionists; they did not embrace Fuller's view of the atonement but merely declined to call it heresy. This was no policy of tolerance; Powelton Baptist Church excluded members who embraced Universalism, Deism, and General Baptist or Arminian principles. Like other Baptists, they excluded anyone whose beliefs departed significantly from the Baptist system of Calvinist doctrine.[10]

Southern Baptists learned from Fuller's biographers that the members of his church argued for many months over "the abstract question of the power of sinful men to do the will of God, and to keep themselves from sin." And they exhibited the same interest in theological precision. Long Run Church in Kentucky divided in 1804 when they disagreed about theology: "Suppose a man has five children. The Indians come and kill four of them, the fifth one being hidden near by. The savages then ask the father if he has another child. Would he be justifiable in telling them that he had not?" After impassioned debate, the "lying party" withdrew and formed their own church. The Arminian delegates to a joint meeting of Virginia Separate Baptists in 1775 walked out because the association concluded with a Calvinist response an all-day debate over the question of whether Christ made salvation possible for every individual. Virginia's Broad Run Baptist Church excommunicated Nathan Matthew for, among other things, rejecting Calvinism—"cavilling at the doctrines of grace."[11]

Baptists championed the rights of conscience and private judgment in the interpretation of scripture, but people had these rights, they believed, as citizens of the state, not as members of the churches. The state had no right to inflict civil or criminal penalties for religious opinions, but churches had every right to inflict spiritual penalties for erroneous beliefs. The authority to censure members for wrong doctrine was a matter of both freedom and unity. Churches could not fulfill their evangelistic commission unless united in doctrine and morals, but they could establish this unity only if they could exclude anyone who disrupted it by teaching error. Samuel Law explained it in a circular letter: "To deny the right of a Church to take cognizance of the religious Sentiments of its Members, would be to sacrifice the liberty of the Society to the licentiousness of the Individual; and [it would be] to say, no Body of Christians have any right to determine, that they will unite with those only, who are nearly agreed in their religious sentiments. . . . For two cannot walk comfortably together except they be agreed; nor can a Christian Society flourish, where important truth is sacrificed to worldly policy, under the specious name of candor and liberality." Baptists submitted both their behavior and their beliefs to the authority of the congregation.[12]

Democratic Exclusiveness

Baptists saw their unity as evidence that they followed the apostolic pattern. They were a mob, a rope of sand consisting of autonomous local churches, but they agreed on most theological and practical issues. They accorded their common beliefs and practices a presumption of orthodoxy and settled disputed points by appeal to "the common usage of the churches." The unity did not come easily. For their unity to serve as a badge of the apostolic tradition, the churches had to restrain innovations through oversight of their members. They responded quickly to any rumor of departures from Baptist doctrine and usage. The quest for unity required discipline.[13]

Jesse Mercer argued that Christian unity consisted of conformity in theology and ethics. It required "a oneness of sentiment in relation to things spiritual and divine." It did not require perfect unanimity, but Mercer insisted on agreement about "the character and law of God; the nature of sin and the corruption of the heart; salvation by grace, justification, and cleansing by the righteousness and blood of Christ." Unity entailed a union of affections among Christians who loved the truth and loathed error. It also required "agreement in purpose and aim," a desire for God's glory, for holiness, for future reward, and for the salvation of sinners. But it was agreement on doctrine that concerned Baptists most, for they considered theological unity their foundation.[14]

They deplored the strife that plagued southern churches, but they deplored aberrant theology more than strife. "Peace is valuable for its own sake," they held, but "a Christian should ever prefer truth to it." Not every union was Christian union: "Union at the expense of truth and principle, we regard as unchristian, and a greater calamity than even disunion."[15]

Viewing church government as a department of revealed theology, they regarded some differences of church polity as worse than division. The practice of infant baptism, for example, they saw as the root of fundamental errors, for it contradicted the doctrine of the regenerate church. Because sprinkling (unlike immersion) was no baptism at all, moreover, Baptists looked at pedobaptist churches as filled with unbaptized people.

For this reason, Baptists held two doctrines that made them odious to other evangelical Protestants: close communion and the invalidity of alien immersion. *Close communion* meant that Baptists could not join in communion with pedobaptist churches or allow other churches' members to take communion in Baptist churches. Because baptism was prerequisite to communion and pedobaptist churches had no baptism, their members could not properly receive communion. *Alien immersion* meant that even the immersion of believers by pedobaptist ministers was no baptism because pedobaptists erred about baptism. As late as the 1890s, Southern Baptist leaders viewed rejection of these doctrines as grounds for nonfellowship. I. R. Branham, editor of the *Christian Index*, argued against admitting open communionists into the church.[16]

Other denominations scorned them for their exclusivist teachings: "Perhaps nine-tenths of our Pedo-baptist friends," said editor J. C. McMichael, "think and speak of our so-called 'close communion' as an unquestionable evidence of Baptist prejudice and bigotry." A Methodist lay member claimed that in practice Baptist churches had a simple constitution: "Art. I.—Baptism by immersion. Art. II.—Close communion. By Laws—1. Be very bigoted. 2. Be very exclusive." David Butler spoke for many Baptists when he reflected on the fact that many persons considered Baptists to be uncharitable and illiberal: "Is it bigotry to maintain the truth?"[17]

Exclusiveness in doctrine was unpopular, Baptists said, but "in the hands of the apostles, Christianity was intensely exclusive." As church union and dogma-free cooperation became the Protestant mottos of the Gilded Age and the Progressive Era, Baptists were inclined more and more "to call attention to the exclusiveness of Christianity." While they did not insist on unanimity as a condition of fellowship, they staked out a large territory of required agreement. Without "making every difference of sentiment a ground of non-fellowship," they still believed that "on fundamental principles, agreement is necessary to fellowship." Baptists defended their exclusivism with the Old Testament sentiment that "two cannot walk together except they agree."[18]

Late in the nineteenth century, when many American Protestants rallied for "Christian union," Southern Baptists adhered to their doctrinal exclusivism. A nondoctrinaire union of churches, H. H. Tucker pointed out, required every group to sacrifice its creed, "and thus a union is formed of men, every one of whom has deserted his colors." When advocates of church union said that doctrine should not keep Christians apart, Tucker retorted that "they forget that dogma is all that can possibly keep them together."[19]

Heresy

Functionally, Baptists defined *heresy* as any belief incompatible with membership in a Baptist church. Samuel Boykin, editor of the *Christian Index*, defined it as "a departure in some essential particular, either from the doctrine of Christ or from the practice he enjoined." The term covered a wide field from atheism to the doctrines of Free Will Baptists. Baptists felt some ambivalence regarding their posture toward Presbyterians, Methodists, and other varieties of Baptists; they were sometimes reluctant to call their errors "heresy." Beyond the circle of traditional Protestantism, however, they felt no such ambivalence. They expelled members for Deism, Roman Catholicism, Christian Science, Mormonism, Spiritualism, and Swedenborgianism.[20]

Deists, who denied miracles and supernatural revelation, did not long remain in Baptist churches. Samuel Parr held "Deistical Principles." John Zachary did also and spoke "reproachfully of revealed religion." Brother Starr said he "did not believe the Scriptures to be the Word of God, and that, if in his power, he would destroy the Bible." Their fellow Baptists excommunicated all of them and anyone who agreed with them. Universalists, who believed that all persons would in the end be saved, met the same fate.[21]

They also expelled careless Calvinists who rejected any major article of the Calvinist creed. Phillips Mill Baptist Church "agreed not to Commune with any person Who Does not believe In the final perseverance of the Saints in Grace." Powelton refused to retain fellowship with anyone who believed that "a real Christian may loose his Christianity and finally fall from Grace." The same church withdrew fellowship from Milly Lord and Nancy Thompson for betraying Arminian convictions when they "joined the General Baptists."[22]

Southern Baptists excluded persons for a wide variety of false beliefs. Penfield excluded J. L. Tarwater for "having denied the divine mission of our Saviour Jesus Christ." Newnan accused H. F. Smith of denying the resurrection of the dead; only his assurances to the contrary spared him from exclusion. Atlanta Second Baptist revoked the license of preacher W. B. Smith for believing that "the impenitent dead were annihilated." In the early 1880s, Greensboro excluded four persons for adopting a "creed inconsistent with the existence of the Baptist church" and for "false views in relation to doctrine as well as church organization."[23]

In 1860, Penfield Baptist Church appointed a committee to investigate a report "in regard to certain fundamental changes in the religious views of Br. Thos. D. Martin," former editor of the *Christian Index*. Although Martin first rebuffed the committee as "inquisitorial," he finally confessed that he had adopted the teachings of Emanuel Swedenborg. The committee summarized his heresies:

> After some delay and reluctantly he professed now to disbelieve the following doctrines which he formerly entertained, and which this Church holds: The doctrine of three persons in the Godhead, called the Trinity, of the general resurrection, of election, of salvation through the imputed righteousness of Christ, and faith in his name; . . . and does not hesitate to teach, that there is an intermediate state called Purgatory, that *all* men will eventually be saved, whether they have, or have not, the Gospel, and that the lost Spirits in Hell, and even the Devil himself, after suffering adequately in penal fires, will be developed from the germ of good that remains undestroyed, into perfect and holy beings, and will then be transferred to Heaven.

Although the church endorsed him as "a high-minded and strictly honorable gentleman," they excluded him because "the promulgation of such doctrines, called the Swedenborgian faith, in general, would be injurious to the cause of religion, [and] that it would be wicked in us as a Church to endorse any one who entertains them." The church found the punishment painful but believed it to be God's will that they preserve doctrinal purity.[24]

Defecting to the Denominations

Although other evangelical denominations in the South practiced doctrinal discipline, Baptists made it a badge of honor. They distinguished themselves partly by their strictness and partly by their tendency to see Arminianism as an error that endangered the salvation of church members. The practice that caught the eye of other denominations, however, was the Baptist custom of expelling members who wanted to join non-Baptist churches.

There were only two ways to get out of the Baptist church: excommunication and death. The Hightower Association tried to prevent churches from merely "erasing" or "dropping" names from membership rolls; it ruled that "a member cannot disconnect himself from the Church of Christ in any other way than, 1st, by death, or 2nd, by regular expulsion, under a charge, and the vote of the church." Adiel Sherwood expressed the consensus: Exclusion is "the only door out of the Church."[25]

Baptists believed that to belong to any group defined by its beliefs, one had to accept those beliefs. When Christians changed their theological views, they therefore often sought to change their church relations. This included Baptists, who sometimes joined other denominations because they changed their minds about Baptist doctrine. A. B.

Corley changed his mind in 1842 and decided to join the Methodists; the Newnan Baptist Church had no option but to expel him because "he did not believe in the Baptist faith." Phillips Mill Baptist Church likewise excluded Patsy Moore for declaring "a nonfellowship with doctrines held by this Church."[26]

Other members withdrew without joining other denominations—merely because they now disagreed with Baptist doctrine. In 1873, Richard Webb, a minister, requested that Savannah Baptist Church drop his name from the roll because he had experienced "a change of mind on the communion question." He had accepted open communion, rejecting the belief that pedobaptist denominations could not share in Baptist communion observances. This theological fastidiousness accorded with the advice of the Hightower Association that churches should admit no one "who has avowed open communion sentiments." The topic of communion was one of several that drove ministers and laity from the denomination. Some could simply no longer "subscribe to the faith of this church."[27]

The churches agreed that differences in belief constituted grounds for separation. The Chattahoochee Association announced in 1826 that it was not "good order for a church to hold members in fellowship who do protest against the principles & faith she was constituted upon. . . . When all the proper means have been used or made use of & fail such an one should be proceeded against as an offender." The Ebenezer Association advised churches not to grant letters of dismission to members who denied "part of the articles of faith on which said Church was constituted."[28]

In 1842, William Moore requested that "his name should be erased" from the church book: "I do not beleive [*sic*] as you do." The church appointed a committee to convince him of his errors. Having failed, it could not agree to erase his name—this would form an unscriptural third way out of the church—and excommunicated him. When Moore returned two years later desiring readmission, the church still showed no disposition to tolerate his theological disagreement. It would receive him back only "by Recantation."[29]

Just as some members thought it disingenuous to remain in a church if they disagreed with its doctrine, so some felt it deceitful to stay if they did not feel truly converted. Several requested to have their names removed because they did not believe they were Christians, had "never been born again of the Spirit," or had "never experienced religion": Pope Mangum told the Savannah Baptist Church that he had joined "under an excitement and did not feel that he could continue a member without practicing hypocrisy." Baptists believed that churches should have no unconverted members; the doctrine of regeneration by the Spirit shaped their doctrine of the church. They thought that they alone practiced this truth, for they alone required a narrative of conversion before all baptisms. Members who felt unregenerate withdrew because Baptist doctrine seemed to require it. But the churches did not allow them merely to withdraw: It was not "according to Gospel order to arrace [erase] a Members name." They rather expelled them for "renunciation of the faith."[30]

The most common reason for leaving was love: woe to the Baptist who married an outsider. Recently married women suffered exclusion if they joined a church of another denomination, though they often returned when their husbands died. Eliza Gilbert assured her former church that despite her recent Methodism she had "always been a baptist at heart."[31]

Others left because they disliked Baptist discipline or became dissatisfied with Baptist worship. Sarah Sargent left when her church refused to buy an organ. Although some found the church unrefined, others found it too refined. When Savannah Baptist Church asked Emiline McClean why she had joined the Methodists, she answered that "she was made Sport of by some of the Members of the [Baptist] Church, and She presumed for no other cause than that they were finer dressed than what she was."[32]

When members joined other denominations, their churches tried to convince them of their error, for to leave a Baptist church was to leave the faith. Savannah excluded Rebecca Stilwell in 1833 because "she had positively attached herself to a body who professed the Doctrine of Alex. Campbell which we believe to be Herrisy." Campbell's group held that faith was intellectual assent and that baptism regenerated the soul. When Elza Cameron asked LaGrange Baptist Church for a letter of dismission because she was joining the Presbyterians, the church excommunicated her and ordered the pastor and clerk to explain why: "the principal [*sic*] upon which Baptist Churches are organized as a reason why her request can not [be] granted & Express to her our entire confidence in her as a christian." The expulsion of members who joined other denominations did not consign them to hell; error did not automatically entail damnation. Some errors, after all, were worse than others. But Baptists had to maintain a church pure in doctrine, so they could not endorse the errors of other denominations. They had to censure members who turned away from orthodoxy toward the corrupted creeds of other communions.[33]

They justified the censures by recalling their duty to oppose error. Newnan Baptist Church recorded a spate of such cases. It charged Mary Jane Swint with "having departed from the Faith of the Gospel and the Scripture rule laid down for the government of the Church by Christ and the Apostles by attaching herself to the Methodist Society." It excluded Sarah Skeen for "having united herself to the Methodist organization, and by that act having as we believe departed from the faith of the Gospel." It excluded Sarah Sargent for "having joined the

Presbyterians and thereby subscribing to doctrines unsound and unscriptural." It expelled Elizabeth Rainey for having "united herself to the Presbyterians and thereby having embraced fundamental errors in religion."[34]

Some Baptists charged defectors with heresy, though others disliked this use of the term. There were murmurs even within the Newnan Baptist Church. In 1854, shortly after the church had expelled Moses Westbrook for joining the Methodists, Jonathan Wood requested dismissal. He explained that he harbored "dissatisfaction with the action of this Church in excommunicating Moses Westbrook for *heresy*[,] stating [that] this Church had made a charge that it could not establish." But he failed to gain any support for his position. Baptists had a suspicion of arguments for tolerance and liberality. They feared that charity toward doctrinal differences concealed hidden heresy. When Wood criticized his church's intolerance, the conference questioned him "in regard to his faith" and sniffed out "fundamental errors." It expelled him "for Heresy; that is for embracing a fundamental error in the faith of the Gospel."[35]

After the Civil War, Newnan tempered its language when excluding defectors. In 1867, James Bohanan and his wife joined the Methodist church. A member brought a resolution of excommunication charging them with heresy. "After considerable debate," the church adopted a substitute resolution, excluding the pair merely for having "joined a church of a different faith and order from this Church." It showed a reluctance to label Methodism as heretical. And such ambivalence may have been widespread even before the war. Some postwar churches continued to equate defection with heresy, or at least to suggest such an equation. Benevolence Baptist Church excluded Martha Wilson in 1878 "for heresy" when she joined a "church of different faith & order." In 1882, Powelton excluded Isabella Jackson for "departure from the faith" when she defected to "a church of a different faith." In 1897, Crawfordville expelled Maggie Slack, who had "united with the Methodists and departed from the faith." But most churches made no explicit reference to the heretical character of the offense, either before or after the war.[36]

It made little difference, for in practice they treated members who departed as heretics. When Atlanta Second Baptist Church cleaned its membership roll in 1896, it refused merely to erase the names of the twenty-two members who had joined other denominations; it excluded them. When Helen Culp joined her new husband's church and asked "that her name be erased," the Athens Church "excluded" her. When Sister Johnson joined the Episcopalians, Atlanta Second Baptist Church voted twenty-nine to five to exclude. Only in Baptist congregations was the truth unadulterated.[37]

Southern Baptists had no trouble identifying truly heretical denominations. The Roman Catholic church, the Mormon church, the Christian Science church, and the New church (Swedenborgian) taught doctrines so far afield from Baptist views that Baptists had no qualms about excluding them. But such evangelical denominations as Methodists and Presbyterians posed a dilemma. Southern Baptists viewed them as colaborers in the gospel and often cooperated with them in local initiatives. All but Landmarkists occasionally allowed other evangelical ministers into their pulpits, and they shared preaching duties at camp meetings and other gatherings. They sometimes shared the same meeting house, and their pastors warmly received one another in ministerial councils.

Although evangelicals often cooperated, they just as often engaged in strife. Baptists attacked Methodist and Presbyterian infant baptism. Methodists attacked Baptist and Presbyterian Calvinism. Presbyterians attacked Methodist and Baptist church government. Denominational papers supported the warfare. Controversy was a test of religious truth, and evangelicals felt obligated to engage in it.[38]

Crowds gathered for live combat. The controversialist typically showed up at the appointed preaching service of his foe, and proffered debate. In 1851, Benedictine priest J. J. O'Connell arrived at his appointment near Charlotte, North Carolina, to find a Presbyterian minister waiting to draw him into public debate. Methodist circuit rider James Jenkins many times rebutted recent attacks of Baptist and Presbyterian preachers and was always ready for public debate. Baptist preacher William C. Crane debated a Universalist preacher for five hours in a Georgia courthouse. Disputation sometimes degenerated, as when a young Presbyterian gladiator reduced an elderly Baptist debater to tears. Would-be disputants sometimes agreed to train their sights on sinners rather than each other, but partisans went away disappointed when their heroes declined debate.[39]

Methodists and Presbyterians did not excommunicate members who joined Baptist churches; they deplored the Baptist practice. But Baptists bristled when other evangelicals accused them of bigotry for expelling defectors. A few Baptist churches chose merely to erase the names of departing members. The Sunbury Association began recording erasures in 1841. Baptist leader James M. Pendleton conceded in his 1867 *Church Manual* that some churches—presumably including a few in the South—had begun dropping members because it "is less disgraceful than exclusion." But most refused to take this path.[40]

In refusing, the southerners distinguished themselves from northern Baptists. Northern Baptist associations began recording erasures around 1820, and the practice became widespread in the 1840s. By the time of the Civil War, it was nearly universal in the North. In the South, it made little headway until the turn of the century. Still rare in 1900, it became common in the late 1920s.

Southern Baptists in the nineteenth century believed that such a practice sacrificed theological principles. Choosing a church was not like choosing clothes—a matter of taste and comfort. Church membership implied assent to the doctrines of the church. To change denominations was to change religious belief. To join the Christian church of Alexander Campbell was to subscribe baptismal regeneration. To become a Presbyterian was to accept infant baptism. To become a Methodist meant embracing the Arminian doctrine that everyone had sufficient grace to decide for salvation. Baptist members who embraced Methodist or Presbyterian beliefs therefore abandoned correct doctrine and departed from the faith.

Even when members did not understand the theological differences, Baptists believed that membership implied the duty of supporting the doctrines. When Sister Ball left Savannah Baptist Church to join the Methodist church, the committee asked her "if she approved the doctrines of the Methodist Church, particularly in relation to 'Baptism,' and the 'final perseverance of the Saints.' " She answered that she did not understand them. The committee reproved "the inconsistency of her conduct" because she joined a church when she did not believe, or at least did not understand, its doctrines.[41]

Adiel Sherwood explained why Baptist churches felt obligated to exclude members who joined denominations that practiced infant baptism. For Baptists, Sherwood attested, it was a matter of obedience to Christ's commands, no matter how illiberal the practice appeared to others:

> A church is not a society for interest or curiosity and connexion with it to be made and dissolved at pleasure; but it is formed to promote the glory of God and joined as a matter of duty in obedience to the general tenor of instructions contained in the New Testament. . . . I consider a Baptist church which allows its members to depart and join Pedobaptists as accessory to the following errors and irregularities: . . . 2d. It admits that pouring and sprinkling are baptism or that the ordinances as positive institutions are trifling concerns. 3d. It allows there is a door out of the church in fellowship, when the Bible knows of none; for no door is recognized except exclusion. . . . All through the New Testament the duty is incumbent on the church to watch over and reprove its members for errors in faith or practice. If one joins a people, not recognized in the N.T. [New Testament] the duty is plain to reclaim from the error; if it cannot succeed, the only course is exclusion. The N.T. allows no other course how harsh soever this may appear to those who whine about liberality, but who are governed by false and erroneous feelings, rather than Scripture requirements.

Toward the end of the century, when Baptists more frequently joined other denominations, excommunication became a routine affair, especially in town and city churches, which handled most of these cases in the press of other matters. But even when excommunications were pro forma, most churches continued to resist any suggestion that joining another denomination was acceptable. Although they were more reluctant to call it heresy, they persevered in the determination to make it an occasion of discipline. Democratic religion meant doctrinal unity.[42]

7

Associations, Creeds, and Calvinism

In the 1850s, the churches of Georgia's Flint River Baptist Association endured considerable strife in defense of creeds, Calvinism, and associational authority. It began in 1851 when two churches complained that Bethlehem Baptist Church in Jasper had "discarded her Articles of Faith." The association interpreted Bethlehem's action as divisive and doctrinally subversive. It convinced the pastor, Willis Jarrill, "to get Bethlehem Church to bring us a system of belief at our next Association." In return, it agreed to delay action.

The following year, Bethlehem Baptist Church presented as their creed a few scripture phrases: "The Baptist Church of Christ at Bethlehem Believing fully that the scriptures of the old and new Testaments are all sufficient to regulate the faith and practice of all Christians We have resolved to take the Bible and the Bible alone for our guide.—But as a matter of convenience to us & that we may the better be enabled to keep the unity of the spirit and the bond of piece we have selected and set forth as a basis of Christian Union the—following Truths 1st There is one body 2nd One spirit 3rd one Hope 4th One Lord 5th One Faith 6th one Baptism & 7th one God—and father of all." To further elucidate their "system of Belief," the church added two pages of scripture verses grouped according to traditional topics in theology. The association took offense and resolved that "our own self-protection requires us now to declare Bethlehem church no longer a member of this body, until she conforms to our established usage, which is to require of churches to have a plain and unequivocal system of belief, which will locate and define their notions of the Bible."[1]

Shortly after the 1852 association meeting, the Tirzah Baptist Church, in which the pastor Willis Jarrill held his membership, divided over the creedal issue. The creedal faction complained that Jarrill had for years agitated against creeds. When members confronted him, "he would then with soft words, say that he believed every sentiment contained in the Creed; and farther, that he was not understood." But he persisted in abusing creeds as "the relics of Popery, the Devil's Clipping Shears, and the Clipping Shears of Fellowship." The creedal group in the Tirzah Church therefore expelled him, mainly for "renouncing our creed."[2]

The 1852 Flint River Association anticipated the church's action. A delegate moved to declare Jarrill a heretic, and the association appointed a committee to consult with him. Jarrill answered "no" to three questions: "1st. Do you believe that our confession of faith is only a synopsis of our views upon the Bible? 2nd. Do you believe that that synopsis can be supported by the word of God? 3rd. Are you willing to continue in our organization, and will you assure us that in the future you will maintain the sentiments of our confession of faith, as able to be proven by the scripture, and cease comparing it to the relics of Popery, and calling it the devil's clipping shears of fellowship?" On hearing Jarrill's answers, the association declared him a "schismatic man," resolving "that we cannot any longer recognize him as an orderly, orthodox minister of our body." He rejected both the idea of creeds and the Calvinist content of Flint River's creed.[3]

Undaunted, Jarrill secured the support of majorities in the Tirzah and Holly Grove Baptist Churches and became the pastor of the Teman Baptist Church. These churches in 1853 protested the resolution against Jarrill as an "unauthorized stretch of Associational power" and accused some of the "most respectable" ministers of exercising "inquisitorial power." The association cast out the three churches.[4]

Associational Authority and Church Autonomy

Baptist churches cooperated with one another in large part in order to define and protect the boundaries of primitive democratic religion. When Baptists organized new churches, they invited "helps"—ministers of other congregations, who examined the applicants, assessed their proposed constitution, and evaluated their orthodoxy. Similarly, local churches refrained from ordaining ministers on their own authority but sought help from other churches, which sent their ministers to form a "presbytery" to examine the candidate and issue a recommendation.

Baptist tradition permitted local churches to act alone, but in the interest of unity they sought the endorsement of other churches.[5]

They also exercised mutual oversight when they had problems with discipline or government. When County Line Church had disciplinary problems, they requested neighboring churches to send "helps, to adjust some difficulties Existing between the church . . . & Brother Thomas Rhodes their Pastor." The helping churches typically sent two or three leading members on an appointed date, and they formed a council to hear the case and make a recommendation. Although a church could reject the advice of the council, few did.[6]

If a church became "disorderly," neighboring churches might call a council. In 1834, Mount Zion accused the LaGrange Baptist Church of fomenting division by receiving members who once belonged to schismatic congregations. Dissatisfied by the response from LaGrange, it announced that it had "called on our Sister Churches at Sardis and Bethlehem as helps to meet us on Saturday . . . at LaGrange to labour with us to try and convince you of your error so that the union of the Churches may be preserved." LaGrange, obstinate at first, eventually agreed to discontinue the practice.[7]

When rumors arose that Bairds Baptist Church allowed a member to rent his property "for a place of retail of ardent spirits," Penfield Baptist Church appointed a committee "to visit our sister church and labor with her in the spirit of christian faithfulness and love." When a member at LaGrange charged the church with "tolerating dancing," the church agreed to request three nearby churches "to send, each, three members as helps to the church to consider this charge."[8]

This mutual oversight was a form of interchurch discipline. Though the churches abjured any right to excommunicate other churches or their members, they declared a right to "disfellowship" each other. To disfellowship a church was to announce that it had departed too far from scriptural norms to retain its status as a New Testament church. It had broken union; it was schismatic.

Interchurch discipline followed the pattern of congregational discipline. Joseph Baker, editor of the *Christian Index*, explained that "before we declare, by word or act, non-fellowship with a sister church, we should use every lawful means within our power to convince her of what we conceive to be her departures from the gospel of Christ." Churches typically sent an investigating committee to the offending church, and if it failed to receive repentance or adequate proof of innocence, the investigating church called for a council. Offending churches that ignored the advice of councils could expect disfellowship.[9]

The primary means by which Baptist churches exercised mutual oversight was through controlling the membership of associations. In England, Particular Baptists were organizing associations as early as

1652. Baptist immigrants brought the associational concept to the American colonies. The Philadelphia Association was the first, organizing in 1707. The first in Georgia, the Georgia Association, formed in 1784. By 1829, there were seventeen in the state. Baptists consistently refused to call associational oversight "discipline," however, lest the authority to determine membership in associations be confused with the authority of the local church to determine its membership. The churches were "independent in matters of discipline—so that one Church has no power over another." An association, composed of autonomous churches, had "no power to enforce her recommendations on the churches."[10]

Baptist associations could "withdraw from any church or churches, whom they shall look upon to be unsound in principle, or immoral in practice, till they be reclaimed." This power to exclude any church that deviated from "the orthodox principles of the Gospel" gave the association an effective authority over the doctrine and practice of member churches. In 1836, the Washington Association appointed a committee to labor with Mount Olive Baptist Church, which had closed the church doors to several ministers who favored missions. The church denounced the association's meddling as tyranny, whereupon the association resolved that it must "in consideration of the disorderly conduct of Mount Olive Church . . . withdraw from her, in terms of the Constitution, and she is no longer considered a member of this body."[11]

Although such events were not common, the associations showed a determination to oust refractory congregations. The Hightower Association threatened to expel any churches that admitted members on the basis of alien immersion. It expelled six churches for refusing to recognize baptisms performed by an immoral minister. The Ocmulgee Association expelled a church for Arminianism. The Middle Association withdrew fellowship from Rocky Ford Baptist Church because, against the advice of the association, it admitted a member excommunicated by another church.[12]

The discipline usually restored the wayward churches to soundness. When Nails Creek Baptist Church failed to excommunicate its minister for immorality, the Sarepta Association requested it to reconsider and report to the next meeting. When the church delayed, the association concluded that it had disrupted the union, injured the reputation of the association, and undermined the cause of Christ. It resolved "to withdraw her connexion with such Church." Eventually, the church ejected the minister and gained readmission.[13]

Because associations disclaimed power to enforce their advice, churches sometimes defended themselves by asserting their independence. This rarely discouraged the associations. They did not deny that the churches were independent and free to do as they pleased, but churches could not retain membership in the association while they deviated from orthodoxy: "We can never place truth and error on the same footing."[14]

The editor of the *Christian Index*, David Shaver, grew incensed when advocates of open communion, appealing to the idea of freedom, demanded membership in the associations.

> They tell us that by virtue of "the time-honored Baptist principles of church independence and the right of private judgment," our people everywhere "must receive evangelical Baptist churches into associational fellowship, without restrictions on the question of communion." . . . Can that be true Independency which would compel churches, whether they will or will not, when forming Associations, to enlarge the bounds of fellowship until it embraces practices false to their own fundamental principles and fatal to their very being? . . . We, at least, shall content ourselves with the Independency, which leaves churches free to draw the lines of "associational fellowship" in consonance with their convictions as to scriptural order. . . . We shall, therefore, turn a deaf ear to the pleas of that false Independency which means, first church-slavery, and then church extinction.

Appeals to private judgment and religious liberty provided straying churches no more protection from associational discipline than they did straying individuals from church discipline. The associations denied accusations of intolerance or persecution. They did not excommunicate members or dissolve churches, much less compel churches by force: "We utter no threats of pains and penalties—we exhibit no fire and faggot." They merely announced to a disorderly church that "if you will pursue a course contrary to that which we conceive the scriptures prescribe, you must pursue it alone."[15]

Calvinism and Authority

To many southern Baptists, Calvinism and discipline went hand in hand. Calvinism encouraged them to believe that although the painful pruning might seem to harm the church, God's secret providence and predestination would prevail. The discipline, in turn, protected Calvinist doctrine by expelling its critics. Georgia Baptists kept up with the divisions among Calvinists at home and in England and were familiar especially with the works of Andrew Fuller, John Gill, and Calvinist hymn writer John Newton.

Georgians drew on a long tradition that reached directly back to John Calvin, the sixteenth-century Geneva reformer whose teaching emphasized the sovereignty of God and the primacy of scripture. His teaching spread widely in Europe and was further developed by his successors Theodore Beza and Francis Turretin. In 1610, some Dutch followers of Jacob Arminius objected to Calvin's views of human salvation. The

Arminian Remonstrants summed up their doubts in five points. The Dutch church hosted the Synod of Dort, a gathering of the leaders of Europe's Reformed churches, which answered each point: It affirmed total depravity (fallen humans are unable to turn toward God), unconditional election (God elected persons apart from any consideration of their actions), particular redemption (Christ's atonement was for the elect only), irresistible grace (God's grace always effected conversion), and the perseverance of the saints (the elect will not fall away). These became known as the "five points of Calvinism."[16]

Arminianism did not prosper in the Netherlands but attracted many followers in England and America. John and Charles Wesley promoted Arminian ideas and ensured that Methodist churches in England and America preached an Arminian gospel. The first English Baptists were the Arminian General Baptists, as were many early American Baptists. Although General Baptists in America became a small minority among Baptists by 1800, other Baptists took up Arminian ideas. In New England, Benjamin Randall began converting Calvinist Baptist churches into Arminian ones, leading in 1827 to the formation of the Freewill Baptist General Conference, which grew to 1,586 churches by 1910. Freewill Baptist churches in the South were less numerous (limited largely to North and South Carolina) and did not join the northern body but formed associations that organized a general conference by 1921.[17]

Despite pockets of Arminian or freewill sentiment among Baptists in the South, few southern Baptists embraced Arminianism before the twentieth century. As early as 1800, most Arminian Baptists in the South had either died or been converted to Calvinistic ideas. The first enduring Arminian Baptist churches in Georgia appeared around 1830, under the leadership of Cyrus White. By 1846, Arminian Baptists numbered almost 2,000, but accounted for only 3 percent of Georgia's 58,000 Baptists. By 1870, of some 115,000 Georgia Baptists, only 808 were members of Arminian churches. Late into the nineteenth century, pastors could still expect the approbation of their colleagues for boasting that their church was "perfectly sound in doctrine, especially Calvinistic."[18]

Regular Baptist churches undoubtedly harbored a number of members who held Arminian ideas. As long as they did not embrace full-blown Arminianism and kept their opinions to themselves, many churches left them in peace. Joseph Baker argued that no one "who relies wholly on the Lord Jesus for salvation, should be excluded from the church because of errors in doctrine, so long as his christian character is good, and he holds his errors as private property."[19]

The most visible display of Baptist Calvinism appeared in the confessions of faith adopted by Baptist churches and associations. Virtually every church creed affirmed the two fundamental tenets of Calvinism: that human nature was radically depraved due to original sin and that

God was the absolute author of salvation, electing individuals for salvation before the creation of the world and creating faith by the operation of the Holy Spirit.

Some of the creeds were expansive. Members of Hopeful Baptist Church professed their belief in "the fall of Adam and the imputation of his sin to his posterity in the corruption of human nature, and the impotency of man to recover himself by his own free will ability" and in "the everlasting love of God to his people, and in the Eternal Election of a definite number of the human race to grace and glory, and there was a covenant of grace or redemption between the father and the Son befoure the world began, in which their Salvation is Secure, and that those in particular are Redeemed."[20]

A few churches, rejecting such creeds as insufficiently detailed, adopted the lengthy Second London Confession of 1689, which had been adopted by many northern associations. English Particular Baptists produced the First London Confession in 1644 to show Parliament that they were orthodox Calvinists. In 1677, they approved a Baptist version of the Westminster Confession, the Second London Confession. When they met again in 1689, they republished it with a new preface. Elias Keach, son of a leading English pastor, brought the 1689 edition with him when he immigrated to the colonies. Adopted by the Philadelphia Association, it became the basis of most Baptist confessions. When Greensboro Baptist Church formed in 1821, the members adopted a brief confession of faith and then added that "this Church adopts the confession of faith published by the Baptist ministers in London in the 17th century and acknowledged by the Philada. & Charleston associations." Others adopted it, too.[21]

The shortest creeds confessed belief in "the fall of Adam, and the imputation of his Sin to his posterity, the Corruption of human nature, the Impotency of fallen man to do that which is Spiritually Good, the Everlasting love of God to his people, the Covenant of Grace, the Doctrine of Election, Particular Redemption, Justification by the Righteousness of Christ Imputed, pardon & Redemption thro[ugh] his Blood, Regeneration and Sanctification by the Influence and operations of the holy Spirit, the final perseverance of the Saints in Grace." Even creeds that made a virtue of brevity affirmed belief "in particular and unconditional election."[22]

Associations adopted confessions on the same pattern as the church creeds. The Georgia Association and others wrote creeds virtually identical to the confession of Hopeful Baptist Church. Association creeds typically emphasized "eternal and particular election" or "the Eternal Election of a Definitive Number of the Human Race." Some associations praised the Second London Confession and formulated their creed as a synopsis of the longer confession, introducing it therefore as "An Abstract of Principles Held by the Baptists in general, agreeable to the confession of faith adopted by upwards of one hundred congregations in England, published in Philadelphia in 1742, which is a Standard for the Baptists." A small number of southern associations adopted the London Confession itself.[23]

Baptist apologists were proud that their summaries of faith came from the "Old Confession, published in England, first in 1643 [1644], and subsequently in 1689." Jesse Mercer saw the London Confession as the basis of all associational creeds, claiming that "some Associations have adopted it in part, some as a whole." Because other creeds were merely "abstracts" of this one, Baptists often spoke as if there existed only one Baptist creed.[24]

Calvinism found other expressions: Jesse Mercer was not the only editor of the *Christian Index* who reassured subscribers by advertising his Calvinist orthodoxy. When Samuel Boykin and Sylvanus Landrum took over the paper, they recommended themselves as "Calvinistic, strict communion Baptists." When T. P. Bell assumed editorial responsibilities, he pledged that the paper would "stand, as it has done in years gone by, for the 'Old Theology.' " So frequently did the editors write and publish articles on Calvinist theology that a pledge to propagate Calvinism seemed almost a prerequisite for holding the editor's chair. As late as 1899, the paper ran a six-month series on Calvinism's "doctrines of grace."[25]

When ministers and deacons gathered to promote unity among the churches, they often discussed theological and practical questions designed to confirm them in Calvinism. At one meeting, delegates affirmed the limited atonement: Asked whether "the sins of all mankind were imputed to the Lord Jesus Christ, when he hung and died on the cross, or for as many as should in the end be saved," the session answered, "for as many as shall in the end be saved." At a different meeting the delegates affirmed that "the doctrine of eternal and particular election" is "a bible doctrine."[26]

Although voices now and then called for an Arminian theology, Calvinists after 1800 had little fear that Arminianism could spread. For one thing, the associations maintained vigilance: The Hightower Association spoke for a united Calvinist front when it resolved that it "would consider any Church denying the doctrine of imputed righteousness, and human depravity, heterodox in doctrine."[27]

Regular southern Baptists would not maintain fellowship with Arminian churches, or approve the sending of letters or visitors to Arminian associations. The non-Calvinist United Association tried in 1842 to open formal correspondence with the Central Association, which declined, concluding that "we can see no way in which a permanent correspondence can be opened, except upon those principles received as orthodox by our denomination generally." The Chattahoochee Association instructed churches to defrock any minister "who publicly denounces the doctrine of human depravity, Salvation by grace, and makes general war on the doctrine of Election." The Sarepta Association told them to refuse church office even to anyone who did not "believe it to be expedient to preach and contend for the doctrine of predestination and election."[28]

One after another, associations counseled their churches to expel any preachers who taught "that Christ atoned for the whole human family," denied a "special, and eternal election," or refused to proclaim "the doctrine of Election." They advised them to punish laity who dared suggest "that Christ died indiscriminately for all men." The Tugalo Association said that believers baptized by "free will" preachers had to be baptized again. As late as 1891, Baptist leaders argued that "an applicant for admission [to church membership] who rejects the doctrine of election should not be admitted." For most nineteenth-century southern Baptists, to reject Calvinism was to deny the gospel of grace.[29]

Churches dismissed members to join another Baptist church with letters of dismission certifying their good standing. Some included in these letters a testimony of the church's orthodoxy: "Whereas our Beloved Brother John Bigar, & our Beloved Sister Mary Bigar, his affectionate consort, both members of us, the Savannah Baptist Church, holding Believers Baptism, Eternal & particular [election], Effectual calling, Sanctification by the Spirit, & the Saints final perseverance thro' grace to glory, Have requested . . . to grant them letters of dismission, . . . do hereby dismiss" them. Other churches certified themselves in these letters as "holding particular redemption," or "holding the doctrines of grace."[30]

The Exclusivism of Orthodoxy

Not every Baptist refused fellowship to Arminians. Jesse Mercer acknowledged that most churches had a few members with Arminian notions and thought they "should be borne with and admonished," not excommunicated, "unless they become contumacious." Joseph Baker agreed that the denial of "eternal and unconditional election" should not debar them from membership, but, like Mercer, he insisted that if they tried to "make proselytes to their faith and create a party in the church, we should feel bound to vote for their exclusion; not because of their faith but because of their schismatic conduct."[31]

In 1843, Baker even suggested associational fellowship with Georgia's small companies of Arminian Baptists, though with no apparent impact on denominational sentiment. Although the leaders of these groups could be full-blown Arminians, their churches and associations normally adopted creeds that were more traditional. Baker thought that these creeds, Calvinistic except for their denial of unconditional election, made closer union possible.[32]

Baker's toleration of disagreement did not go far. Even he urged separation from proponents of a general atonement. He commended the example of Christ, who cautioned his listeners "against the self-righteous, or—what would be called in the present day—the Arminian doctrines of the Pharisees." Baker believed that Arminians preached salvation by human merit and declared that it was sinful to associate with such preachers.[33]

In 1874, J. S. Lawton, moderator of the Rehoboth Association and co-owner of the *Christian Index,* urged an almost latitudinarian tolerance of divergent beliefs. Reflecting a trend that was just beginning to emerge, he argued that if Baptists united "on the great Baptist principles of regeneration, immersion, and strict communion," further differences in theology should form no barrier to church fellowship. "Hyper-Calvinist" antimission Baptists, "moderate" Baptists, and "even Arminian" Baptists should be tolerated, Lawton urged, because "none of us are infallible." He thought that practice was more important than belief, but he was a generation or two ahead of his time.[34]

Although Arminianism was not widespread, complaints could be heard by the 1830s that too many "Baptists nowadays are afraid to preach the doctrines of Grace" because church members complained about "the doctrine of eternal and particular election." William Holcombe worried that other denominations were noticing the neglect: "some of the Pedobaptists are saying that Baptists are becoming ashamed of Predestination and Election, and that they will soon quit preaching it." Calvinist doctrines were unpopular outside the church, and some ministers would not "preach the doctrine of election, lest they should suffer persecution." Later in the century, some Calvinists feared that neglect of their doctrines—combined with Methodist successes—was infecting churches with notions of free will and general atonement. They complained that election was ignored in "pulpit performances" and that preachers glossed over "eternal election" and "predestination."[35]

In many instances, southern Baptists saw Arminianism even in mild departures from high Calvinism. Sharon Baptist Church, in the Arminian United Association, professed belief in original sin, depravity and inability, perseverance, and in the necessity of the Holy Spirit for conversion. Its statement on election nettled Calvinist Baptists, however, for it described election as "according to foreknowledge." It was not surprising that Arminianizing Baptists sometimes abjured the name "Arminian."[36]

The response was renewed calls for fidelity to Calvinist doctrine in pulpit, print, and assembly. When P. H. Mell, perennial president of the Southern Baptist Convention, took charge in 1852 of Antioch Baptist Church in Oglethorpe County, he concluded that "a number of the members were drifting off into Arminianism." Mell decided that a Baptist church should have Baptist doctrine, and therefore he "preached to them the doctrines of predestination, election, free-grace." So popular was his Calvinist preaching during his twenty-five year pastorate that a Methodist preacher called the region "Mell's Kingdom."[37]

From one corner of the state to another, churches and associations defrocked preachers for questioning Calvinist doctrines, criticized even slight alterations in Calvinist creeds, and blocked fellowship with doctrinally careless congregations. Just as the Georgia Association disfellowshiped Jeremiah Walker and his Arminian followers in 1790, so the Sunbury Association refused fellowship to four Arminian churches in 1880. Associations refused to alter their creeds from "eternal election of a definite number" to "election according to the Scriptures." Throughout the nineteenth century, the Calvinists won victory after victory. They held Georgia for Geneva.[38]

As late as 1885, Baptist leaders still proclaimed that "the Arminian doctrine . . . is one of the most deadly heresies." It was so damaging because it robbed preaching of its power and religion of its pure doctrine. Jesse Mercer thought that the more Calvinistic the preaching, the deeper and more enduring the impression on sinners. If salvation was by grace, added his father, Silas, the doctrine of election was "the very foundation of our faith" and the basis of revival. Arminianism, warned Baptist apologists, was a halfway house on the road to unbelief. Its end result was "cold, irreverent, dreary Rationalism." Calvinism sustained moral purity; Arminianism tolerated "hypocrites."[39]

Calvinists felt that the attraction of Arminianism was its popularity with people outside the true church, whether Methodists or unbelievers. In 1890, the editors of the *Christian Index*, expressing shock at reports that most Baptist ministers in northern cities were Arminians, attributed the decline of Calvinism in the North to its unpopularity. In the South, by contrast, Baptists knew that "doctrinal purity is more and better than popular favor."[40]

Freedom and Creeds

The widespread belief that Baptists have always opposed creeds is wrong. Historians have been misled by attending only to what Baptists said—and only to part of what they said—rather than to what they did. Baptists berated other denominations as creedal and called for "no creed but the Word of God," but they encountered creeds every time they entered their churches and association meetings.[41]

Early Baptists were not liberal individualists. They maintained that the right of individual conscience in religion was inalienable and that creeds did not infringe that right. They balanced the individual's need to follow conscience with the community's need to define truth and morality. They did this by establishing voluntary, creedal churches.[42]

Baptist denunciations of creeds were only rarely outright rejections. When they objected to creeds, they were objecting to religious confessions enforced by a civil government, imposed on churches by a hierarchy, corrupted by unscriptural doctrines, or serving as a legal authority in place of the scriptures. They disliked creeds that claimed independent authority, for the Bible alone, they argued, could bind the conscience.

In practice, they placed great stock in creed making. When a Mississippi church excommunicated Georgia missionary Lee Compere for holding Arminian notions, he demanded scriptural evidence against his views. The moderator of the conference replied that "any sort of doctrine" could be proved by biblical texts, that the church judged the meaning of scripture, and that they must be governed by the views embodied in their confession. Baptists taught that all persons were free to believe what they wished, but churches were free to exclude those who rejected Baptist doctrine.[43]

Churches expected applicants to agree with their creeds. Although they did not usually require public subscription to the creed, they did demand submission to the doctrines in it. Joseph Baker explained that the confessions embodied scriptural doctrine, and the scriptures, not the confessions, regulated belief. But creeds were vital, Baker wrote, for without them the churches could not preserve doctrinal unity. Applicants should not join unless they agreed with the creed. Baker described the usual practice: "The question we have generally heard asked on this subject, is, in effect, this: 'Do you believe in the doctrines of the gospel as generally held by Baptists, as far as you understand them?' . . . Every one wishing to unite with a Church ought to know what are the views entertained by those with whom he seeks to unite; for how can two walk together except they agree? One that cannot fellowship with our views of scriptural doctrine, certainly should not seek to have church fellowship with us."[44]

Some churches read their confessions to prospective members and required assent, even when they brought letters of dismission from other Baptist churches. Newnan Baptist Church received a husband and wife from a Baptist church in Tennessee, but only "after our faith being read and acknowledged." The same church received "Harry a servant" only upon his "adoption of the articles of our Faith."[45]

Associations would not admit churches unless they had adopted an orthodox confession. The Tallapoosa Association received churches "after hearing their Articles of Faith read," and it examined the orthodoxy of other associational creeds before agreeing to open correspondence with them. As late as 1908, applicant churches could expect associations to examine their creeds. When Battle Hill Baptist Church applied to the Stone Mountain Association, it attached "a copy of our Articles of Faith as adopted at the organization of the church October 13th, 1907, and respectfully request the same be examined by your usual method." Churches usually secured admission, but associations were not accommodating when they discovered an unsound creed. The Ebenezer Association objected to Hartford Baptist Church's articles of faith and did not admit it until it adopted the association's creed. The Western Association rejected the application of Antioch Baptist Church until it exchanged its "defective" creed for "the constitution of this Body."[46]

Associations refused fellowship with other associations that had unsound confessions. In 1880, a number of churches formed the Gillsville Association, which adopted the New Hampshire Confession and prepared to join the Georgia Baptist Convention. Georgia Calvinists opposed fellowship with any association with a creed as vague as the New Hampshire Confession, which could accommodate both Arminians and Calvinists. New Hampshire Baptists, smarting from the success of Benjamin Randall and his Freewill Baptists, sought to soften their Calvinist identity to prevent additional churches from defecting. They adopted a new confession in 1833 that expunged or obscured such Calvinist distinctives as human depravity, imputed righteousness, and eternal election. With later modifications back toward Calvinism, it became the most popular Baptist confession by the early twentieth century. C. D. Campbell, pastor of Athens First Baptist Church, pledged opposition to the Gillsville Association's application for membership.[47]

Southern Baptists suspected groups that adopted the New Hampshire Confession not only because the creed contained error but also because it failed to distinguish clearly between error and truth, especially the truth of election. Why would any group adopt it in place of abstracts of the London Confession unless it was to move toward Arminianism? The petition of the Florida Association for admission in 1846 to the Georgia Baptist Convention caused a "protracted debate" over its use of the New Hampshire Confession. The convention granted membership after Florida delegate James McDonald assured everyone that the association was not Arminian, but Florida Baptists sent no delegates the next year.[48]

His experience at the convention induced McDonald to reconsider the New Hampshire creed. In 1847, he criticized it for being ambiguous about depravity, election, and perseverance. Joseph Baker also pleaded with the Florida churches to abandon the New Hampshire Confession, and finally they did, adopting in its place an abstract affirming "the doctrine of eternal and particular election." They had evidently adopted the New Hampshire Confession because it was easily at hand in the *Encyclopedia of Religious Knowledge*, not because they wished to tolerate Arminian doctrine, though Arminian sentiments lurked behind one Florida apologist's statement that the New Hampshire Confession at least moved beyond the "old Popish doctrine of original sin."[49]

Opposition to Creeds

If confessions were so important, why did Baptists decry them? Why did they so often insist that they had none? Francis Wayland, president of Brown University, declared that "an established confession of faith . . .

is impossible" with Baptists. Virginia Baptist editor Henry Keeling spoke of "Baptist churches, with no creeds." Tennessee Baptist professor A. S. Worrell admitted that Baptists had creeds, but he called for "the abolition of all creeds except the New Testament."[50]

Jesse Mercer faulted creedal churches for not making "the Bible the all-sufficient rule of faith and practice." In place of the Bible, they substituted their "excellent standards," assuming that the common people and the ministers would err if they exercised their own judgments. Baptists placed "the inspired Volume into the hands of the reader" and trusted that it would not fail "under the guidance of the Spirit, to lead him into all necessary truth." Mercer argued that Baptists had "always professed to take the Bible as our standard, our creed, our confession."[51]

Historians have mistaken such anticreedal statements as evidence of Baptist commitment to individual autonomy. They have taken them to mean that Baptists opposed an enforced doctrinal conformity. Baptist confessions were not, the consensus says, statements of what must be believed and could not serve to discipline or exclude dissenting views. They have concluded that Baptists rejected creeds because they espoused individual freedom.[52]

Yet Mercer almost persuaded the Georgia Association to adopt the most robust of all Baptist creeds, the Second London Confession. In 1808, Mercer introduced a resolution to this effect, though in the end the association agreed that its original confession was adequate. Most Baptists imitated Mercer's approach—touting the Bible as the only creed of Baptists while insisting on the need for explicit confessions of faith. At bottom, Baptists rejected creeds that seemed to claim authority independent of the Bible. In the same breath, they abjured any "standards" except the Bible and insisted that they had always had "a confession of Faith." The difference, as they saw it, was that other denominations appealed to their creeds, whereas Baptists appealed to the scriptures that authorized their creeds.[53]

The rhetoric against creeds reflected the Baptist sense of democracy. Other denominations imposed their creeds from above: from civil governments, as in European churches, or from church hierarchies, as in Presbyterian and Methodist churches. Baptists adopted them voluntarily from below, each church voting democratically to embrace the form of scriptural truth. They jointly had the authority to determine what the scriptures taught, and they formed their creeds from "the pure democracy of the New Testament." Baptist anticreedalism was a rejection of creeds imposed on local churches from above.[54]

Some baptists associated "creeds" with state churches, which tolerated such "human elements" as infant baptism because they wanted to include all citizens. State churches therefore replaced membership based on conversion and purity with one based on assent to creeds. They promoted an "implicit faith" in creeds that precluded the testing of human traditions by scripture. Baptists commended their own creeds as being void of human teachings and containing only scriptural truth. "It has been our peculiar glory," wrote William J. Hard, pastor of Augusta Baptist Church, "to take the scripture as our guide: . . . the constitution of our churches, their ritual discipline, and creed, accord with the New Testament."[55]

The Baptist cry of "no creed but the Bible" was not so much anticreedal as antipedobaptist, antihierarchical, and anti-Erastian. They attacked the "no-creed" doctrine, associating it with the errors of Alexander Campbell. Asa Chandler conceded that "some zealously contend against all human creeds and confessions," but he asked in response: "What harm can creeds do, if they contain the truth? Is the truth less valuable because it is published, or declared in a creed? . . . Creeds that do harm, are those that contain error—not those that are founded upon Bible truth."[56]

The distinctions between Baptist and non-Baptist use of creeds created confusion. In the spring of 1842, W. H. Stokes wrote two articles alleging that the divisions of Christianity resulted from deference to creeds: Christians should adopt the Baptist principle—"put the people, even all the people, upon the business of examining for themselves that they might know what the Bible does teach; it would foster an independence in these investigations which never can co-exist with a blinded deference to creeds." He scorned the Episcopalians' Thirty-nine Articles; the Presbyterians' Excellent Standards, and the Methodists' Most Excellent Discipline. The Baptists were different: "Our motto is, the Bible—the Bible as God gave it—nothing suppressed, nothing transferred!"[57]

Some readers asked him whether he intended to say "that everything like a confession of faith should be set aside by religious denominations." Stokes explained that he objected only to the improper use of confessions. Baptists had confessions, he conceded, but required no subscription to their articles as a condition of membership and imposed no obligations on ministers to conform to anything but biblical truth. Stokes was, in fact, so taken with the Second London Confession that he wished to "furnish every Baptist family in America with a copy" and urged every association to adopt it.[58]

Baptists demanded that individuals understand scripture for themselves not because they privileged individualism but because they believed that saving faith had to be exercised individually. Their populist approach to Bible interpretation was based on a conviction that lay Bible study and public instruction would lead to basic uniformity of belief. Creeds expressed that uniformity; discipline enforced it.

Creeds and Discipline

Baptists adopted creeds for two main reasons: First, creeds bore testimony to their orthodoxy and prevented misinformed criticism. Christian diversity, said James Armstrong, gave rise to "many false representations, and injurious calumnies, which are heaped upon the different sects without just grounds." Creeds protected churches and their doctrine from slander. Second, creeds offered a plain statement of an understanding of scripture, so that none who disagreed would sow division by joining the creedal community. By the adoption of creeds, Armstrong reasoned, "each particular denomination will then be circumscribed within proper boundaries; and individuals holding opposite sentiments, will unite with that sect whose principles are most congenial with their views." If dissenters joined the denomination, strife and division would result. Creeds were necessary for harmony and cooperation.[59]

Associations often listed these two justifications in the preambles to their confessions: "And as we are convinced, that there are a number of Baptist churches, who differ from us in faith and practice; and that it is impossible to have communion where there is no union, we think it our duty, to set forth a concise declaration of the faith and order upon which we intend to associate." Churches likewise included similar preambles: "Whereas there is very Different Opinions in the world about Religion, therefore many Denominations Cannot see Eye to Eye with Each other; we think it wright to point out Sum particular articles of our faith to this End, that we may bee of the same minde with Each other, that peace, union, and true fellowship, may abound amonst us without a jar."[60]

Critics of confessions, who professed only "their adoption of the Bible in general terms," were often seeking, W. H. Stokes argued, "a sort of shield for heterodox opinions." Many Baptists saw opposition to creeds as a disguised threat to Calvinist orthodoxy. And crypto-Arminians often did express their discontent with Calvinism by attacking the principle of creedalism. When Brother Hamrick of the Tallapoosa Association rejected in 1868 its confession of faith, his real objection was evidently to the doctrine of election. When Marietta First Baptist Church endured five years of controversy and a schism over the article on election in its creed, the "Anti-Predestinarian" party included a group "preferring the abolition of all Creeds."[61]

The 1850s struggle in the Flint River Association revealed the complexities of the battles over creeds. Willis Jarrill claimed not only that creeds were Satanic and divisive but also that the Baptist creed "did not contain a single Bible sentiment." He opposed it because of its Calvinism. One of his allies confirmed this when he lambasted the association for investing so much energy in "an unimportant difference of opinion." Comparing the dispute to a disagreement over the color of the whale that swallowed Jonah, he observed that "while a portion of the Baptist Church believe that there is only a certain few who were elected and foreordained to go to heaven from the beginning of all time, another portion believe, most conscientiously it appears, that all men can inherit this greatest of all blessings, by strictly complying with our Biblical mandates."[62]

The association had suspected all along that Jarrillite anticreedalism was a blanket for some heresy. At the 1852 meeting, the association so admired Virginian Eli Ball's speech against anticreedalism that they placed it in the minutes, an unusual action. Ball tried to demonstrate that "the no creed system is paralyzing in its influence, and dangerous in its tendency" and that Baptists who pretended to oppose all creeds and to take only the Bible as their guide were on the path to Unitarianism, Universalism, Arianism, or atheism. To advocate anticreedalism was "to abandon long established doctrinal sentiments, under the pretext of throwing away human creeds for the bible." Ball reasoned that a creed defined an understanding of the words of revelation. Baptists therefore founded their faith not on the creed but on the Bible. Yet the creed was the expression of the faith: "It expresses to others what we believe the word of God teaches." Every Christian had a creed, an understanding of what the Bible taught. Those who opposed creeds were unwilling to write down what they believed. They could never be "safe guides for the church as teachers."[63]

Ball's arguments repeated the Baptist commonplace that "desire for the destruction of creeds arises among such as have very little regard for the Bible teaching." When in 1837 Arminian James Willson argued that it was inexpedient for the Georgia Association to retain its articles of faith because they caused strife, he proposed that each Baptist explain the Bible for himself. Jesse Mercer assailed Willson's position: "This charity rejoices in iniquity; as it admits the amalgamation of every sentiment, for which its holder finds a foundation in the Bible, according to his own explanation. It would harmonize predestinarians, arminians, unitarians, antinomians and universalists, &c. All these would come in, and claim the Bible, as the foundation of their different creeds, each explaining for himself." The Georgia Association refused to abandon its creed.[64]

Such eminent leaders as Adiel Sherwood and David Shaver warned in the 1860s that opposition to creeds threatened the integrity of the church. Shaver contended that opposition to creeds was one of the tendencies of a latitudinarian Gilded Age. Rationalists, liberals, and "the broad Evangelical school" warred against creeds because they thought that Christianity aimed at spiritual life rather than doctrine. The result of such "credophobia" was always error. Aversion to creeds concealed the hatred of divine truth that sinfulness fostered. The strategy of error was to prepare the way "by an outcry against creeds." Ultimately, anticreedalism was a rejection of the gospel of grace; it was a gospel of salvation by human effort. So he exhorted Baptists to protect their creeds and their orthodoxy. If orthodoxy ever fell, "the secret spring of mischief" would be found not among unbelievers but in the lack of "definite, uncompromising, faithful testimony" from pulpits professing orthodox belief. He remained confident: "Baptists, as friends of creeds, will not be likely to abandon them."[65]

Baptists believed that orthodox belief divided the church from the world. Creeds protected that belief, especially the Calvinist doctrines that alone could "humble the pride of man, and exalt the Lamb of God." To surrender creeds was to relinquish the truth, which would entail the loss of piety, the dissolution of the churches, the loss of the Bible, and the abandonment of hope for salvation.[66]

At the end of the century, they were still guarding their churches against the depreciation of doctrine. While inclusivist values won the hearts of other American denominations, Baptist leaders in the South continued to praise "the principle of exclusion as a factor in the formulation of doctrine." In accepting creeds based on the Second London Confession, churches drew a "sharp defining line" that shielded the flocks.[67]

In a sense, Willis Jarrill was correct: Baptist creeds did function in many ways as "Clipping Shears of Fellowship." In Jarrill's view, this made creeds demonic, for they fomented unjustifiable schism over doctrinal differences. But in the view of most Baptists, creeds signified a divine duty to obey Christ, who commanded his church to preserve purity in life and doctrine. Creeds protected the doctrines that formed the "walls and bulwarks of the Church." The exclusivism of southern democratic religion demanded a populist creedalism.[68]

8

Democratic Religion Transformed

In many ways, Southern Baptists succeeded in their struggle against the "age of progress." Early in the twentieth century, Baptist churches in the South still showed few signs of accepting progressivist and modernist agendas for the church. They were unmoved by the assured results of the higher criticism of the Bible, by the alleged scandal of miracles, or by the supposed offensiveness of a wrathful God requiring propitiation. But Baptists embraced other forms of progress. Many Baptists were captivated by the ideals of the New South. They sought to incorporate scientific methods of social organization into their communal piety. In time, commitment to the ideals of the New South would transform Southern Baptist views of individual freedom and ecclesiastical authority. The clearest indication of change was the loss of church discipline.

By the 1920s, Southern Baptist church discipline had disappeared. Although a few isolated churches kept up the practice into the 1940s, the fate of Southern Baptist discipline had been sealed by 1900. Many Baptists knew it. In a report of the Western Association in 1910, pastor J. A. Bell lamented the loss: "When have you heard of a church vindicating her righteous claims by an effectual arraignment of her malicious or delinquent members? Church discipline, it seems, must be reckoned as a thing of the past, belonging to the fossil remains of bygone ages." In 1915, the Ebenezer Association confessed that "the matter of arraigning our disorderly members before the Church in Conference is very much a thing of the past. We have ceased to require our members to live, at least, a decent Christian life."[1]

Although preachers in every decade had warned of the decline of discipline, the twentieth-century Jeremiahs were right. In Georgia, Baptist churches began a steady pattern of declining discipline in the 1840s, despite a brief reversal in the 1870s. In the 1840s, they excommunicated annually an average of 201 persons per 10,000 church members. By the 1940s, church discipline had fallen by more than 90 percent, with churches excluding an annual average of only 18 per 10,000 members.

Northern Baptists, who had never achieved the southern levels of strictness, began a similar decline in the 1850s. In the North, discipline fell from a peak of 143 average annual excommunications per 10,000 members in the 1850s to only 7 in 1910 to 1920. Southern Baptists, although lagging behind the northerners, transformed their heritage of communal authority and relinquished the right to judge the moral behavior of individuals. Democratic religion took on new meaning.[2]

Jeremiads of Decline

Few Baptist preachers in any period were satisfied that the churches faithfully practiced discipline. In church meetings, associational gatherings, and denominational newspapers, critics exhorted the churches to faithful, strict discipline. Complaints could be heard in every era, but beginning around 1850, the laments became more frequent, until by the 1890s they were commonplace.[3]

Careful observers could notice changes as early as the 1840s, when the statistical decline began. Antebellum reports occasionally decried "neglected discipline," failure "to enforce the laws of Christ in regard to discipline," a standard of church discipline "too low in most of our churches," and a church "accustomed to indulge a very loose reign of discipline." In 1846, Joseph Baker observed that "our churches in Georgia are entirely too lax in discipline, and we fear they are growing more and more so." But these were changes in the texture of discipline; changes in its fabric occurred after the Civil War.[4]

By the 1870s, an array of Southern Baptists agreed that something was terribly wrong with the discipline of the churches. The cry of the day was for a "revival of discipline." Preachers issued warnings that "church discipline has become deplorably lax" or that "we are without discipline." Associations fretted that "the great needed work among the churches is discipline" and urged pastors "to insist upon a stricter discipline." North Carolina preacher J. A. Stradley suggested in 1873 that the best way for Southern Baptist churches to grow would be for them to shrink: "If the Baptists of North Carolina would, during the present year, exclude from their churches 10,000 unworthy members, they would do far more to increase their real strength and true prosperity than if they were to add the same number."[5]

By the 1890s, such jeremiads were standard in discussions on the condition of Southern Baptist churches. Recognizing that "the discipline of members is a much neglected duty of our churches," churches passed resolutions to enforce discipline. "So far have our Churches already departed from primitive piety," LaGrange First Baptist Church lamented in 1890, "that not one in twenty perhaps will enforce Scriptural discipline." Such laments were out of step with the optimism of the New South.[6]

The urbanization of the South accelerated after the Civil War. The number of villages doubled from 1870 to 1880 and again by 1900. Towns and cities burgeoned in 1880s, southern urban growth nearly doubling the national average. In the New South era, railroads expanded their lines faster in the South than in the nation as a whole, which stimulated commerce and industry. In the 1880s, capital, wages, and product value all more than doubled, outpacing the growth of New England's industrial revolution fifty years earlier.[7]

This New South nurtured exuberant optimism. Such southern boosters as Louisville's Henry Watterson and Atlanta's Henry Grady spread the gospel of the New South in newspapers and lecture halls. The South was the proud equal of the North, Grady told New York's elite in 1886. It had "nothing for which to apologize" and "nothing to take back," and it was glad to exchange slavery for the commerce, industry, and racial cooperation that now characterized the region, Grady exaggerated. Capitalism promised to remedy the South's ills.[8]

The laments also seemed to ignore the phenomenal growth of the denomination, from under 1 million in 1870 to more than 3.6 million in 1926. In 1870, Methodists led southern churches with 42 percent of all adherents, compared to 30 percent for Baptists. By 1926, Baptists claimed 43 percent and Methodists only 28 percent. But the laments served an explanatory function. Whenever Southern Baptists experienced slow growth or spiritual torpor, the reason was ready at hand: The churches did not exercise discipline.[9]

Delegates to a special meeting of western Georgia churches in 1851 had resolved that they could not "reasonably expect the blessing of God upon us, as a Denomination, until we return again to the 'old paths,' and reinstate in our churches, that soundness of faith, purity of practice, and vigor of discipline, which once characterized us." Such observations continued through the rest of the century. Baptists blamed the absence of discipline for declensions in spirituality, interest, and efficiency. The decline of discipline explained why the church seemed powerless. Pastor E. V. Baldy ascribed the rise of aberrant theologies to the loss of discipline. "Holiness" movements emerged in postwar

Methodism to restore emphasis on purity and spawned groups like the Salvation Army, which came to Georgia's villages by 1890. "Would it not be well for our churches to consider whether or not the 'Holiness' heresy, and 'Faith-cure' movement are not both a rebuke and a warning to our churches," Baldy asked, "a reaction occasioned by the general looseness on the part of our churches in the matter of discipline, and a low standard of morality and faith, which satisfies so many professed Christians?"[10]

Nothing availed to restore discipline to its former rigor, and Baptists feared that God would withhold the blessings of revival and piety. Churches no longer able to protect their purity would become infested with worldliness; they would lose the title of "Church of Christ." The only consolation was that Baptists had a rational explanation for instances of spiritual declension, an explanation that retained its power into the twentieth century.

Obstacles to Discipline

The wonder is not that Baptist discipline fell on hard times but that it ever flourished at all. As David Butler acknowledged, "Discipline, as administered by the church, is seldom, if ever, a pleasant duty." Members found it distasteful. "It is not always a pleasant task," W. H. Stokes noted, "to admonish a brother—to point out his delinquencies and urge him a speedy amendment." Churches sometimes shrank from discipline to avoid hurt feelings. Pastor Benjamin Roberts commented on the frequency with which "tenderness" became an excuse for neglecting discipline. The agents of discipline in a local church had to expect resentment, especially from the family and friends of the accused. They sometimes faltered: "It is not popular, or it is cruel, or it is distasteful."[11]

Discipline committees sometimes dragged their feet and had to be rebuked for their negligence. In reply, they decried the mortification they endured in carrying out their commission. They appended to their verdicts the lament that their task was a "painful duty," a source of "unqualified regret." Basil Manly Jr., pastor of a church that was about to exclude a young woman for fornication, expressed to a fellow pastor his anguish: "I presume that our Church will take action next Sat. at the regular church meeting. The young lady had expressed the greatest penitence; and much sympathy is felt for her, together with no small indignation against Mr. Schreiber [her partner]. My own feeling is one of profound grief."[12]

They also found discipline difficult because it created "much trouble." W. H. Stokes confessed that churches sometimes avoided pursuing discipline because "we know if we begin, we shall be under the necessity of prosecuting a long course of dealing, and this is so unpleasant, that rather than go into it, we suffer sin upon our brethren." It was troublesome to endure extended discussions in successive conferences, especially for the investigating committees. The Powelton Baptist Church excluded Sister Allen for falsely accusing Sister Frazier of having borne illegitimate children. The case took two months of "considerable investigation" on the part of the committee, which met with the alienated parties, witnesses, and other concerned parties but failed to resolve the difficulty. Two months later, the church agreed to reconsider the case and persevered through three conferences filled with "considerable conversation." At an impasse, the church called in "helps" from other churches. After six months, it decided to stand by its excommunication of Sister Allen.[13]

Some churches observed the rule "that whoever makes a motion that results in the formation of a committee shall be appointed chairman of that committee." This meant that whoever initiated discipline against a member would have to lead the investigation and make the report. Since many cases, like that of Sisters Allen and Frazier, involved "extended and unpleasant investigations," members hesitated long before they would "place themselves in a position, of accuser and voluntary and active prosecutor of their delinquent brethren."[14]

The distress was especially great when the accused were influential or well connected. The churches did discipline influential members, but the impediments were well-known: "It is no easy matter to carry a disciplinary process through, where the offender is obstinate and has influential friends in the church and congregation." Samuel Henderson acknowledged that "we all have known persons tolerated in neighborhoods, nay, kept in churches for years on account of their relationships to worthy people" because their kindred and friends interposed a barrier to protect them from exclusion. Disciplinary action against prominent members could be a special sign of church fidelity. A young Adiel Sherwood noted it in his journal when Mars Hill Baptist Church "assembled in conference and excluded a valuable member."[15]

When a wealthy member transgressed, the brethren were "pretty sure to 'make haste slowly.' " It was noticeable that the man who paid $100 toward the pastor's salary "can go farther into the world without danger to his church relations, than a poor man." Wealth sometimes overcame piety in disciplinary proceedings. Pastor A. L. Moncrief described a case in which a pious Sunday school superintendent accused the wealthiest and most influential member of the church with drunkenness. Attempting to evade censure, the offender won a majority in his favor, and at the next conference it rejected the charge against the wealthy member and excluded the superintendent "on false charges."[16]

By the late nineteenth century, however, such difficulties were halting the exercise of moral authority in the churches. They never renounced the goal of purity or the duty of discipline, but in the end they preferred sinners in the flock rather than "vexatious discipline."[17]

Dancing and Worldly Amusements

The most distressing issue was "popular amusements," especially dancing. Jesse Mercer referred to it as the "vexed question." It was the rock on which discipline foundered. Baptists had invented nothing new in their proscription of dancing. A statute of pre-Reformation Zurich had outlawed dancing "in order that the Lord God will protect us, that our crops may flourish in the fields, and that there may be good weather." Baptists had little reason to expect that growing numbers of members would balk at discipline against dancers and effectively jeopardize the ecclesiastical authority on which discipline stood.[18]

Antebellum American culture was divided on the moral character of dancing and other amusements. Many of the amusements denounced by evangelicals constituted the staple enjoyments of the southern gentry. Countless Americans, not just the affluent, adopted the ideals of aristocratic gentility, in which dancing transformed the awkward carriage of youth into the graceful, refined movement of adults. But dancing did not find universal favor. Many colleges prohibited it, as did the University of Georgia under the presidency of Presbyterian minister Moses Waddell.[19]

Since many southerners danced, Baptists had to remind their members that it was prohibited behavior. In 1794, Phillips Mill Baptist Church resolved that it was not "lawful" for Christians to "attend on publick Meetings of Dancing and other Vain amusements." Savannah Baptist Church adopted new bylaws in 1835, pronouncing that "we hold the assembling together of persons of any age or character for dancing and other discipation, as highly improper for professors of religion." The Washington Association in 1837 counseled the churches that it was not "consistent with Gospel order, for Church members to attend balls or dancing parties."[20]

Early Americans viewed dancing as part of the education of children, so the Baptists criticized dancing schools more frequently than dancing. In 1799, a member of Powelton Baptist Church asked whether it was "right for a member of a Baptist church to enter or suffer to be entered his children that are under his jurisdiction to a dancing school?" The church answered unanimously in the negative. Christian parents should not, churches urged, allow their children "to attend and danc[e] at baals [balls] or parties" or "to visit houses where there is fiddling." Associations reminded churches to excommunicate parents who "allow their children & wards to frequent balls, or be scholars at dancing schools."[21]

In the early nineteenth century, all the evangelical churches censured their members who danced or abetted dancing. Methodist circuit rider Peter Cartwright once recalled that early Methodist parents "did not allow their children to go to balls or plays; they did not send them to dancing schools." Presbyterians resolved that their members should not permit their children to attend balls, dances, and other worldly amusements. Among Protestants, Episcopalians had the dancing to themselves: One of them observed that "gay society seems to have been relegated to the Episcopalians," who alone "supported the race course, dancing master, and theater." Eliza Andrews complained when the evangelical preachers of Washington, Georgia, attacked dancing: "I wish we had an Episcopal Church established here to serve as a refuge for the many worthy people who are not gamblers and murderers, but who like to indulge in a little dancing now and then."[22]

In large part, the churches succeeded in keeping their members off the dance floors. Every revival of religion diminished dancing's stock. When evangelist George Whitefield promoted the Great Awakening in the South in 1740, the dancing masters began "to cry out that their craft is in danger." Itinerant dancing master Nelson Mount had a prosperous school in Monticello, Georgia—filled with "back sliding Methodists"—but he had to reconsider his plan to set up a school in Macon when "a great revival" occurred there. Conversely, Dorothy Shorter confessed that her attendance at dancing school had hardened her heart against religion. Dancing and evangelical religion did not mix.[23]

When antebellum Baptists ventured to dance, their churches cured them of the practice. Baptist leaders could almost always convince the laity that dancing was immoral. As late as 1858, Newnan Baptist Church prosecuted five men for sanctioning a dancing school and persuaded all five of their error. One by one, the five confessed their actions "wrong" and admitted that dancing was unchristian. It was the same with other fashionable amusements, which included the theater and circus, cards and other games of chance, and billiards. Before the Civil War, the churches usually succeeded in enforcing discipline against all of them.[24]

A revival in 1837 in Greensboro steeled its inhabitants against the theater. The protracted meeting in the Presbyterian church was held over for a fifth night, when a theatrical company advertised it would begin its show. As the church bell signaled the beginning of the service, the theater musicians took up a melody beckoning the citizens to come to the show. The thespians shipped out the following day, for young and old filled the church, while "the theatre room had not its first visitor!" In 1841, the Protestants of Talbotton accomplished the same feat, for two nights furnishing no customers for a theatrical troupe.[25]

By the 1840s, Presbyterian and Methodist churches found it increasingly difficult to dissuade members from worldly amusements. There were instances of Presbyterian elders resigning in frustration and Presbyterian ministers battling reluctant congregations. In 1847, B. M.

Palmer wanted to keep the members of the Columbia, South Carolina, Presbyterian Church away from dances, the theater, the opera, and the racecourse. The elders refused to allow him to announce his intention to apply "wholesome discipline" until Palmer threatened to resign on the grounds that "his conscience would not permit him to be the pastor of a dancing church."[26]

Methodist minister Moses Henkle, editor of the Nashville *Christian Advocate,* complained at midcentury that Methodist discipline had run aground on the indulgence of fashionable amusements: "In every place, we hear complaint, that members . . . trample on the rules, by direct and open acts of violation. How many theatre-going members are hanging, as dead weights, on the Church! How many have danced away their last 'desire to flee from the wrath to come.' . . . And all this takes place among people who have solemnly subscribed to these very stringent rules of holy living."[27]

The years following the Civil War brought a crisis in Southern Baptist discipline. For the first time in their history, the churches encountered sustained resistance to discipline. Somehow the war had changed the churches, and they noticed the difference. One observer, looking back in 1866 at the war, saw it as a time of changing moral standards: "Vice and immorality of almost every kind have been rapidly on the increase during the last five years, and, what is still worse, public sentiment has become so much demoralized that many things are now thought right, or at least admissable, which formerly all men agreed in pronouncing wrong."[28]

In 1868, the Ebenezer Association blamed the war for neglect of discipline: "The war and its results have largely demoralized many of our church members, and as such, there is too much intemperance, profanity, neglect of church duties, heresies, dissensions, and general unchristian conduct, tolerated by the followers of Jesus. Many, perhaps all, of our churches need purifying, and the only way to secure the strength and efficiency of the churches is to keep them pure." In 1866, Penfield Baptist Church blamed the increase in dancing on the ill effects of the war, for it had effaced "the lines of distinction between the Church and the world" and produced "a conformity to practices and amusements not sanctioned by the word of God."[29]

The Civil War had given a jump start to southern "civil religion." After the war, southern churches would find more to bless in the society, and the society would find the religion more congenial. The society became more religious as the churches became less hostile to the society. Although some Southern Baptists resisted, the denomination followed the cultural trend. The earliest sign that Baptists would transform their piety appeared in their ineffectual opposition to dancing and amusements.[30]

Even before the war, there were rare instances of opposition to disciplining dancers. In 1857, LaGrange Baptist Church excluded George W. Chase when he confessed that "he had danced at different times in public and private, that he saw nothing wrong in doing so and intended doing so again whenever he had an opportunity." In 1859, Penfield Baptist Church forgave Brother and Sister Morgan when they pledged to abstain from dancing in the future, in spite of the fact that Brother Morgan said he "did not consider that they had sinned thereby [in dancing] against God, or Christ, or the Bible."[31]

After the war, more and more Baptists made their peace with dancing. Hue Gibson earned exclusion in 1866 when he "persisted in the belief of the charge [dancing] being no harm in his view of the scripture." Ira Reid suffered the same outcome when he "stated that he had attended dancing parties, and had danced, that he did not think it a Sin and was not sorry for dancing." Rosa Howell gained her freedom from the church in 1894 when she charged herself with dancing, adding that "she expected to continue to dance." Eunice O'Brien eluded exclusion only when she recanted her former opinion that "she does not consider dancing a sin." Powelton Baptist Church forgave G. W. Stewart's dancing when he pledged to desist, even though Stewart admitted that "he did not believe dancing to be a sin."[32]

Dancing Baptists multiplied in the 1860s and 1870s. Contrary to the downward trend for most actionable offenses, the average annual rate at which Georgia churches tried members for dancing offenses rose from 8.4 trials per 10,000 members between 1785 and 1860 to a rate of 18.1 between 1861 and 1880, more than doubling the prewar rate. Still, the churches were much more reluctant to exclude the dancers. Georgia Baptists accused of dancing between 1861 and 1880 received exclusion less than half as often as those accused of dancing between 1785 and 1860. Most churches held that promiscuous dancing was wrong in principle, but in practice they relaxed their strictness.[33]

In response, Baptist leaders attacked dancing and other amusements on every front: in the churches, in the associations, and in the press. Denunciations proliferated in church meetings. An early proclamation admitted that Baptists were beginning to see no harm in worldly amusements. In 1857, LaGrange Baptist Church resolved:

> Whereas a question seems to exist in some minds in relation to the fitness and propriety of certain popular amusements as theater going, attendance of the circus, and patronising dancing and dancing Schools—a fact which in its manifestation in our own midst has been a subject of deep regreat to members of the church, Whereas we are convinced that the interests of religion are suffering . . . and whereas we as a church are unwilling to have any complicity with such a sentiment, Therefore resolved that it is the sense of this church, that such practices are of

> unchristian and immoral tendency, and inconsistent with Gospel order. 2nd Resolved that we cannot find it in our conciences to connive at persistence on the part of any in these practices.

The Washington and Athens churches passed resolutions against dancing in 1864, Atlanta First Baptist Church in 1866, and Newnan Baptist Church in 1869. So did numerous other churches for several decades: They decried the "worldly tendency" of dancing and amusements, "which though they may be approved of by the world have ever been regarded by the most devout and pious as unfriendly to the growth of vital Godliness." The associations repeatedly issued the same warning.[34]

They opposed not only dancing but also all other forms of worldly amusements. In 1851 the Rehoboth Association summarized the illicit amusements that drew the flood of postbellum resolutions. It announced that neither members nor their children should attend "Theatres, Circuses, Balls, Dancing Schools, Horse Races, fashionable card-parties, or . . . any other similar places of amusement." Dancing almost always appeared in such lists, and card playing appeared often. The Greensboro Baptist Church approached a complete list in 1870, condemning "the patronage of bar rooms, billiard Saloons, card tables, circuses, and dancing parties." Yet the list went on. Churches proscribed shooting matches, chess, drafts, and backgammon. One clerk tried unsuccessfully to bar baseball.[35]

Young people invented various "plays" and "games" that provided some of the pleasure of dancing without the name. The churches found the dancing games just as objectionable, censuring youth who "dance and play those games equivalent thereto." Associations advised churches to discipline any member who engaged in "the modern fashionable dances under the various sham names of 'Stealing Partners,' 'Twistification,' 'Wild Irishman,' etc." Powelton Baptist Church forgave a number of young members who "confessed to the charge of playing after violin, [who] did not know until [that] time this was dancing." The popularity of these games induced one church to define dancing as "any amusement at Social gatherings requiring music or the Calling of figures in its performance." Others were content to prohibit "dancing . . . or anything bordering so near to dancing." The Hightower Association denounced broadly "plays, such as carrying on, after the Fiddle, a kind of dance called Twistification—Grind the Bottle—or any other such idle plays."[36]

Yet the churches became more permissive. They became uncertain about any discipline for worldly amusements. They thought worldly amusements evil, but they hesitated to address the evil by means of discipline. One difficulty was that young people were the main offenders. The churches tried to censure parents who allowed children to dance or "play," but this did not solve the problem. The dilemma was that the churches were growing mainly through an influx of younger converts, and they were unwilling to cut off the younger generation. Dancing and other amusements appealed primarily to the youth. Churches tried to explain that the amusements were "injurious to youth," devices to "entrap the young." But the LaGrange Baptist Church recognized the dilemma: "The idea is so prevalent that if we enforce church discipline and exclude members they will be lost," and the churches balked at losing the youth.[37]

As Baptists began to doubt the propriety of discipline for dancing church members, they responded in ambivalent ways. On the one hand, they drummed out resolutions against amusements; on the other, they sometimes expunged those resolutions. In 1871, Georgia's former governor Joseph E. Brown, a member of Atlanta Second Baptist Church, submitted a resolution that members who frequented "Theatres or places of Worldly Amusement where exhibitions immoral in themselves or indecent or offensive to good taste or good manners, are witnessed" should be subject to discipline. The resolution passed, but only "after considerable discussion." A portion of the church, irritated by this action, secured a unanimous passage of a compromise resolution the following month in which the church abrogated "all Rules heretofore adopted as a basis of disciplinary action." The church did not pledge to refrain from discipline for amusements, but the more liberal party ensured that each case would require an assessment of culpability of the amusement, which would entail the need for "considerable discussion." The church left its position shrouded in ambiguity.[38]

A decade after resolving to prohibit "dancing in any of its forms," Crawford Baptist Church voted in 1885 to "expunge its definition of dancing as it now stands on the minutes." On the eve of the Civil War, Newnan Baptist Church agreed unanimously that dancing was contrary to "the principles and spirit of Christianity" but refused to adopt a resolution that made "attendance of balls and cotillion parties . . . a subject matter of [disciplinary] dealing." The next year the church could not agree on what action they should take toward members "who patronize dancing schools." It continued to express its "disapprobation" of dancing, but its indecision about disciplinary action gave dancers a measure of immunity.[39]

Powelton Baptist Church rescinded in 1878 its article against dancing and card playing. "Our reason for advising that this article be struck out," the committee explained, "is not that we have any doubts of dancing or card playing being immoral amusements, but we think the teaching of the new Testament sufficient to guide us in the disposition of all cases." LaGrange Baptist Church likewise repealed its rules that required discipline for amusements, substituting "the Old and New Testaments [as] its only rule of its faith and practice." The argument was essentially the same as the one made by Arminian Baptists who struggled against creeds. But if the Bible prohibited dancing and card playing, what was the harm in writing it down?[40]

The churches split into three factions on the question of dancing and amusements. The conservatives remained convinced that scripture forbade dancing and that dancers should be subject to discipline. The liberals accepted the complete innocence of dancing. The moderates felt that dancing was unspiritual and unscriptural but were unwilling to exclude Baptists who felt differently. By way of compromise, churches repealed the resolutions requiring discipline while continuing to denounce the activity.

When dancing liberal F. M. Cleveland stood before his church to answer the charge of dancing, he admitted attending a dancing party, but the moderate faction's tolerance prevailed. Cleveland felt he had done nothing wrong, so the church "agreed to drop the case and relieve Brother Cleveland from any charge of unchristian conduct." The Georgia Association recognized the existence of the liberal faction: Since "fiddling and dancing" had become so popular in southern society, "some members of the Church profess to believe them to be harmless practices." In LaGrange Baptist Church, the moderates blocked discipline against dancers, prompting a conservative member to prefer "a charge against the church for neglect of duty in tolerating dancing."[41]

Only the predominance of the moderate view explains both the denunciations of dancing and the evidence that churches were "delinquent in reporting the names of such members as . . . do injury to the cause of Christ by participating in the amusements of the world." Many churches followed the policy of Savannah Baptist Church, urging self-restraint and a "be ye kind" toleration of those who indulged. By the 1890s, Southern Baptist opposition to worldly amusements was mostly baying at the moon. By then, the rate at which Georgia churches brought members to trial for dancing offenses had fallen well below antebellum levels; the rate at which 1890s churches actually excluded members for dancing offenses had fallen by more than 70 percent. Resolutions against amusements became plaintive cries of congregations that had lost the resolve to discipline.[42]

Urban Religion

Although the South long remained a predominantly rural area, its rapid urbanization after Reconstruction shaped southern culture. The promise of the New South was not rural cotton, the price of which remained low because of overproduction, but urban industry and commerce. Every village hoped to become the next Birmingham, whose coal and iron operations spurred growth from 3,000 inhabitants in 1880 to 133,000 in 1910. The lure of the city attracted educated professionals and ambitious illiterates.[43]

In 1886, New South aspirations brought the first electric streetcars in the nation to Montgomery, Richmond, and Atlanta. Electric lights and telephone systems spread yet more rapidly. The region's 11 percent of the nation's urban population had 18 percent of the nation's municipally owned power stations and 22 percent of its telephone systems. Urban religion prospered as well. As railroads connected county after county to urban areas, rural life, including church life, began to follow the fashions and values of the city. Baptists noticed the change.[44]

During the antebellum period, urban congregations labored under a dark cloud. Several cities had difficulty establishing Baptist congregations, and the urban churches often remained smaller than many rural congregations. The growth of Baptist work in New Orleans and Mobile was painfully slow. Jesse Mercer wondered aloud why "our brethren have so much trouble getting pastors in Southern Cities."[45]

The explanation came from Baptist ambivalence about urbanity. In addition to their reputation as centers of wickedness, cities inspired awe. The cool refinement of city dwellers intimidated the poorly educated Baptist preachers. They shrank from city pulpits in part because city churches would not accept them. Conscious that their Presbyterian and Episcopalian neighbors considered them unworthy of respect, urban Baptist congregations sought well-educated preachers who could attract the more "respectable" classes. The same consciousness impelled aspirations for an educated clergy. Urban Baptist preachers attracted the notice and respect of their peers and acquired the salaries and wealth to go along with it. They commanded salaries five to ten times higher than their rural counterparts and attained wealth four times above the national average.[46]

Basil Manly Sr., president of the University of Alabama, declined to accept a pulpit in Richmond, explaining that the labor was too demanding and "the people in a city are sermon-ridden. They grow hard, insensible, if not carping and surly." Jesse Mercer recalled his visit to Charleston, South Carolina: "I went to the place with many prejudices against the brethren in that place, taking it for granted, that as they lived in a large city, they were a proud, formal, fashionable people, and had very little religion." Although Mercer went away impressed by Charleston piety, prejudices against urban Baptists did not die easily. In 1877, an African-American Baptist preacher commended Atlanta pastor Frank Quarles, who was "a good servant of God, even if he does live in a city, and in Atlanta at that; and he has just as much good practical religion in him as if he was born and raised in the country. The truth is, I am beginning to believe that a great many of our city brethren are very nearly, if not quite, as good as our country brethren, any way."[47]

Country Baptists after the war began to believe the same thing—or, at least, to believe that if city Baptists were not quite as good as country Baptists, they were nonetheless worthy of emulation. By 1870, the leadership of the southern denomination had passed to the city pulpits. In 1868, the Western Association, denouncing the spread of worldliness and popular amusements, placed the heaviest burden on "city and town churches, which are look[ed] up to as examples."[48]

S. G. Hillyer recalled in 1869 the time "when the strength and wealth of our denomination were in the country. The planters, and their families, formed a large and influential membership, which gave tone to public sentiment, and regulated, in a great degree, the state of Christian morality." But a revolution had occurred: "The churches of our large towns and cities are generally stronger. The superior influence is now with them. . . . The intelligence, wealth, and social position, and able ministry, with which they are so highly favored, must necessarily make them conspicuous in the ranks of our denomination, and give their opinions and practices a power for good, or for evil, which is almost irresistable." On city churches rested the burden of conserving doctrinal fidelity and moral purity for the denomination, Hillyer argued, because "it is a fact, the country imitates the city, and country churches imitate city churches."[49]

Although many Baptists considered the ascendancy of urban churches a mixed blessing, for traditionalists it was a catastrophe. Urban churches proved incapable of sustaining discipline and the exclusivist vision on which it stood. On a per member basis, postbellum town and city churches in Georgia brought their members to trial at about one-third the rate of their village and rural counterparts and excluded their members at about one-half the rate. The difference was not that urban Baptists committed fewer transgressions but that urban churches were more tolerant.

The city churches retained the policy of exclusion when members joined other denominations. They maintained their opposition to recognizing alien immersion. They adhered to the principle of close communion. Indeed, they were more likely to exclude those members whom they managed to bring to trial. Town and city churches excluded 57 percent of defendants in the 1860s, increasing to 69 percent in the 1890s. Village and rural churches showed the opposite trend, declining from 50 percent in the 1860s to 33 percent in the 1890s.

The sagging exclusion percentage in rural churches indicated some relaxing of discipline, but the rising exclusion rate of the urban churches may not indicate sustained strictness. Much postwar urban church discipline consisted of lopping off defectors to other denominations, often by sweeping clean the membership roll. More than half of all trials in urban churches between 1861 and 1900 involved offenses against the church, most by members who joined another denomination.[50]

Conservatives bemoaned the failure of the urban churches to provide leadership. F. M. Law urged the need to trim the church because drunkenness, fighting, gambling, and dancing often "pass unnoticed" and congregations exhibit "little or no difference between the church and the world." This was true "especially in our towns and cities," where immorality was "more tolerated . . . than in the country churches." J. B. Gambrell, the president of Mercer University, argued that country churches exercised "something like New Testament discipline"; city churches did not. Urban Baptists were more generous and less prejudiced, but many of them were "so broad and attenuated, that they amount to little or nothing in a moral or spiritual way. And, as to prejudices, they have none, no, not even against the Devil or his agents and enterprises. . . . Many a city Baptist church is over trained in form and breadth till the rugged integrity of the New Testament is trained out." The exclusiveness that undergirded discipline withered before the inclusivism of the urban environment.[51]

The soft spot in urban discipline, observers thought, was tolerance of worldly amusements. S. G. Hillyer accurately predicted that once urban Baptists extended the walls of the church enough to include members who pursued worldly amusements, all Baptist discipline would collapse. "If therefore, our city churches relax their discipline, and tolerate irregularities of behaviour, inconsistent with a pure christian morality, these irregularities will be sure to find apologists and even advocates among the people of the country. Sooner or later, discipline will be relaxed everywhere." The offenses that posed a clear and present threat, fretted Hillyer, were "rafflings, card-playing, dancing, attending the theatre, and opera, &c. . . . Thus the blandishments of wealth, the power of fashion, and the subtle relations of society, (so-called,) conspire to carry the church along with the world, in the giddy pursuit of pleasure." The barriers of discipline were "broken down."[52]

Another observer excoriated city churches for setting a bad example. When country churches attempted to discipline members for dancing, the dancers pleaded that city pastors "favor dancing, regard it as innocent, allow it in their houses and qualify their daughters to attend. And then, too, the practice of the large city churches and the expressions of their pastors, from the seaboard to the mountains, are minutely and forcibly detailed, with the question accompanying, 'Why shall not this church do likewise? And why should our pastor propose to be more righteous than these learned, pious city preachers?' The result is, church discipline is trampled under foot."[53]

Urban churches did not hold the line against worldly amusements. Whereas almost one in four discipline cases in rural churches between 1861 and 1900 included charges of worldly amusements, barely one in twenty urban cases did. In the town and urban churches, discipline for dancing declined by 60 percent after the antebellum period. Rural and village churches between 1861 and 1900 prosecuted members for dancing at a rate twenty-three times higher than that of urban churches in the same period; they excluded dancers at a rate eleven times higher.[54]

Although town and urban churches occasionally announced their opposition to dancing and amusements, they showed little resolve to address the issue by means of discipline. Rural and village churches entered a similar decline a little later. Urban Baptists blazed the trail that the rest followed. Many began to view dancing, within proper bounds, as an innocent pursuit. In addition, they were developing better, more efficient methods of promoting spirituality than through corrective church discipline.

Efficiency and Progress

Before the late nineteenth century, Baptists defined the church in terms of its purity. The preacher explained and proved pure doctrine, which carried power for conversion and piety. Praise and prayer proceeded according to the pure example of the apostles. Church government conformed to the pure pattern of the primitive church. Membership was reserved for the pure and was guarded by discipline.

By the late nineteenth century, the paradigm of the pure church seemed less compelling. It was the vision of the efficient church that captivated Baptists of the Gilded Age. Baptists by no means abandoned the quest for purity, but it no longer gave the policies and principles of Baptist churches their shape. The search for the efficient church transformed traditional notions of purity. Baptists were not alone. Churches across the nation were abandoning old models of congregational life. They instituted more efficient systems of church finance and transformed themselves into centers of social life and recreational activity. Efficiency became the watchword of a new generation.[55]

The ideal of the efficient church informed the labors of postbellum pastors, especially in city pulpits. In 1872, the members of Atlanta Second Baptist Church, not satisfied with their level of piety, called a meeting "to promote a more efficient church organization." Baptists of an earlier generation might have considered such a goal presumptuous because the pattern of church organization revealed in the New Testament was the true one and, if true, then most efficient. Now efficiency meant something else.[56]

Savannah Baptist Church in 1873 appointed a committee on "Systematic Effort." The committee took it for granted that its goal, and the goal of lay Bible study, was "church efficiency." Athens Baptist Church sought to remedy meager attendance at meetings in 1867 in order "to ensure the efficiency of the church." The Georgia Association urged its churches to adopt means "for making each and every member efficient in the discharge of that particular line of duty for which he has talent."[57]

Where antebellum southern churches might have honored the disciplinary abilities of their pastors, postbellum churches sought efficiency.

Barnesville Baptist Church, expressing appreciation for pastor R. J. Willingham at his resignation, praised him first as "an efficient servant." Newnan Baptist Church voiced their esteem for J. H. Hall upon his resignation from a pastorate that he "so efficiently and acceptably filled." Efficiency headed the list of virtues for New South pastors.[58]

The success of postbellum churches, especially in the cities, compelled them to seek new methods of organization. Missionary and educational enterprises established before the war required broader financial support from the churches. Town and city churches expanded and built tasteful new buildings to house their larger congregations. Carpeted and furnished to suit refined tastes, churches introduced instrumental music, ordered expensive organs from New York firms, and employed organists and professional quartet choirs to thrill their audiences. The prominent churches required prominent preachers and had to pay $2,000 or $3,000 annually to attract and keep them.[59]

The unintended result of such trappings of success was that discipline was squeezed out of its traditional home, the monthly church conference. Urban church conferences, already swelled with the press of financial business necessary to address perennial fiscal straits, reached such size that merely keeping up with the admission and dismission of members proved a burden on conference time. Harried meetings shoved disciplinary business on sidings to attend to more urgent concerns. In this way, Atlanta First Baptist Church neglected to dispose of a profanity charge for sixteen months, a fraud charge for twenty-nine. Urban Baptists could do little more by way of discipline than visit peremptory excommunication on notorious offenders and defectors.[60]

The efficiency of the churches had two components: system and activity. To achieve efficiency, the churches sought a system that would produce generous financial giving. When Atlanta Second Baptist Church recorded church revenues three times greater than in any previous year, Baptist editor H. H. Tucker concluded that "system is the secret of the whole of it." The plan that postbellum southern churches adopted was "the System Known as the Envelope System."[61]

Traditionally, Baptist churches had raised money with the subscription method. At the beginning of each year, members put their names on the subscription list, pledging a certain sum toward the pastor's salary. They relied on the same method when erecting or improving their buildings, contributing to missions, or aiding impoverished church members. In the postwar economy, Baptist churches experimented with pew rents, assessments based on income, or a system of church dues, sometimes with a paid dues collector.[62]

Eventually, most raised part or all of their budget with the envelope system, in which members pledged to give a small amount weekly or monthly, remitted in an envelope. Athens Baptist Church adopted the plan in 1868, Atlanta First in 1871, Atlanta Second in 1872, Savannah in 1873, LaGrange in 1888, Crawfordville in 1896, and Newnan in 1897. William Strickland endorsed the sentiment of the Stone Mountain Association, which recommended in 1870 that the "*Envelope System* be adopted by the churches."[63]

In the drive toward efficiency, churches also organized the membership into a system of standing committees. Baptist churches were moving in this direction by the 1850s, but it was in the 1870s that the movement achieved its final form. Macon Baptist Church led the way, appointing in 1877 standing committees on visitation, social visitation, the sick, the poor, strangers, absentees, Sunday schools, and missions. Other churches, especially those in towns and cities, followed suit. The committees realized the second component of the Baptist pursuit of efficiency—activity. With "the whole church" divided into committees, "the aim is to give every member of the church something to do," producing "a tender-hearted, happy, united and enthusiastic band of workers, going about doing good." One of the great purposes of Christian training, Baptist leaders urged, was "to increase the efficiency of the church by calling into useful activity every member."[64]

The pursuit of system and activity entailed a new conception of the pastor. Traditionally, Baptist pastors viewed themselves as custodians of orthodoxy and purity. They expected orthodox preaching to create right belief and pure behavior. Pastors in the New South supplanted the priority of proclaiming truth with that of efficient management of pious workers. "Without organization there would be no system; without system there would be no efficient work. . . . Much of the pastor's time must be given to the arrangement of the work and the appointment of workers."[65]

Notions of the mission of the church underwent a similar transformation. A church aiming at efficiency valued orthodoxy and purity as secondary objectives. The primary goal was action—"The essence of Christianity is activity," Baptist preachers began to feel. The goal was to make every member "available and useful," because "Christianity must be progressive, and to be progressive must be aggressive. It must not wait for something to be, but must do something." Activism became the crowning virtue of Baptist piety in the twentieth century.[66]

The churches applied their activism to missions and evangelism, but no longer did they conduct evangelism only to save sinners and establish pure, orthodox churches. Baptists found a larger vision that transformed the evangelistic task itself. J. B. Gambrell, Progressive Era president of the Southern Baptist Convention, goaded Baptist pastors to the task of "getting everybody in the church to do something," in order that Baptists might achieve their highest goal—to "gather in and dominate all the forces in this widening, intensifying, complex civilization, by a masterful spirit of evangelism." Evangelism would establish a pure social order.[67]

Belief in the inevitability of progress fueled the transformation of Southern Baptist churches from asylums of the sanctified to efficient labor clubs. As early as the 1840s and 1850s, Baptists thought they could discern moral progress in "this age of improvement." Late-nineteenth-century Baptists, still eschewing the notion of progress in doctrine, embraced the idea that "the one universal law of this nineteenth century is progress." The century was, pastor S. M. Provence declared, "remarkable for its progress."[68]

The organizers were not dismayed by the "great number of unorganized Baptists in our midst." Despite such inefficient congregations, they discerned "a spirit of progress in almost all our churches." They ascribed this moral advance primarily to the efficient labor of the laity: "the brethren . . . are feeling more than ever their individual responsibility." Baptists paraded the new progress in their yearly associational gatherings. The Middle Association changed the name of its annual report on the "State of Religion" to the "Progress and Development of the Churches," reporting triumphantly that "within the last ten years our churches have increased the number of members more than one thousand; they have more than doubled their contributions to the various mission fields and other benevolent work. . . . The salaries of our pastors have been greatly increased and more than fifty thousand dollars has been added to the value of church property. Much progress has been made in our Sunday school work. . . . The greatest progress, however, has been in woman's work."[69]

The progress had two foci: First, Baptists were giving more money to missions, to the support of the clergy, and to the improvement of church properties. In 1870, Georgia Baptists reported no state missionaries and contributions to missions of $4,151. In 1880, they reported 24 missionaries and $16,829 given to missions. By 1895, the numbers grew to 54 missionaries and $57,417. Second, they were proliferating organizations for efficient labor, such as Sunday schools and Sunday school unions, young peoples' unions, and women's missionary unions. LaGrange Baptist Church praised pastor J. W. Ford primarily for his abilities in advancing the financial support and efficient activity of church members. "The improvement of the church property, increased effort in the benevolent enterprises of the church, larger attendance upon public worship and the devotional meetings of the church," the church resolved, attested to his "spiritual power."[70]

The New Form of Democratic Religion

In turning to the efficient church, Southern Baptists did not repudiate the need for discipline and purity, but they did subordinate them to a new agenda. Church discipline did not long survive service to its new master. In theory, church discipline had a significant place in producing an efficient church. The leaders of LaGrange Baptist Church felt that "our declension in moral power and spirituality and our loss of interest and efficiency in all departments of church work" could be attributed to a neglect of discipline. The "only way to secure the strength and efficiency of the churches," the Ebenezer Association urged, was to "keep them pure" through discipline. The Georgia Association reminded its churches of the "importance of exercising strict, Godly discipline, that our members may become more and more efficient." Church efficiency increased, some Baptists urged, in the unlikely soil of discipline.[71]

In practice, Baptists could not overcome complacency about discipline. If they grew alarmed at the decline of discipline, their confidence in progress assuaged their fears. B. M. Callaway, looking back over the history of Sardis Baptist Church in 1888, speculated that the decline of discipline was evidence of spiritual advance. Noticing that "cases of discipline are becoming less frequent," Callaway concluded that "church members are generally better now" and "the moral tone of professing Christians is on rising ground." He predicted that "improvements in the future would tend to further elevate the Christian character of church membership and diminish crime and the necessity of discipline in the churches." The deacons of Savannah Baptist Church took the same view of their congregation's infrequent recourse to discipline: "Our membership as a whole is orderly in christian walk and conversation, and but little occasion has existed, and does exist, for arraignments of our members for misconduct."[72]

Pastor J. H. Fortson took the sanguine view that progress in the church meant transforming discipline from correction into nurture: "We know the churches are not so strict in discipline as in former years, yet we hope there is more formative discipline. If it is true that corrective discipline is not so good, but formative discipline is better, we hope this indicates growth. There is certainly less dram drinking and, therefore, less drunkenness among our members. We believe also that our members are less inclined to join the dancers." Traditionally, Baptists thought of discipline as "corrective discipline," the censure of transgressions among members. Antebellum Baptists recognized that the church also had the task of "formative discipline," the spiritual training of its members. Basil Manly Sr. could explain in 1843 that "discipline means instruction. It therefore includes the whole order of a christian church. Preaching is discipline; the administration of the ordinances is discipline; the infliction of church censures is discipline; and all the ways in which the edifying of the body of Christ is promoted, constitute discipline." But in the vast majority of cases, antebellum Baptists reserved the term *discipline* for "the infliction of church censures."[73]

By the end of the century, *discipline* was redefined. Manly and his antebellum colleagues saw corrective discipline as a component of formative discipline. For many New South Baptists, formative discipline displaced corrective discipline. In 1894, Baptist editor J. C. McMichael, asserting that "the fundamental idea of church discipline should not be to lop off dead limbs," urged instead that "it should have more especial reference to taking the new members and training and developing them into strength and usefulness." Church discipline, McMichael argued elsewhere, "denotes a process of teaching and training." McMichael pushed corrective discipline aside, reasoning that true discipline "is a process which, if faithfully carried forward along all the lines of church-life, will in great measure prevent the offences that ever make exclusions necessary."[74]

The old church discipline did not promote efficiency very well; it cut off members who might otherwise have been mobilized for church work. The new church discipline sought to turn dead weight into efficient laborers. Pastor J. B. Parrott, promoting young people's unions in the churches, argued that the answer to any "lack of efficiency" rested in "discipline and training." The churches, he observed, housed "a vast amount of raw undeveloped material. . . . These are to be reached and developed and utilized by teaching them their duty and training them in a discharge of it. . . . In the neglect of this important duty lies the secret of the failure of many Christians and the inefficiency of many churches." The design of discipline was to engage every church member in activity, "to increase, concentrate, and direct the agency of Christians in the conversion of the world."[75]

Some Baptists did not feel that the demise of discipline was a great loss. They urged attenuating the penalties. Pastor M. J. Webb sought to restrict exclusion to cases in which the offender did not repent, in place of the former practice of excluding all gross offenders, penitent or not. A few postbellum Baptists went further still, holding "that when a man is once brought into the church, he should never be excluded for any cause." Many churches had factions who were "not satisfied that the church has the right to proceed to extreme disciplinary measure."[76]

To some extent, this lack of enthusiasm for traditional discipline derived from the prior commitment to efficiency. Strict discipline would damage the ability to carry out the reforming mission because it would mean the loss of workers and their contributions. Churches hesitated "lest the exercise of wholesome discipline result in injury to the church." Editor M. B. Wharton, worrying that traditional discipline would weaken the denomination, found in the exigencies of a changing world a demand that "we suit our policy to its ever-varying necessities." Early Georgia Baptists, Wharton admitted, "exercised rigid discipline, but to do that now would be to exclude our strongest members, especially from a financial point of view, while other denominations, witnessing the pruning, stand ready with open arms to receive the falling branches." Efficient evangelization of the world depended as much on the generous offerings of church members as on their organized activity—neither of which could endure the exclusivist moral discipline of earlier decades.[77]

Other Baptists felt the attractions of individualist and subjectivist ideas. At the end of the century, Baptists emphasized as never before "Baptist distinctives," doctrines such as believer's baptism by immersion and soul liberty. J. L. D. Hillyer, pastor of a Florida church, taught his congregation that "no one has a right to judge a servant of Christ. Each one must account for himself before God. This is the basis of that doctrine of 'Soul liberty,' for which Baptists have always contended." Although Hillyer probably did not intend to undermine the authority on which discipline rested, such doctrines extended the reach of individualism and subjectivism in the churches. Lacking confidence in their moral authority over one another, members grew reticent to initiate disciplinary proceedings, being "afraid the culprit will rise and say, 'physician, heal thyself.'"[78]

With members equal before the throne of God, none could judge another. Baptists had traditionally understood the democracy of Baptist churches to mean that all church members exercised ecclesiastical authority jointly, including authority over belief and behavior. By the Progressive Era, Baptists began to embrace the idea that a democratic church meant that all were equally free from ecclesiastical authority. Pierce Simms, facing charges of dancing, sought to avoid exclusion by appealing to the individual liberty conferred by church democracy: "He thought the Baptist church was a democratic body and according to his opinion each member should enjoy personal liberty & that no one had a right to interfere with his pleasures." Although Simms did not elude exclusion, his argument was gaining wider acceptance. The appeal to individual liberty undermined older notions of congregational authority. New ideas of tolerance, linked to new understandings of "soul liberty," gained entrance to the pantheon of Baptist virtues and made room for the coexistence in Baptist churches of wide doctrinal differences. There was a new form of democratic religion.[79]

The elevation of toleration as an ecclesiastical virtue was a necessary condition for the Southern Baptist controversy in the late twentieth century. Baptists had always tolerated a measure of doctrinal difference, but until the twentieth century, they had also enforced doctrinal unity, believing that orthodoxy was a source of church life more important than tolerance. Once the vision of the efficient church replaced that of the pure church as the goal of Christian community, Baptists could no longer afford rigid exclusivism. Tolerance improved efficiency in cooperative evangelism and missions. The tolerance of the efficient church gave shade to varied theological opinions, so that once the denomination belatedly confronted modernism, serious differences emerged.

Southern Baptists did not reject all exclusivism when they individualized their democratic religion. The ecclesiastical authority to enforce purity eroded, but the less institutionalized authority of a morally conservative southern society and a fundamentalist clergy ensured that Southern Baptist churches retained a measure of commitment to exclusivism. Although informal, this exclusivism secured considerable consensus on right doctrine and right living for two or three generations after the disappearance of church discipline. Even in the late twentieth century, Southern Baptists' commitment to exclusivist orthodoxy and purity remained strong enough to challenge successfully the proponents of tolerance and an inclusivist church.

Conclusion

The transformation of democratic authority was a long process. The churches experienced a revolutionary change between 1850 and 1950. In 1850, Southern Baptists understood democracy largely in terms of ecclesiastical authority. In 1950, they understood it primarily in terms of individual freedom. The revolution gained momentum from individualist trends in American culture, but it also contributed to new forms of individualism in the churches. The changing character of individualism is an important part of the story of the transformation of American evangelicalism. The church-oriented evangelicalism of early nineteenth-century American Protestantism continued the Puritan pursuit of the pure, primitive church. Twentieth-century American evangelicalism preferred pietism's traditional approach: the promotion of an individual spirituality that was loosely connected to the institutional churches. Evangelicals were no longer convinced that there was a divine mandate to establish pure churches as the kingdom of God on earth. The kingdom was within. Individual piety required no mediation of the ecclesiastical institutions. The role of the church changed.

The story of the Southern Baptist heritage of democratic authority is a part of the larger story of the transformation of Western culture. Modernity's reverence of the individual reshaped the social and intellectual landscape of the northern hemisphere. Southern Baptists resisted the change. Although they embraced aspects of individualism—persons had to exercise faith individually and possessed inalienable human rights as individuals—they rejected its privatizing currents. John Dewey described how modernity's new individualism rested on a confidence in the moral and intellectual discernment of individuals. In modernity, Dewey said, "there is a gradual decay of the authority of fixed institutions . . . and a growing belief in the power of individual minds, guided by methods of observation, experiment and reflection, to attain the truths needed for the guidance of life."[1] Each reasoning soul discovered truth and morality privately.

Southern Baptists were latecomers to this aspect of modernity. Although they recognized that human reason was prone to error, they preferred to entrust the definition of truth and morality to the congregation rather than to the individual. When a woman who had been baptized by immersion by a Presbyterian minister sought membership in a Baptist church in 1856, Basil Manly Sr. refused to privilege her conviction that her baptism was sufficient for admission. "Even if she has no sense of the defectiveness of her Pedobaptist immersion," Manly argued, "this does not prove that it was infallibly right and sufficient. It is only an opinion of hers, which may be as apt to be wrong as the opinion of other people. Especially, why should she set up her judgment against that of the whole body of churches of the only people under heaven who are striving to keep the ordinance of baptism as Christ delivered it?"[2] Southern Baptists privileged corporate responsibility for truth and morality. It was the basis of their democratic religion.

A significant residue remains. In the Southern Baptist denomination, churches occasionally exclude an adulterer, but usually prefer to sentence offenders of different kinds to private therapy rather than communal discipline. More commonly, perhaps, Baptist associations agitate to disfellowship churches that ordain women, tolerate homosexuality, or recognize alien immersions as valid baptisms. Although selectively applied and attenuated, the heritage of democratic authority continues to make its presence felt in American evangelicalism.

Notes

Abbreviations Used in Notes

EU	Special Collections, Pitts Theology Library, Emory University, Atlanta, Ga.
GDAH	Georgia Department of Archives and History, Atlanta, Ga.
MU	Special Collections, Main Library, Mercer University, Macon, Ga.
SBTS	Special Collections, James P. Boyce Centennial Library, Southern Baptist Theological Seminary, Louisville, Ky.

Introduction

1. Bradley J. Longfield, *The Presbyterian Controversy: Fundamentalists, Modernists, and Moderates* (New York: Oxford University Press, 1991), 132. This was Longfield's description of Presbyterian moderate Charles R. Erdman.

2. Cecil E. Sherman, "An Overview of the Moderate Movement," in *The Struggle for the Soul of the SBC: Moderate Responses to the Fundamentalist Movement*, ed. Walter B. Shurden (Macon, Ga.: Mercer University Press, 1993), 40, 42.

3. Robert G. Torbet, *A History of the Baptists* (Philadelphia: Judson, 1950), 15.

4. See H. Leon McBeth, *The Baptist Heritage* (Nashville: Broadman Press, 1987), 32–48; Torbet, *History*, 59–62.

5. McBeth, *Baptist Heritage*, 123–152; Torbet, *History*, 220–238.

6. McBeth, *Baptist Heritage*, 206, 203.

7. Robert B. Semple, *History of the Baptists in Virginia* (1810; reprint, Lafayette, Tenn.: Church History Research and Archives, 1976), 98–101, 449–452; Torbet, *History*, 222–226, 239–252.

8. Jesse Mercer, *History of the Georgia Baptist Association* (Washington, Ga: n.p., 1838; reprint, Washington, Ga.: Ga. Baptist Association, 1980), 16, 140; Robert G. Gardner, et al., *A History of the Georgia Baptist Association, 1784–1984* (Washington, Ga.: Wilkes Publishing Company, 1988), 537.

9. Although most non-Landmarkists believed in Baptist successionism, they did not elevate it to the same status. For Graves, succession determined the validity of the churches; for other Baptists, validity derived from following the apostolic example more than from apostolic succession.

10. Robert Gardner, *Baptists of Early America: A Statistical Study* (Atlanta: Georgia Baptist Historical Society, 1983), 35; Adiel Sherwood, *A Gazetteer of the State of Georgia* (Charleston, S.C.: W. Riley, 1827; reprint, Athens: University of Georgia Press, 1939), 132, 130–131, 117–120, 129–131; J. R. Graves, *The Southern Baptist Almanac and Annual Register, for the Year of Our Lord, 1852* (Nashville: Tennessee Publication Society, [1851?]), 15; "Statistical Table of the Denomination in Georgia, for 1860," *Minutes*, Georgia Baptist Convention, 1860, 46–47; *Minutes of the Annual Conferences of the Methodist Episcopal Church, South, for the Year 1860* (Nashville: Southern Methodist Publishing House, 1861), 259; James Stacy, *A History of the Presbyterian Church in Georgia* (Elberton, Ga.: n.p. [1912?]), 285.

11. William W. Sweet, "The Churches as Moral Courts of the Frontier," *Church History* 2 (1933): 3–21.

Chapter 1

1. Church Book, Savannah First Baptist Church, Savannah, 2 May 1806, 6 and 13 June 1806, 31 August 1806, 12 and 14 September 1806, MU.

2. I recorded 33,383 excommunications from association records. For each year from 1846 to 1860, I multiplied the church members not in my association sample by the average annual exclusion rate of the sample, rendering an additional 4,319 exclusions. I estimated 2,500 to 5,000 additional exclusions from churches outside my sample from 1785 to 1845.

3. Matt. 18:15–17; 1 Cor. 5.13; Justin Martyr, *Apology*, I.66; Tertullian, *Apology*, 39.3–4, 46.17. See also O. D. Watkins, *A History of Penance*, 2 vols. (1920; reprint, New York: Burt Franklin, 1961); R. S. T. Haselhurst, *Some Account of the Penitential Discipline of the Early Church* (New York: Macmillan, 1921).

4. Martin Bucer wrote that "the corruption of discipline ruins the entire ministry of teaching and sacraments, and the devil fills their place with superstitions" (*The Common Places of Martin Bucer*, ed. and trans. D. F. Wright [Appleford, England: Sutton Courtenay Press, 1972], 205). Calvin argued that without discipline the "Church cannot retain its true condition" and that "the safety of the Church is founded and supported" by "doctrine, discipline, and the sacraments" ("Articles concerning the Organization of the Church and of Worship at Geneva," in *Calvin: Theological Treatises*, ed. and trans. J. K. S. Reid, Library of Christian Classics [Philadelphia: Westminster Press, 1954], 51; "Reply to Sadolet," in ibid., 232). See also Robert M. Kingdon, "Peter Martyr Vermigli and the Marks of the True Church," in *Continuity and Discontinuity in Church History: Essays Presented to George Hunston Williams*, eds. F. Forrester Church and Timothy George (Leiden: E. J. Brill, 1979), 199–201; Jeffrey P. Jaynes, " 'Ordo et Libertas': Church Discipline and the Makers of Church Order in Sixteenth

Century North Germany" (Ph.D. dissertation, Ohio State University, 1993); Wolfgang Dobras, *Ratsregiment, Sittenpolizei und Kirchenzucht in der Reichsstadt Konstanz 1531–1548* (Gütersloh, Germany: Gerd Mohn, 1993).

5. Increase Mather, *The Order of the Gospel, Professed and Practised by the Churches of Christ in New England . . .* (Boston, 1700; reprinted in *Increase Mather vs. Solomon Stoddard: Two Puritan Tracts* [New York: Arno Press, 1972]), 3. See also John Cotton, *The Way of the Churches of Christ in New-England* (London, 1645; reprinted in John Cotton, *The New England Way* [New York: AMS Press, 1984]), 304; Edmund S. Morgan, *Visible Saints: The History of a Puritan Idea* (New York: New York University Press, 1963), 9–16. On Separatist discipline, see Timothy George, *John Robinson and the English Separatist Tradition*, National Association of Baptist Professors of Religion Dissertation Series 1 (Macon, Ga.: Mercer University Press, 1982), 136–148. On early Baptist discipline, see T. Dowley, "Baptists and Discipline in the 17th Century," *Baptist Quarterly* 24 (1971): 157–166; James Lynch, "English Baptist Church Discipline to 1740," *Foundations* 18 (1975): 121–135. On New England Puritan discipline, see Emil Oberholzer, Jr., *Delinquent Saints: Disciplinary Action in the Early Congregational Churches of Massachusetts* (New York: Columbia University Press, 1956); Morgan, *Visible Saints*, 22–25.

6. See Rhys Isaac, *The Transformation of Virginia, 1740–1790* (New York: Norton, 1988), 161–205.

7. Quoted in Bertram Wyatt-Brown, *Southern Honor: Ethics and Behavior in the Old South* (New York: Oxford University Press, 1982), 23. See also pp. 90–97, 272–361.

8. Mrs. B. H. Gammell, Letter to Mrs. Marion Baber Blackshear, 5 August 1867, Baber-Blackshear Collection, Special Collections, University of Georgia at Athens; *Minutes*, Georgia Baptist Association, 1818, 4. Baptist pastor James Perryman expressed a view common in eighteenth- and nineteenth-century America: "It cannot then be denied, that the public prosperity of our land depends upon the virtue of the people" (*The Christian Index*, 12 December 1839, 801).

9. John Asplund, *The Annual Register of the Baptist Denomination in North America* (1791; reprint, Goodlettsville, Tenn.: Baptist Banner, 1979), 47; Minutes, Philadelphia Baptist Association, 1761, in A. D. Gillette, ed., *Minutes of the Philadelphia Baptist Association, from A.D. 1707 to A.D. 1807* (Philadelphia: American Baptist Publication Society, 1851), 85; Jesse Mercer, "Comprehensive Commentary," *The Christian Index*, 24 February 1835, 3.

10. *Minutes*, Sunbury Baptist Association, 1830, 8.

11. Church Book, Bethesda Baptist Church, Greene County, Ga., 17 April 1824, in *Conference Minutes of Bethesda Baptist Church: August 1817 to December 1865*, transcribed by Vivian Toole Cates (Tyler: East Texas Genealogical Society, 1991); Church Book, Powelton Baptist Church, Hancock County, Ga., 25 November 1848, 1 April 1866, MU. In the late nineteenth century, churches began to dismiss the congregation prior to the observance of communion. See Church Book, Newnan Baptist Church, Newnan, Ga., 23 June 1855, MU; Church Book, Athens First Baptist Church, Athens, Ga., 7 January 1877, MU; A. W., "Is It Right?" *The Christian Index*, 22 June 1871, 97.

12. John Asplund, *The Universal Register of the Baptist Denomination in North America* (Boston: John Folson, 1794), 5.

13. Church Book, Bethesda Baptist Church, Greene County, Ga., 24 August 1834, MU; Church Book, Savannah First Baptist Church, 19 April, 1807; Church Book, Athens First Baptist Church, 17 October 1852; Church Book, Springfield African Baptist Church, Augusta, Ga., 2 January 1881, MU; Stokes, "Baptism in Rivers," *The Christian Index*, 16 April 1841, 249. Second (Wentworth Street) Baptist Church in Charleston, S.C., planned to construct a baptistry in their new building (Thomas F. Curtis, "Extracts from Dr. Curtis Discourse," *The Christian Index*, 12 August 1842, 500).

14. J. H. Campbell, "Revival Scenes and Incidents," *The Christian Index*, 18 September 1879, 2.

15. Ministers' Meeting, "Condensed Statement," *The Christian Index*, 27 July 1837, 475–476; Whilden, "State of Religion," in *Minutes*, Rehoboth Baptist Association, 1870, 16.

16. William Rabun, "Circular Letter," Georgia Baptist Association, 1809, in Jesse Mercer, *History of the Georgia Baptist Association* (Washington, Ga.: n.p., 1838), 187; Jesse Mercer, "Circular Letter," Georgia Baptist Association, 1806, in ibid., 167; Jesse Mercer, "Circular Letter," Georgia Baptist Association, 1811, in ibid., 196. See also W. D. Lane, "Circular Letter," Georgia Baptist Association, 1805, in ibid., 164.

17. Church Book, LaGrange First Baptist Church, LaGrange, Ga., 28 September 1890, MU.

18. S. G. Hillyer, "A Converted Church Membership," *The Christian Index*, 18 February 1892, 2. See also Jesse Mercer, "Circular Letter," Georgia Baptist Association, 1816, in Mercer, *History*, 227–228.

19. Ripley, "An Essay on the Mutual and Distinct Duties of Christians in Governing the Churches," in *Tracts Read before the General Association of Georgia* (Augusta, Ga.: William J. Bunce, 1825), 7, 6; Basil Manly Jr., Letter to Rev. M. B. Wharton, 12 February 1873, Basil Manly Jr. Collection, SBTS.

20. James Perryman, "No. 1," *Christian Index*, 9 December 1842, 770. The same phrase appeared in a speech given before the national Baptist Triennial Convention ("An Address to the Baptist Denomination of the United States," *Christian Index*, 21 July 1836, 435).

21. Conference meetings were called "days of discipline" twice in the Savannah's Church Book (6 June 1806, 12 April 1811). For a number of years, the church met in conference weekly.

22. Church Book, Athens First Baptist Church, 19 November 1853. Attendance at conference meetings could fail for various reasons, including inclement weather, epidemic, or warfare.

23. "Receiving Members to the Church," *The Christian Index*, 27 May 1842, 323; Stokes, "Faith," *The Christian Index*, 20 May 1842, 313. See also A Bible Baptist, "Relating Christian Experience," *The Christian Index*, 18 August 1870, 125.

24. Church Book, Bethesda Baptist Church, 15 November 1834. Church clerks probably did not ordinarily record such instances, which represented no official action on the part of the church. In this case, the clerk noticed the action ex post facto, for on this date the objection to Charles's character was removed, and he was received into membership. But see Church Book, Powelton Baptist Church, 2 September 1867, 5 October 1867.

25. Church Book, Powelton Baptist Church, 7 July 1839, 2 August 1839; Mercer, quoted in Charles D. Mallary, *Memoirs of Elder Jesse Mercer* (New York: John Gray, 1844), 65–66.

26. Morgan, *Visible Saints*, 64–112.

27. In some cases, the articles of faith were embedded in the covenant. Some churches did not adopt a decorum. Some eighteenth-century churches may have adopted covenants after they constituted. In the nineteenth century, the clergy called to help constitute a church would not proceed without some written statement of the church's doctrine and practice.

28. Morgan, *Visible Saints*, 17, 36–40.

29. Champlin Burrage, *The Church Covenant Idea: Its Origin and Development* (Philadelphia: American Baptist Publication Society, 1904), 26–33, 85–94, 125, 156, 173–209; Charles W. Deweese, *Baptist Church Covenants* (Nashville: Broadman Press, 1990), 24–59; David Lowes Watson, *The Early Methodist Class Meeting* (Nashville: Discipleship Resources, 1985), 36–37, 83–84, 107–108.

30. Church Book, Phillips Mill Baptist Church, Wilkes County, Ga., 10 June 1785, MU. The same covenant, or one very similar, can be found in the church books of Athens First Baptist Church, 15 August 1840; Beaverdam Baptist Church, Wilkes County, Ga., 18 March 1836, MU; Washington First Baptist Church, Washington, Ga., 29 December 1827, MU; Atlanta First Baptist Church, Atlanta, 1 January 1848, GDAH; Crawfordville Baptist Church, Taliaferro County, Ga., 24 August 1802, MU; Powelton Baptist Church, 1 July 1786; Antioch Baptist Church, Oglethorpe County, Ga., 14 July 1813, GDAH; Atlanta Second Baptist Church, Atlanta, 1 September 1854, GDAH.

For a discussion of the various kinds of covenants adopted by Baptist churches, and for a number of covenant texts, see Charles W. Deweese, "The Origin, Development, and Use of Church Covenants in Baptist History" (Th.D. dissertation, Southern Baptist Theological Seminary, 1973).

31. Church Book, Phillips Mill Baptist Church, 10 June 1785.

32. Church Book, Atlanta First Baptist Church, 3 August 1861.

33. Church Book, Atlanta First Baptist Church, 4 October 1856. Similarly see Church Book, Newnan First Baptist Church, 22 May 1841. Cases could continue for some time: A case unresolved after about five months was long; one such case dragged on for two years and four months (Church Book, Powelton Baptist Church, 31 August 1792, 3 January 1795).

34. Church Book, Poplar Springs Baptist Church, Stephens County, Ga., 23 June 1827, 23 February 1833, 6 July 1839, MU; Church Book, LaGrange First Baptist Church, 12 February 1831.

35. Church Book, Penfield Baptist Church, Greene County, Ga., 7 September 1839, 10 March 1849, MU. See also Church Book, Savannah First Baptist Church, 24 September 1832.

36. Georgia Baptists excommunicated annually 186 persons per 10,000 church members 1781–1850, or 1.86 percent. My sample counted 21,468 excommunications and 1,154,147 member-years. Northern Baptists excommunicated annually 118 persons per 10,000 church members 1761–1850, or 1.18 percent. My sample counted 24,357 excommunications and 2,058,793 member-years. Emmanuel Episcopal Church in Athens, Georgia, did not entertain a single charge from 1837 to 1900 (Vestry Minutes, Emmanuel Episcopal

Church, Athens, Ga., GDAH). Presbyterians censured members at a rate perhaps one-tenth that of Baptists. W. D. Blanks cataloged 1,150 trials in 61 Presbyterian churches 1800–1899 ("Corrective Church Discipline in the Presbyterian Churches of the Nineteenth Century South," *Journal of Presbyterian History* 44 [1966]: 99). Assuming that the churches averaged 50 members and that 50 percent of trials resulted in either suspension or excommunication, Presbyterians would average 19 censures per 10,000 members annually, about one-tenth the Baptist rate. The combined censure rate of Atlanta First Presbyterian and Mount Zion Presbyterian, Hancock County, is much lower, about 9 censures per 10,000 members annually (Session Records, Atlanta First Presbyterian Church, Atlanta, 1858–1900, GDAH; Session Records, Mount Zion Presbyterian Church, Hancock County, Ga., 1813–1900, GDAH). Georgia Methodists expelled 48 members per 10,000 annually, combining all reported expulsions, drops, and withdrawals (Covington Circuit, Athens District, 1836–1838, 1843–1852, EU; Gainesville Circuit, Cherokee District, 1834–1835, EU; Grantville Circuit, LaGrange District, 1869–1877, EU; Gwinnett Circuit, Lawrenceville District, 1836–1853, EU; Louisville Circuit, Augusta District, 1836–1864, EU; Macon Station, Macon District, 1841–1849, EU; Newton Circuit, Athens District, 1838–1842, EU; Suwanee Circuit, Athens District, 1831–1833, EU; Trinity Charge, South Atlanta District, 1887–1890, EU). Membership figures were obtained from published annual conference records. The records included 184 ejections and 38,536 member-years.

37. Dealing(s): Church Book, LaGrange First Baptist Church, 3 April 1895; Church Book, Kiokee Baptist Church, Columbia County, Ga., 16 January 1790, 12 August 1870, MU; Church Book, Powelton Baptist Church, 3 May 1845, 27 May 1850; Church Book, Newnan First Baptist Church, 26 December 1829, 24 January 1857; "Decorum," Church Book, Antioch Baptist Church, Forsyth County, Ga., front of Church Book dated 1849–1865, GDAH.

Church dealing(s): Church Book, LaGrange First Baptist Church, 12 February 1831 (quote in subheading); Church Book, Powelton Baptist Church, 5 June 1830.

Trial: Church Book, Poplar Springs Baptist Church, Stephens County, Ga., 6 July 1839; Church Book, Powelton Baptist Church, 5 July 1788; Church Book, Newnan First Baptist Church, 22 May 1841; Church Book, Greensboro First Baptist Church, Greensboro, Ga., 12 September 1824, GDAH.

38. Church Book, LaGrange First Baptist Church, 13 August 1831, 9 October 1831; Church Book, Kiokee Baptist Church, 16 May 1829.

39. Church Book, Poplar Springs Baptist Church, 2 March 1839.

40. Church Book, Poplar Springs Baptist Church, 6 July 1839; Manuscript Minutes, Tugalo Baptist Association, 1833, 60, MU.

41. Quoted in Mallary, *Memoirs*, 446.

42. *Minutes*, Hephzibah Baptist Association, 1812, 2. The query is followed by four dots and the words "voted out." See Thomas R. R. Cobb, *An Inquiry into the Law of Negro Slavery in the United States of America* (Savannah: W. Thorne Williams, 1858), 1:230; and George M. Stroud, *A Sketch of the Laws relating to Slavery in the Several States of the United States of America* (Philadelphia: Kimber and Sharpless, 1827), 65–76.

43. Church Book, Savannah First Baptist Church, 5 January 1816; Church Book, Atlanta First Baptist Church, 1 May 1851.

44. Church Book, Crooked Creek Primitive Baptist Church, Putnam County, Ga., 23 January 1819, MU; Church Book, Kiokee Baptist Church, 16 May 1829 (similarly, 15 August 1829), January 1815, and 15 March 1823; Church Book, Powelton Baptist Church, 3 July 1819; Church Book, Bethesda Baptist Church, 20 April 1845; Church Book, Phillips Mill Baptist Church, 11 June 1808; Church Book, Powelton Baptist Church, 5 July 1788, 1 August 1788.

45. Church Book, Benevolence Baptist Church, Crawford County, Ga., 28 September 1878, MU; Church Book, Kiokee Baptist Church, February and March 1806. See also William Innes, "Of the Improper Treatment of Offences," *The Christian Index,* 12 October 1833, 55. Most churches discouraged initiating public dealings for private offenses but had no compunction about receiving such "disorderly" accusations. Once they had been made public, churches treated them as "public" offenses.

Chapter 2

1. G. E. Thomas, "Rev. Jesse Mercer and His Ecclesiastical Court," *The Christian Index,* 13 July 1863, 4; Church Book, Powelton Baptist Church, Hancock County, Ga., 6 September, 4 October, and 1 November 1817, MU.

2. W. B. Johnson, quoted in Charles D. Mallary, *Memoirs of Elder Jesse Mercer* (New York: John Gray, 1844), 410; Richard Wood, "A Request," *The Christian Index,* 24 March 1836, 163; Adiel Sherwood, "Life and Times of Jesse Mercer," *The Christian Index,* 4 September 1863, 4. See Learner, "Heads of a Discourse," *The Christian Index,* 10 March 1836, 133; Deacon, *The Christian Index,* 2 June 1835, 3; Inquirer, *The Christian Index,* 27 October 1835, 3; and Mallary, *Memoirs,* 256.

3. Thomas, "Rev. Jesse Mercer," 4; 24 July 1863, 4. Powelton Church may have experienced a revival of piety, purity, family devotions, and benevolent activity, but they did not experience a rush of new converts. Powelton's baptisms in this period were at an average rate and did not approach the number they witnessed in the revivals of 1801–1803, 1812–1814, or 1828–1829.

4. Mercer, "Hear What the Spirit Saith to the Churches, No. II," *The Christian Index,* 6 August 1841, 506. See Mercer, "The Importance of an Elevated Standard of Christian Morality," quoted in Mallary, *Memoirs,* 256.

5. J. M. P., "Constitution, Government and Discipline of the Primitive Churches," *The Christian Index,* 18 February 1836, 92; Jesse Mercer, "Church Policy," *The Christian Index,* 15 September 1836, 562; Jesse Mercer, in [William H. Stokes], "Brother Mercer's Late Sermon at Washington," *The Christian Index,* 23 July 1841, 473; Wm. J. H—d [William J. Hard], "To the Georgia Baptists—Greeting," *The Christian Index,* 18 January 1838, 24.

6. See Richard T. Hughes and C. Leonard Allen, *Illusions of Innocence: Protestant Primitivism in America, 1630–1875* (Chicago: University of Chicago Press, 1988), 53–187; and Nathan Hatch, *The Democratization of American Christianity* (New Haven, Conn.: Yale University Press, 1989), 68–81.

7. Joseph S. Baker, "The Christian Church—No. 3," *The Christian Index,* 30 June 1843, 411; Joseph S. Baker, "The Christian Church," *The Christian Index,* 16 June 1843, 379. See also Isaac Backus, *A History of New England with Particular Reference to the Baptists* (1777–1784; reprint, New York: Arno Press, 1969), 2:405–406. By contrast, Landmark Baptists taught that by practicing infant

baptism, pedobaptists renounced any proper claim to be churches at all. Infant baptism was no baptism, and no baptism, Landmarkists urged, meant no church.

8. J. L. Dagg, "Brief Discussions of Important Doctrines: Church Action," *The Christian Index,* 21 August 1863, 1; William H. Stokes, "Legislating for the Church," *The Christian Index,* 18 June 1840, 400. See also Church Book, LaGrange First Baptist Church, LaGrange, Ga., 8 May 1857, MU.

9. Adiel Sherwood, "Extracts from Sherwood's History of Georgia Baptists, No. 2: Religious Liberty," *The Christian Index,* 2 June 1843, 341; Mercer, "Reply to H.—No. 1," *The Christian Index,* 11 February 1836, 67–68; Sherwood, "Life and Times," 4. See also Clio, "Masonry," *The Christian Index,* 28 October 1834, 3.

10. Church Covenant, Church Book, Atlanta First Baptist Church, Atlanta, 1 January 1848, GDAH; J. H. Taylor, *The Christian Index,* 19 March 1841, 171; Church Book, Phillips Mill Baptist Church, Wilkes County, Ga., 7 July 1785, MU; Jesse Mercer, *History of the Georgia Baptist Association* (Washington, Ga., 1838), 30–31. The Sandy Creek Baptist Association, the oldest in North Carolina, adopted an identical statement in 1816 ("Principles of the Sandy Creek Association," in William Lumpkin, *Baptist Confessions of Faith* [Valley Forge, Pa.: Judson Press, 1969], 358).

11. Clio, "Masonry," 3; *Minutes,* Bethel Baptist Association, 1840, 4. On public and private offenses, see P. H. Mell, *Corrective Church Discipline* (1860; reprint, Athens, Ga.: E. D. Stone Press, 1912), 10–24; Jesse Mercer, "Circular Letter," Georgia Baptist Association, 1806, in Mercer, *History,* 169–171; Melancthon [Adiel Sherwood], "Offences," *The Christian Index,* 28 October 1834, 3; Micajah Fulgham, "Circular Letter," *Minutes,* Ebenezer Baptist Association, 1816, 7–8; Church Book, Kiokee Baptist Church, Columbia County, Ga., July 1806, MU; Church Book, Newnan First Baptist Church, Newnan, Ga., 26 December 1829, MU.

12. *Baptist Confession of Faith and a Summary of Church Discipline* (Charleston, S.C.: W. Riley, 1831), 148–156; Joseph S. Baker, "Church Discipline," *The Christian Index,* 1 March 1844, 1; Church Book, Savannah First Baptist Church, Savannah, Ga., 2 May 1806, MU; James M. Pendleton, *Church Manual, Designed for the Use of Baptist Churches* (Philadelphia: American Baptist Publication Society, 1867), 142–144. Some churches employed a third class of censure, *suspension,* entailing a temporary loss of office, voting rights, and communion participation but not membership.

13. Melancthon [Adiel Sherwood], "Is Discipline an Internal Right of the Church?" *The Christian Index,* 14 September 1833, 2; Jesse Mercer, *The Christian Index,* 12 October 1833, 54; Adiel Sherwood, "To 'A Young Member,'" *The Christian Index,* 29 October 1833, 63.

14. Roberts, "Circular Letter," *Minutes,* Washington Baptist Association, 1829, 5; Church Book, Newnan First Baptist Church, 26 February 1831; Church Book, Antioch Baptist Church, Oglethorpe County, Ga., 13 November 1831, GDAH.

15. Jesse Mercer, "Circular Letter," Georgia Baptist Association, 1816, in Mercer, *History,* 224.

16. Sylvanus Landrum, "Church-Discipline," *The Christian Index,* 23 June 1858, 2; J. L. Dagg, "Brief Discussions of Important Doctrines: Church Action," *The Christian Index,* 21 August 1863, 1. See also Jesse Mercer, "Circular Letter," Georgia Baptist Association, 1806, in Mercer, *History,* 171; and Jesse

Mercer, "Circular Letter," Georgia Baptist Association, 1821, in Mercer, *History*, 244.

17. Jesse Mercer, "Circular Letter," Georgia Baptist Association, 1801, in Mercer, *History*, 153, 154; Jesse Mercer, "A Dissertation on the Resemblances and Differences between Church Authority and That of an Association," *The Christian Index*, 10 December 1833, 86.

18. W. O. Wyer, Letter to Jesse Mercer, 15 February 1830, MU.

19. Jesse Mercer, "Circular Letter," Georgia Baptist Association, 1806, in Mercer, *History*, 172.

20. Backus, *History*, 2:74; Silas Mercer, *Tyranny Exposed and True Liberty Discovered; Wherein Is Contained the Scripture Doctrine concerning Kings* (Halifax [North Carolina?]: Thomas Davis, 1783), 57.

21. Leonard W. Levy, *The Establishment Clause: Religion and the First Amendment* (New York: Macmillan, 1986), 46–49.

22. See Bertram Wyatt-Brown, "The Antimission Movement in the Jacksonian South: A Study in Regional Folk Culture," *Journal of Southern History* 36 (1970): 501–529.

23. Manuscript Minutes, Echaconnee Primitive Baptist Association, 1837, 65, MU; Luke Robinson, *The Christian Index*, 19 October 1837, 672; Mercer, *The Christian Index*, 9 June 1835, 2; Jesse Mercer, "Unanimity of Sentiment among the Baptists," *The Christian Index*, 16 December 1834, 5. The Ocmulgee Baptist Association resolved that "the churches have put their keys into the hands of the Association," giving the association authority to regulate the discipline of the churches (quoted in Mercer, *History*, 106–125).

24. Nathan Hatch, "The Christian Movement and the Demand for a Theology of the People," *Journal of American History* 67 (1980): 564; *Minutes*, Shaftesbury Baptist Association, 1817, 7. See also John Leland, *The Writings of the Elder John Leland*, ed. L. F. Greene (New York: n.p. 1845), 59–60; and Hatch, *Democratization*, 97, 101, 163.

25. John Cooper, *The Christian Index*, 8 February 1838, 69; Jesse Mercer, *The Christian Index*, 8 February 1838, 69–70.

26. J. L. Dagg, *A Treatise of Church Order* (Charleston, S.C.: Southern Baptist Publication Society, 1858), 274. See also Jesse Mercer, "Circular Letter," Georgia Baptist Association, 1806, in Mercer, *History*, 167.

27. Church Book, Antioch Baptist Church, Oglethorpe County, Ga., 1 August 1852, 8 August 1853, 5 August 1860. In these instances, the church's annual meeting turned into a protracted meeting. The annual meeting was a quarterly communion meeting to which was added settling church finances, choosing the pastor for the coming year (they were generally elected to one-year terms), and the reading and revision of the church roll. See its church book for 2 February 1814 and 11 June 1814.

28. C., *The Christian Index*, 12 November 1833, 71. See Adiel Sherwood, "Sharon Camp Meeting," *The Christian Index*, 12 November 1833, 71. Sherwood wrote that Georgia Baptists did not much employ the new measures until after 1820 (Sherwood, "Life and Times of Jesse Mercer," *The Christian Index*, 15 June 1863, 1). Sherwood, from upstate New York, may have played an important role in introducing them.

29. Elias Hibbard, *The Christian Index*, 3 December 1833, 82; Jesse Mercer, "From Correspondents," *The Christian Index*, 18 August 1836, 497; Jesse Mercer, "Circular Letter," Georgia Baptist Association, 1806, in Mercer, *History*, 167.

30. Joseph S. Baker, "Eastern Louisiana Baptist Association," *The Christian Index*, 16 February 1844, 3; J. C. Solomon, "Friendship," *The Christian Index*, 6 March 1890, 5; W. D. Atkinson, "Elements of Church Prosperity," *The Christian Index*, 31 January 1878, 3.

31. Landrum, "Church-Discipline," 2; Church Book, Washington First Baptist Church, Washington, Ga., 2 January 1869, MU.

32. James J. Davis, "How Can We Best Promote the Spirituality of the Churches?" The Christian Index, 9 June 1887, 2; J. H. Kilpatrick, quoted in W. L. T. P., "Seminary Commencement," 11 June 1885, 4; *Minutes*, Stone Mountain Baptist Association, 1874, 11. See also *Minutes*, Central Baptist Association, 1892, 12; and J. M. Hurst, "Georgia Baptists," *The Christian Index*, 13 March 1890, 2–3.

33. Jesse Mercer, "From Correspondents," *The Christian Index*, 22 December 1836, 785; Mercer, "Reply to H.—No. 1," *The Christian Index*, 11 February 1836, 67. See also A. T. N. Vandivere, "Circular Letter," Manuscript Minutes, Sarepta Baptist Association, ca. 1845, 286, MU; S. Rowe, "Circular Letter," *Minutes*, Bethel Baptist Association, 1843, 7; Samuel Henderson, "Undisciplinable Offenses," *The Christian Index*, 15 January 1880, 1; "Hindrances to the Advancement of Religion," *The Christian Index*, 22 July 1847, 237; Joseph S. Baker, "Trimming Lights," *The Christian Index*, 27 January 1848, 29; and Mercer, "Circular Letter," Georgia Baptist Association, 1806, in Mercer, *History*, 167.

34. Jesse Mercer, "Circular Letter," Georgia Baptist Association, 1806, in Mercer, *History*, 167; A Layman, "Backsliding Church-Members," *The Christian Index*, 11 September 1851, 146. See also *Minutes*, Western Baptist Association, 1901, 13.

35. Jesse Mercer, "From Correspondents," *The Christian Index*, 22 December 1836, 785; Mercer, "Circular Letter," Georgia Baptist Association, 1821, in Mercer, *History*, 244. See Mercer, "Circular Letter," Georgia Baptist Association, 1806, in Mercer, *History*, 167; J. F. Reeves, "Revival," *The Christian Index*, 3 March 1892, 13; "Prompt Discipline," *The Christian Index*, 12 August 1852, 129; W. H. Robert, "Atlanta Baptist Church," *The Christian Index*, 21 April 1853, 82; William Henry Strickland, "Salem Church, Rockdale County, Ga.," *The Christian Index*, 9 March 1871, 38.

36. T. H. Stout, "Bethel, Randolph County, Ga.," *The Christian Index*, 21 September 1871, 146.

37. Robert Gardner, *Baptists of Early America: A Statistical Study* (Atlanta: Georgia Baptist Historical Society, 1983), 35; Robert Gardner, et al., *A History of the Georgia Baptist Association, 1784–1984* (Washington, Ga.: Wilkes, 1988), 12; *Minutes*, Georgia Baptist Convention, 1861, 31. One million Baptists is a conservative estimate: 649,528 Southern Baptists in 1860, 435,471 northern Baptists in 1867; 118,000 Primitive and Free Will Baptists in 1852 (W. W. Barnes, *The Southern Baptist Convention, 1845–1953* [Nashville: Broadman, 1954], 306; *American Baptist Yearbook, 1868* [Philadelphia: American Baptist Publication Society, 1868], 101–111; J. Lansing Burrows, ed., *American Baptist Register for 1852* [Philadelphia: American Baptist Publication Society, 1853], 495). Joseph Wilson counted 1,020,442 Baptists for 1860 (Wilson, *The Presbyterian Historical Almanac, and Annual Remembrancer of the Church, for 1861* [Philadelphia: Joseph M. Wilson, 1861], 327). The U.S. population grew from 3,929,214 in

1790 to 31,443,321 in 1860, a rate of 800% (U.S. Bureau of the Census, *Historical Statistics of the United States, Colonial Times to 1970, Bicentennial Edition, Part 2,* [Washington, D.C.: The Bureau, 1975], 1:8). Baptist increase was 1,493%. Georgia's population grew from 83,000 in 1790 to 1,057,000 in 1860, a rate of 1,273% (U.S. Bureau of the Census, *Historical Statistics,* 1:26). Georgia's Baptist increase was 2,970%.

Chapter 3

1. Bertram Wyatt-Brown, *Southern Honor: Ethics and Behavior in the Old South* (New York: Oxford University Press, 1982), 34.

2. Church Book, Bethesda Baptist Church, Greene County, Ga., 20 December 1828, 19 June 1830, MU.

3. Ibid., 17 January 1835 (first and second quotes), 18 July 1835.

4. See, for example, John A. Broadus, *Should Women Speak in Mixed Public Assemblies?* (Louisville, Ky: Baptist Book Concern, 1880).

5. "A Summary of Church Discipline," Charleston Baptist Association, 1774, in James Leo Garrett, *Baptist Church Discipline* (Nashville: Broadman, 1962), 31; Church Book, Powelton Baptist Church, Hancock County, Ga., 1 June 1792, MU; Church Book, Benevolence Baptist Church, Crawford County, Ga., 28 September 1878, MU. The discipline manual, which prohibited female voting, was adopted by Charleston First Baptist Church and Savannah First Baptist Church.

6. Church Book, Kiokee Baptist Church, Columbia County, Ga., 20 June 1830, MU. Another slave member introduced a charge in the same meeting; likewise in the minutes of 15 December 1832. For an instance in which a black member was present at a conference (without being "subpoenaed" as a witness, plaintiff, or defendant): Ben, a slave, was charged with adultery, and "Ben being present" denied the charge (Church Book, Phillips Mill Baptist Church, Wilkes County, Ga., 12 November 1790, MU).

7. Church Book, Poplar Springs Baptist Church, Stephens County, Ga., 21 May 1814, MU. See George M. Stroud, *A Sketch of the Laws relating to Slavery in the Several States of the United States of America* (Philadelphia: Kimber and Sharpless, 1827), 76–77.

8. Church Book, Bethesda Baptist Church, 16 June 1827; see also 19 September 1829. A charge of absence from church elicited a confession of backsliding, profanity, hostility, and other improprieties (ibid., 18 July 1835, 17 September 1835).

9. Ibid., 18 October 1828, 18 January 1834, 15 March 1835, 19 April 1835.

10. Clerks recorded the response of defendants in 2,128 cases out of 3,776: 130 defendants acknowledged their guilt merely; 64 confessed their guilt but excused their conduct; 1,544 confessed their guilt and repented; 228 confessed their guilt but refused repentance; and 162 denied their guilt.

11. Church Book, Mount Olive Baptist Church, Mitchell County, Ga., 23 December 1877, MU.

12. This sample excludes those cases in which absence from church conference constituted the only charge.

13. Church Book, Powelton Baptist Church, 5 July 1806; see also 1 February 1806.

14. Church Book, Poplar Springs Baptist Church, 27 February 1819.

15. Church Book, Penfield Baptist Church, Greene County, Ga., 12 March 1859, MU.

16. Church Book, Little Ogeechee Baptist Church, Screven County, Ga., August 1806, MU; Church Book, Hopeful Baptist Church, Burke County, Ga., February 1851, MU; Church Book, Powelton Baptist Church, 1 August 1823, 1 November 1823.

17. Church Book, Vernon (formerly Mount Pleasant) Baptist Church, Troup County, Ga., 6 August 1853, MU; Church Book, Poplar Springs Baptist Church, 1 June 1839; Church Book, Penfield Baptist Church, 13 December 1840. See also Church Book, Vernon Baptist Church, 5 July 1851, 3 September 1853, 1 October 1853.

18. Wyatt-Brown, *Southern Honor*, 450–453.

19. Church Book, Powelton Baptist Church, 1 November 1823; Church Book, Kiokee Baptist Church, July 1808, July 1811, 17 July 1838; Church Book, Powelton Baptist Church, 1 August 1823.

20. For example, association minutes included annual statistical tables containing a column that recorded the number of excommunications. The Georgia Baptist Association usually headed this column "Excommunicated" (or its abbreviation) 1803–1851, after which "Excluded" replaced it. In the tables of the New Sunbury Baptist Association (Georgia), "Excommunicated" last appeared in 1862 (except for a cameo in 1885), replaced by "Excluded." In the tables of the Hephzibah Baptist Association (Georgia), "Excommunicated" lasted until 1875, after which it was replaced by "Excluded."

21. The bishop of Arles in the sixth century lamented that among men concubinage before marriage was so pervasive that "the bishop cannot excommunicate all" but must "endure and wait" for God to grant them repentance (Caesarius of Arles, Sermon 288, quoted in O. D. Watkins, *A History of Penance* [1920; reprint, New York: Burt Franklin, 1961], 2:551). The church's excommunication was a "spiritual" penalty. But the medieval church endorsed the idea that secular governors had a responsibility to punish spiritual offenders. Heresy became a capital crime against the state. The church barred them from grace; the state exiled, enslaved, or burned them. See Henry Charles Lea, *A History of the Inquisition of the Middle Ages* (New York: Macmillan, 1922), 1:326–359.

22. R. H. Rivers, *The Life of Robert Paine, D.D., Bishop of the Methodist Episcopal Church, South* (Nashville: Southern Methodist Publishing House, 1884), 192.

23. Church Book, Greensboro Baptist Church, Greensboro, Ga., 9 July 1876, GDAH.

24. E. M. Green, "Life and Letters of Dr. Palmer," *Presbyterian Standard* 47 (May 1907): 5.

25. Church Book, Powelton Baptist Church, 1 December 1804. Later in the century, however, some city churches adopted this kind of publishing because their congregations became large and their conference attendance small and because knowledge of excommunications did not circulate sufficiently among the larger public. See Church Book, Savannah First Baptist Church, Savannah, 1 September 1859, MU; Church Book, Macon First Baptist Church, Macon, Ga., 4 June 1886, MU.

26. "A Monster of Iniquity," *Washington [Georgia] News*, 19 May 1829, 1.

27. Church Book, Atlanta First Baptist Church, Atlanta, 31 July 1852, GDAH; Church Book, Vernon Baptist Church, 1 March 1851. See also Church Book, Antioch Baptist Church, Forsyth County, Ga., 9 May 1856, GDAH; *Minutes*, Tallapoosa Baptist Association, 1868, 5; Manuscript Minutes, Chattahoochee Baptist Association, 1830, 40, MU.

28. Church Book, Penfield Baptist Church, 13 April 1851. See Church Book, Macon First Baptist Church, 2 March 1855.

29. Church Book, Newnan First Baptist Church, Newnan, Ga., 26 February 1831, MU; Church Book, Savannah First Baptist Church, 21 June 1812. See also Church Book, Powelton Baptist Church, 30 December 1791; and the case of William Barnes, discussed previously in chapter 1. Churches that missionaries established in other nations did this also. Adoniram Judson noted that "of the Burman converts eight have been excluded . . . besides three or four in Rangoon, on whom the sentence has not been formally pronounced" (Adoniram Judson, *The Christian Index*, 7 October 1834, 4).

30. Church Book, Powelton Baptist Church, 1 August 1823; Church Book, "Gospel Order," Newnan First Baptist Church, 11 June 1828; Henry Holcombe, "Circular Letter," *Minutes*, Savannah River Baptist Association, 1809, 7; "Covenant," Church Book, Kiokee Baptist Church, beginning of second Church Book, 1820. See also Church Book, Bethesda Baptist Church, 14 June 1851; Church Book, Penfield Baptist Church, 14 December 1852. For expressions of voting as a privilege: voting on leaders, Church Book, Barnesville Baptist Church, Lamar County, Ga., May 1884, MU; voting on discipline, Church Book, Powelton Baptist Church, 31 December 1808. Churches distinguished their poor as "poor Saints" (Church Book, Savannah First Baptist Church, 5 August 1814) and "the poor of the church" (Church Book, Atlanta First Baptist Church, 4 January 1877; Church Book, LaGrange First Baptist Church, 11 July 1868). For examples of aid to poor members, see Church Book, Bethesda Baptist Church, 16 January 1819, 19 December 1840, 15 January 1842, 16 April 1886, 14 May 1896; Church Book, Athens First Baptist Church, Athens, Ga., 30 November 1861, MU; Church Book, Beaverdam Baptist Church, Wilkes County, Ga., 16 February 1861, 15 November 1862, MU; Church Book, Hopeful Baptist Church, May 1818; Church Book, Kiokee Baptist Church, September 1809. See also John L. Dagg, "Brief Discussions," *The Christian Index*, 21 August 1863, 1.

31. Quoted in James Holmes, *"Dr. Bullie's" Notes: Reminiscences of Early Georgia and of Philadelphia and New Haven in the 1800s*, ed. Delma Eugene Presley (Atlanta: Cherokee, 1976), 168.

32. Church Book, Bethesda Baptist Church, 14 April 1849; Church Book, Penfield Baptist Church, 11 November 1854; Church Book, Bethesda Baptist Church, 14 June 1851; Church Book, Poplar Springs Baptist Church, 23 September 1815; Church Book, Newnan First Baptist Church, 26 February 1831. See also Church Book, Penfield Baptist Church, 7 June 1851; Church Book, Powelton Baptist Church, 5 July 1788, 1 August 1788.

33. *Minutes*, Washington Baptist Association, 1832, 2.

34. Excluded for drunkenness, Early gave on different occasions $50 and $10 to missions and contributed $10 of Pastor B. M. Sanders's $85 salary (Church Book, Greensboro First Baptist Church, 26 September 1840, 9 January 1841, 25 September 1841).

35. Church Book, Penfield Baptist Church, 12 May 1855, 9 June 1855, 7 July 1855, 7 June 1856, 8 November 1856; Church Book, Kiokee Baptist Church, 19 June 1835 (James and Susannah Culbreath returned after 35 years), 18 November 1842 (Jacob Few, a slave, returned after 36 years); Church Book, Washington First Baptist Church, Wilkes County, Ga., 20 October 1833, MU; Church Book, Powelton Baptist Church, 5 July 1788, 1 August 1788, 2 August 1788; Church Book, Bethesda Baptist Church, 14 June 1851, 17 November 1855; Church Book, Washington First Baptist Church, 1 October 1859; Church Book, Powelton Baptist Church, 2 January 1790. See also Church Book, Penfield Baptist Church, 18 September 1859.

36. See these minutes in which minorities prevented restoration: Church Book, Powelton Baptist Church, 28 April 1805; Church Book, Penfield Baptist Church, 12 May 1855, 9 June 1855, 7 July 1855. For examples of demand for personal appearance, see Church Book, Kiokee Baptist Church, 21 April 1833, 20 October 1834.

37. Church Book, Penfield Baptist Church, 1 July 1849; Church Book, Poplar Springs Baptist Church, 22 July 1826; Church Book, Washington First Baptist Church, 1 October 1859. See also Church Book, Long Creek Baptist Church, Warren County, Ga., 21 May 1853, 21 October 1853, MU.

38. Church Book, Powelton Baptist Church, 4 April 1795, 2 May 1795.

39. Church Book, Savannah First Baptist Church, 12 April 1811.

40. Ibid., 30 April 1813, 4 March 1814. The church allowed Sister Houver to withdraw and join the Methodist church without censure (18 March 1814, 15 April 1814).

41. Ibid., 21 May 1813, 5 June 1813; *Minutes*, Savannah River Baptist Association, 1813, 5; ibid., 1814, 3.

42. Church Book, Savannah First Baptist Church, 16 October 1814, 23 December 1814, 1 January 1820, 13 December 1823.

43. Ibid., 18 November 1815, 5 and 12 January 1815, and 9, 16, and 23 February 1816.

44. Church Book, Greensboro Baptist Church, 4 February 1860; Church Book, Long Creek Baptist Church, 21 May 1831; Church Book, Savannah First Baptist Church, 1 October 1830, 1 April 1866; Church Book, Greensboro Baptist Church, 4 February 1860, 5 March 1860; Church Book, Savannah First Baptist Church, 8 August 1831.

45. Church Book, Savannah First Baptist Church, 8 June 1822; Carolyn White Williams, *History of Jones County, Georgia, 1807–1907* (Macon, Ga.: J. W. Burke, 1957), 313; Church Book, Crooked Creek Primitive Baptist Church, Putnam County, Ga., 26 December 1818, MU; Church Book, Sharon Primitive Baptist Church, Monroe County, Ga., 5 June 1886, MU; Church Book, Antioch Baptist Church, Oglethorpe County, Ga., June 1830, 7 June 1834, GDAH; Church Book, Atlanta Second Baptist Church, Atlanta, 11 April 1877, GDAH; Church Book, Washington First Baptist Church, 5 September 1857; Church Book, Antioch Baptist Church, 1 June 1867. See also Church Book, Phillips Mill Baptist Church, 12 November 1790; Church Book, Greensboro First Baptist Church, 9 July 1876.

46. Wyatt-Brown, *Southern Honor*, 370, 327–401.

47. *Minutes*, Bethel Baptist Association, 1841, 14–16.

48. Church Book, Penfield Baptist Church, 4 February 1849.

Chapter 4

1. See James Henley Thornwell, "The Christian Doctrine of Slavery," in *The Collected Writings of James Henley Thornwell*, ed. John B. Adger (Richmond: Presbyterian Committee of Publications, 1871–1873; reprint, Carlisle, Pa.: Banner of Truth, 1974), 4:428; James O. Farmer, *The Metaphysical Confederacy: James Henley Thornwell and the Synthesis of Southern Values* (Macon, Ga.: Mercer University Press, 1986), 106–110, 158–159.

2. Morgan Edwards, *Materials towards a History of the Baptists* (Danielsville, Ga.: Heritage Papers, 1984) 63.

3. Nathan Hatch, *The Democratization of American Christianity* (New Haven, Conn.: Yale University Press, 1989), 193. See Isaac, *Transformation*, 172–177.

4. On female voting, see also Randy Sparks, *On Jordan's Stormy Banks: Evangelicalism in Mississippi, 1773–1876* (Athens, Ga.: University of Georgia Press, 1994), 50–51, 153. Antebellum Baptists frequently called ordained ministers *elders*. Some churches also appointed "ruling" elders, who were not ordained ministers (Church Book, Phillips Mill Baptist Church, Wilkes County, Ga., 9 February 1787, 11 May 1787, 10 August 1787, 10 March 1792, MU; Church Book, Powelton Baptist Church, Hancock County, Ga., 5 May 1787, 3 August 1787, 29 May 1811, 6 July 1811, MU; Church Book, Long Creek Baptist Church, Warren County, Ga., membership list, February 1788, MU; Church Book, Atlanta Second Baptist Church, Atlanta, 12 January 1872, GDAH; *Minutes*, Georgia Baptist Association, 1794, 7).

5. *Minutes*, Dover Baptist Association (Virginia), 1802, 10; A. S. Worrell, *Review of Corrective Church Discipline* (Nashville: Southwestern, 1860), 208–216, 219; Sylvanus Landrum, "Should Females Vote in Our Churches?" *The Christian Index*, 8 February 1860, 1.

6. Jesse Mercer, *The Christian Index*, 9 September 1834, 2, quoted in Charles D. Mallary, *Memoirs of Elder Jesse Mercer* (New York: John Gray, 1844), 447–448. See also Eliza C. Allen's article supporting Mercer's position ("Right of Females to Vote in the Churches," *The Christian Index*, 2 March 1837, 140).

7. Henry Holcombe, "Circular Letter," *Minutes*, Savannah River Baptist Association (South Carolina and Georgia), 1809, 7; Martha, *The Christian Index*, 20 October 1836, 642–643; Watchman, "It Is a Contest for Principle," *The Christian Index*, 17 December 1833, 90; I. R. Branham, *The Christian Index*, 26 April 1894, 2. Holcombe did not extend these privileges to include the ministry, for a woman "is not to teach, under any circumstance, as would render her teaching an usurpation over the man" (p. 8).

8. *Minutes*, Hephzibah Baptist Association, 1812, 3; Manuscript minutes, Sarepta Baptist Association, 1828, 113, MU; *Minutes*, Western Baptist Association, 1869, 3, 9.

9. Church Book, Powelton Baptist Church, 31 December 1808, 3 February 1809; A Venerable Minister, *The Christian Index*, 10 June 1834, 90; Church Book, Powelton Baptist Church, 3 July 1845; Church Book, Newnan First Baptist Church, Newnan, Ga., 7 July 1869, MU; Church Book, Savannah First Baptist Church, Savannah, Ga., 21 May 1813, MU. In one controversial case, the church affirmed the right of women to vote in discipline cases, and two women voted in a roll call ballot (Church Book, Atlanta First Baptist Church, Atlanta, 12 December 1888, GDAH).

10. Church Book, Savannah First Baptist Church, 19 February 1855, 27 January 1859.

11. Church Book, Greensboro First Baptist Church, Greensboro, Ga., 12 September 1824, GDAH; Church Book, Powelton Baptist Church, 5 May 1827; Church Book, Greensboro First Baptist Church, 13 January 1833. Similarly, two male blacks voted against restoring an excluded slave, preventing his restoration (Church Book, Powelton Baptist Church, 28 April 1805).

12. James M. Simms, *The First Colored Baptist Church in North America* (Philadelphia: J. B. Lippincott, 1888), 112.

13. A. S. Worrell argued against according slaves voting rights in the churches for the same reasons he opposed the right of children to vote—because of their intellectual immaturity and their restriction from voting in civil elections (*Review*, 219).

14. Church Book, Phillips Mill Baptist Church, 10 March 1860. In some, perhaps most, churches, slaves probably did not vote on government, since white evangelicals considered slaves to be members of the master's household, albeit in minority.

15. Church Book, Little Ogeechee Baptist Church, Screven County, Ga., October 1829, MU; Church Book, Bethesda Baptist Church, Greene County, Ga., 14 February 1818, MU; Church Book, LaGrange First Baptist Church, LaGrange, Ga., 12 May 1866, MU. Similarly, see Church Book, Antioch Baptist Church, Oglethorpe County, Ga., 12 December 1818, GDAH; Church Book, Savannah First Baptist Church, 26 May 1809, 16 February 1812, 1 July 1831; Church Book, Poplar Springs Baptist Church, Stephens County, Ga., 27 June 1829, MU; Church Book, Hopeful Baptist Church, Burke County, Ga., November 1826, MU; Church Book, Long Creek Baptist Church, 20 April 1831.

16. Church Book, Kiokee Baptist Church, Columbia County, Ga., 15 October 1825, MU; Church Book, Little Ogeechee Baptist Church, October 1832. See Church Book, LaGrange First Baptist Church, 29 November 1835, 26 August 1838; Church Book, Greensboro First Baptist Church, 13 January 1833; Church Book, Athens First Baptist Church, Athens, Ga., 2 April 1833, MU; Church Book, Antioch Baptist Church, 14 April 1822, 8 June 1823. Little Ogeechee Church, for example, appointed standing black discipline committees but left no evidence of the existence of a conference for the black members.

17. In the sample, 555 females and 1,114 males sustained excommunication; among whites, the difference was greater still, numbering 315 females and 778 males.

18. A. T. Holmes, "The Duties of Christian Masters," in H. N. McTyeire et al., *Duties of Masters to Servants: Three Premium Essays* (Charleston, S.C.: Southern Baptist Publication Society, 1851), 131; H. N. McTyeire, "Master and Servant," in McTyeire et al., *Duties*, 7.

19. Shaler G. Hillyer, *Manual of Bible Morality: A Text Book for Elementary and Academic Schools and for the Help of Parents in Training Their Children at Home* (Richmond, Va.: B. F. Johnson, 1897), 103; R. B., "The Influence of Novel Reading in Young Females," *The Christian Index*, 29 June 1837, 413. See also Hezekiah A. Boyd, "Circular Letter," Georgia Baptist Association, 1810, in Jesse Mercer, *History of the Georgia Baptist Association* (Washington, Ga., 1838), 193.

20. A Lover of Woman, and a Friend of Decency, *The Christian Index*, 16 July 1840, 463; H. H. Tucker, "Vashti," *The Christian Index*, 28 May 1885, 8;

Macedonia Temperance Society, *The Christian Index*, 6 May 1834, 71 (3); [Jesse Mercer], "Woman's Influence," *The Christian Index*, 14 September 1833, 3.

21. J. Lansing Burrows, ed., *American Baptist Register, for 1852* (Philadelphia: American Baptist Publication Society, 1853), 421–449; Lewis Joseph Sherrill, *Presbyterian Parochial Schools, 1846–1870* (New Haven, Conn.: Yale University Press, 1932), esp. 73–82; Joseph M. Wilson, *The Presbyterian Historical Almanac, and Annual Remembrancer of the Church, for 1861* (Philadelphia: Joseph M. Wilson, 1861), 346, 353. See also Charles D. Johnson, *Higher Education of Southern Baptists: An Institutional History, 1826–1954* (Waco, Tex.: Baylor University Press, 1955), 25–40; and Kendall Brooks, "In General Education," in Lemuel Moss, ed., *The Baptists and the National Centenary: A Record of Christian Work, 1776–1876* (Philadelphia: American Baptist Publication Society, 1876), 77–121. Abel Stevens reported 77 antebellum southern Methodist academies but did not specify which were female; the North had the same number of academies, with 7,299 male and 10,462 female students (*The Centenary of American Methodism: A Sketch of Its History, Theology, Practical System, and Success* [New York: Carlton & Porter, 1866], 170, 214). Episcopalians had at least one female academy before the war, Hannah More Academy in Maryland (James Thayer Addison, *The Episcopal Church in the United States, 1789–1931* [New York: Charles Scribner's Sons, 1951], 121).

22. M., "Delicacy," *The Christian Index*, 8 September 1836; Robert Fleming, "Female Piety: Its Character and Influence," in *The Georgia Pulpit: Or Minsters' Yearly Offering*, ed. Robert Fleming, vol. 1 (Richmond, Va.: H. K. Ellyson, 1847), 327, 329. Barbara Welter, describing antebellum views of womanhood, divided the ideal elements of female character into piety, purity, submissiveness, and domesticity. Although her analysis is based heavily on northeastern sources, it largely holds true for the antebellum South as well ("The Cult of True Womanhood, 1820–1860," in her *Dimity Convictions: The American Woman in the Nineteenth Century* [Athens, Ohio: Ohio University Press, 1976], 3). Novel reading, Baptists urged, produced a dislike of domestic duties and a distaste for Bible reading (R. B., "Influence," 415).

23. J. A. Wynne, "Woman's Place and Work in the Church," *The Christian Index*, 26 April 1894, 2; J. B. Hawthorne, "Paul and the Women," in *Paul and the Women and Other Discourses* (Louisville, Ky.: Baptist Book Concern, 1891), 3.

24. *Minutes*, Georgia Baptist Association, 1829.

25. M. J. Lanier, "Ladies' Charitable Association," *The Christian Index*, 21 January 1857, 10; "Annual Report of the 'Macon Female Tract Society' for 1856," *The Christian Index*, 21 January 1857, 10; R. Pierce Beaver, *American Protestant Women in World Mission: History of the First Feminist Movement in North America* (Grand Rapids, Mich.: Eerdmans, 1968), 15–17. See the church books of Atlanta First Baptist Church, 31 January 1852, 4 September 1852; Athens First Baptist Church, 10 July 1830; LaGrange First Baptist Church, 14 December 1862; Greensboro First Baptist Church, 1 June 1867. The following is a list of those female societies in antebellum Georgia whose existence was recorded (often the contributions from individuals or benevolent societies were not itemized)—from the minutes of the Sunbury Baptist Association, 1839–1850: Baptist Female Sewing Society of Savannah, Savannah Baptist Church Ladies' Foreign Missionary Society, Waynesville Female Baptist Missionary Society; from the minutes of the Washington Baptist Association, 1850–1856: Sisters

of Sparta, Ladies of Darien, Ladies of Powelton; from the minutes of the Georgia Baptist Convention, 1832–1857: Eatonton Female Benevolent Society, a few sisters in Athens, sisters of Milledgeville church, Ladies at Richland church, sisters at Monticello, Columbia County Female Missionary Society, Athens Female Missionary Society, Americus Baptist Female Missionary Society, Crawfordville Female Society for Indian Missions, Female Missionary Society of the Augusta church, Greenwood Female Missionary Society, females of Powelton, Hamilton Baptist Female Society; from the minutes of the Georgia Baptist Association 1830–1846: females of Horeb Church, sisters of Mt. Zion Church, Penfield Juvenile Female Society, Bethesda Ladies.

26. See Luther Rice, "Origin of the Triennial Convention," in I. M. Allen, *The Triennial Baptist Register, No. 2, 1836* (Philadelphia: Baptist General Tract Society, 1836), 46–48.

27. *Proceedings of the General Convention of the Baptist Denomination in the United States* (Philadelphia: Anderson & Meehan, 1817), 137; Monroe Missionary Society, "Worthy of Imitation," *The Christian Index*, 18 May 1837, 309–310; R. Pierce Beaver, *American Protestant Women in World Mission*, 14–37. In 1850, "the females of Powelton Church" contributed $45.10 toward missions in 1850, and the rest of the church gave only $29.75, a circumstance repeated in 1853 (*Minutes*, Washington Baptist Association, 1850, 12; ibid., 1853, 11). See "Woman's Work," *The Christian Index*, 4 June 1885, 4; Mrs. Stainback Wilson, "Women's Mission Work," *The Christian Index*, 6 June 1889, 2; Jesse Mercer, "Greenwood Female Missionary Society," *The Christian Index*, 7 April 1835, 2; Mary Dandy, "The Hamilton Baptist Female Missionary Society," *The Christian Index*, 31 May 1838, 340.

28. E. Vining, "A Decorum for Baptist Churches," *The Christian Index*, 26 February 1852, 34; Church Book, Savannah First Baptist Church, 13 August 1824, 10 April 1825; Jesse Mercer, *The Christian Index*, 8 September 1836, 548 ("Their vote would, in almost all cases, control the vote of the males, and constitute the ruling power"). On required female attendance, see Church Book, Athens First Baptist Church, 31 January 1846; Church Book, Poplar Springs Baptist Church, 24 February 1816 (they later excepted "women and servants" from attendance in the church book of 6 July 1839); Church Book, Atlanta Second Baptist Church, 11 November 1870. For instances noting women's presence and suffrage, see the following church books: Phillips Mill Baptist Church, 9 September 1820, 11 January 1890; Washington First Baptist Church, Washington, Ga., 25 July 1840, MU; Savannah First Baptist Church, 14 January 1869; Athens First Baptist Church, 9 May 1831 (clerk noted women's absence).

29. Martha, *The Christian Index*, 20 October 1836, 642–643.

30. Hawthorne, "Paul," 20, 27; Fleming, "Female Piety," 316, 328.

31. A Lover of Woman, and a Friend to Decency, *The Christian Index*, 16 July 1840, 463; Fleming, "Female Piety," 325.

32. White males: 21 prosecutions per 10,000 white male members; white females: 22 prosecutions per 10,000 white female members.

33. Jesse Mercer, *The Christian Index*, 3 March 1836, 113.

34. Most antebellum churches probably followed the course of Poplar Springs Baptist Church, which resolved that "all free persons of Couler shall sit to themselves" and that "the Free People of Couler ocupy the Back Seats in

the meeting house" (Church Book, 1 May 1852, 1 October 1853). On slave missions, see Albert J. Raboteau, *Slave Religion: The "Invisible Institution" in the Antebellum South* (New York: Oxford University Press, 1978), 96–174; Milton C. Sernett, *Black Religion and American Evangelicalism: White Protestants, Plantation Missions, and the Flowering of Negro Christianity, 1787–1865* (Metuchen, N.J.: Scarecrow, 1975), 36–58; Jon Butler, *Awash in a Sea of Faith: Christianizing the American People* (Cambridge, Mass.: Harvard University Press, 1990), 135–151.

35. Church Book, LaGrange First Baptist Church, 7 January 1860.

36. C. F. Sturgis, "Melville Letters; or, The Duties of Masters to Their Servants," in McTyeire et al., *Duties*, 100; J. S. Law, "Religious Oral Instruction of the Colored Race," in Fleming, *Georgia Pulpit*, 439. Southerners attributed to blacks an inferiority that they at times based on an innate lack of intellectual or moral capacity and at other times based on a lack of opportunity to develop their capacities through education and culture.

37. Law, "Religious Oral Instruction," 440; McTyeire, "Master," 29.

38. *Minutes*, Sunbury Baptist Association, 1830, 7.

39. Robert Gardner, et al., *A History of the Georgia Baptist Association, 1784–1984* (Washington, Ga.: Wilkes, 1988), 188–189; Raboteau, *Slave Religion*, 155; *Minutes*, Sunbury Baptist Association, 1841, 6; *Minutes*, Southern Baptist Convention, 1845, 15; ibid., 1849, 64; ibid., 1853, 57–60; ibid., 1855, 26–28; ibid., 1859, 60–61; Law, "Religious Instruction," 443–444; Church Book, Greensboro Baptist Church, 9 June 1821. On the broader southern effort to teach slaves morality, see Anne Loveland, *Southern Evangelicals and the Social Order, 1800–1860* (Baton Rouge, La.: Louisiana State University Press, 1980), 219–256; Sernett, *Black Religion*, 36–81.

40. Law, "Religious Instruction," 441; Sturgis, "Melville Letters," 119; McTyeire, "Master," 40. See Hezekiah A. Boyd, "Circular Letter," Georgia Baptist Association, 1810, in Mercer, *History*, 194.

41. Church Book, Bethesda Baptist Church, 15 November 1834; Church Book, Kiokee Baptist Church, 19 November 1831; S. G. Hillyer, *Reminiscences of Georgia Baptists* (Atlanta: Foote & Davies, 1902), 185. Penfield Baptist Church in 1842 appointed a committee "to inquire into the propriety of admitting Blacks to membership with us." The church was three years old and apparently had no black members prior to this time; the church comprised largely the faculty and students of Mercer University. It would have been unprecedented to question on principle whether blacks could be admitted to white churches. The question must rather have been an issue of the expediency of admitting blacks to that church at that time. Penfield admitted black members shortly afterward (Church Book, Penfield Baptist Church, Greene County, Ga., 2 July 1842). For a characterization of the common elements in the narrative of conversion experience, see Hillyer, *Reminiscences*, 183. Preacher E. B. Teague asserted that Jesse Mercer was accustomed to say that the narrative should consist of two parts: "I felt very bad, then I felt very good" ("Rev. C. H. Spurgeon and His Theology," *The Christian Index*, 9 October 1856, 162).

42. Quoted in Julia Sherwood, *Memoir of Adiel Sherwood, D.D.* (Philadelphia: Grant & Faires, 1884), 147. For examples of black defendants acquitted after white accusations, see Church Book, Powelton Baptist Church, 25 November 1854 (the white who laid in the accusation in this case was elected moderator pro tem on at least one occasion: 21 December 1854); Church Book, Bethesda

Baptist Church, 7 July 1822. For examples of aid to blacks, see Church Book, Bethesda Baptist Church, 19 December 1840, 15 January 1842 (the church appointed a committee "to see to the support of old bro. Tom and wife Rebecca both free persons of color" and at Tom's death paid his outstanding funeral expenses).

43. E. Brooks Holifield, "Toward a History of American Congregations," in James W. Lewis and James P. Wind, eds., *American Congregations* (Chicago: University of Chicago Press, 1994), 1:23–53.

44. Church Book, Poplar Springs Baptist Church, 25 September 1824; Church Book, Vernon Baptist Church, Troup County, Ga., 2 June 1849, MU.

45. See Mechal Sobel, *Trabelin' On: The Slave Journey to an Afro-Baptist Faith* (Westport, Conn.: Greenwood, 1979), 250–355. Sobel counted 28 Georgia churches; adding Friendship Baptist in Atlanta (constituted ca. 1850) makes 29 out of 119 known southern churches.

46. Church Book, Bethesda Baptist Church, 20 February 1830. Powelton Baptist Church twice temporarily abolished black worship services on account of "the disorderly conduct of the irreligious blacks" who attended along with the pious ones (Church Book, 3 March 1827, 26 May 1855).

47. Sturgis, "Melville Letters," 115. One association, at least, opposed this view, resolving "that as far as practicable, the blacks be organized in separate bodies, subject to the regulation of the Churches." But the motive seems to have been to preach to them a children's sermon, as it were: "Resolved further, That in place of preaching in the usual way, that a system of simple oral instruction be adopted" (*Minutes*, Western Baptist Association, 1847, 5). A separate service, however, was a different matter than separate churches, which many opposed. See *Minutes*, Hephzibah Baptist Association, 1849, 4.

48. Church Book, Powelton Baptist Church, 6 July 1805, 22 April 1804, 31 March 1804, 31 December 1808, 3 February 1809, December 1821; Church Book, Phillips Mill Baptist Church, 9 October 1791, 12 May 1792, 7 February 1800, 8 August 1823.

49. From the following church books: Washington First Baptist Church, 1 August 1835; Greensboro First Baptist Church, 14 July 1822; Kiokee Baptist Church, June 1812; Phillips Mill Baptist Church, 7 February 1800. For an instance in which a black served as moderator, see Church Book, Greensboro First Baptist Church, 7 June 1863.

50. Joseph S. Baker, "Colored Sunday Schools," *The Christian Index*, 29 August 1845, 2; Resolutions on the State of the Country, *Minutes*, Georgia Baptist Convention, 1862, quoted in [Samuel Boykin] *History of the Baptist Denomination in Georgia* (Atlanta: Jas. P. Harrison, 1881), pt. 1, 235. See Samuel Boykin, "Repeal of an Unjust Law," *The Christian Index*, 6 April 1863, 2; Visitor, "Fast Day Exercises in Milledgeville, Georgia," *The Christian Index*, 6 April 1863, 2; [Boykin], *History*, pt. 1, 264–268; Eugene Genovese, *Roll, Jordan, Roll: The World the Slave Made* (New York: Vintage, 1976), 69; Bell Irvin Wiley, "The Movement to Humanize the Institution of Slavery during the Confederacy," *Emory University Quarterly* 5 (1949): 207–220.

51. *Minutes*, Hephzibah Baptist Association, 1849; *Minutes*, Sunbury Baptist Association, 1843, 7; ibid., 1849, 16; ibid., 1856, 17.

52. C., "The Representation of Colored Churches," *The Christian Index*, 10 March 1853, 38; John F. Dagg, "Colored Churches," *The Christian Index*, 10

March 1853, 38; *Minutes*, Sunbury Baptist Association, 1857, 4; ibid., 1858, 8; ibid., 1859, 9.

53. 42 percent (240/576) of black excommunicants applied for restoration; 28 percent (301/1093) of white. Black restorations rejected: 15/240; white: 31/301. Black acquittals: 7.72 percent (67/868) of accusations; white: 7.40 percent (175/2365).

54. White members were prosecuted at an annual rate of 347 prosecutions per 10,000 white members; blacks at a rate of 194 prosecutions per 10,000 black members. Since churches excommunicated black *defendants* at a higher rate than white defendants, the exclusion rates were much closer—whites: 160 excommunications annually per 10,000 white members; blacks: 129 excommunications per 10,000 black members.

55. Alcohol—whites: 48 percent of defendants, blacks: 53 percent; personal speech—whites: 64 percent, blacks: 74 percent; worldly amusements—whites: 53 percent, blacks: 59 percent; sexual—whites: 89 percent, blacks: 83 percent; church—whites: 74 percent, blacks: 57 percent; violence—whites: 38 percent, blacks: 60 percent; property—whites: 51 percent, blacks: 77 percent.

Chapter 5

1. I estimate that the black membership in the churches of my research sample reached an average of 42 percent in the 1840s and 41 percent in the 1850s. The returns of a large portion of Georgia Baptist associations showed black membership at an exaggerated 48 percent in the 1840s (the Sunbury Association, with large numbers of slave members, was overrepresented, since many associations did not report racial statistics in the 1840s) and 40 percent in the 1850s. The statistical tables in the minutes of the Georgia Baptist Convention understated slave membership, reporting 32.4 percent black membership in 1850, 36 percent in 1855, and 36.5 percent in 1860. Many black members went uncounted; as late as 1860, many Georgia churches neglected to report the racial composition of their membership.

2. J. H. DeVotie, "Georgia Baptist Statistics for 1883," *The Christian Index*, 8 May 1884, 5.

3. I examined Springfield's extant nineteenth-century records: 1880–1889, 1896–1900 (Church Book, Springfield African Baptist Church, MU); Gillfield's extant nineteenth-century records: 1827, 1834–1836, 1842–1853, 1857–1862, 1868–1871 (Church Book, Gillfield Church, Alderman Library, University of Virginia, Charlottesville); and the extant antebellum records of two Louisville churches: Green Street, 1845–1860, and First Colored, 1842–1860 (both church books at Archives, Ekstrom Library, University of Louisville, Louisville, Ky.). The sample selected for analyzing African-American church discipline included all the extant nineteenth-century records of Springfield and Gillfield churches and the Green Street church, 1846–1849. The sample recorded 1,789 church trials.

4. The black Baptist associations indicated that their churches excommunicated 299 persons annually per 10,000 members.

5. Antebellum Georgia churches prosecuted 194 black members per 10,000 black members annually and excommunicated 129 per 10,000.

6. H. H. Tucker, "Letter from H. H. Tucker, D.D.," in *History of the First African Baptist Church, from Its Organization, January 20th, 1788, to July 1st, 1888*, ed.

E. K. Love (Savannah, Ga.: Morning News Print, 1888), 322. Jesse Mercer argued in 1837 against the policy of social equality of the races: "Every man who looks at this subject rightly, knows and feels, that if the black man is free, he ought to be in his own country—in the land of his fathers! Amalgamation and promiscuous intercourse, are out of the question. . . . There the free negro can go and act for himself, perfectly untrammeled by the superior advantages of his white neighbor" ("African Colonization," *The Christian Index*, 15 June 1837, 372).

7. Edward L. Ayers, *The Promise of the New South: Life after Reconstruction* (New York: Oxford University Press, 1992), 132–136, 137, 146–149, 153–159.

8. James Melvin Washington, *Frustrated Fellowship: The Black Baptist Quest for Social Power* (Macon, Ga.: Mercer University Press, 1986), 147–150.

9. Tucker, "Letter," 323; E. B. Teague, "The African in Selma," *The Christian Index*, 9 September 1869, 138. Black Baptist leader E. K. Love stated that although he disagreed with some of Tucker's points, "the point touching social equality meets our fullest approval. We have never urged social equality as a prerequisite to negro greatness" (*History*, 326). Love later rejected policies of cooperation with white Baptists and urged strict separation.

10. A. J. Kelly, "Colored Church and Ministers," *The Christian Index*, 28 May 1868, 87. Perry Jones preached twice and Allen Westhorn once for Mount Olive Baptist Church, Mitchell County, Ga. (Church Book, 21 May 1870, 23 July 1870, 23 December 1871, MU).

11. Eric Foner, *Reconstruction: America's Unfinished Revolution, 1863–1877* (New York: Harper & Row, 1988), 314; Basil Manly to S. F. Gano, 10 July 1871, Basil Manly Jr. Collection, SBTS, quoted in Joseph P. Cox, "Study of the Life and Work of Basil Manly, Jr." (Th.D. dissertation, Southern Baptist Theological Seminary, 1954), 230.

12. Foner, Reconstruction, 112, 282, 287, 292; Edward L. Wheeler, *Uplifting the Race: The Black Minister in the New South, 1865–1902* (Lanham, Md.: University Press of America, 1986), 61–83, appendix.

13. David E. Butler, "The Victory—Rejoice!" *The Christian Index*, 19 November 1874, 5; "Colloquy with Colored Ministers," *Journal of Negro History* 16 (1931): 91.

14. A. T. Holmes, "The Colored People," *The Christian Index*, 17 June 1869, 93. See Albert J. Raboteau, *Slave Religion: The "Invisible Institution" in the Antebellum South* (New York: Oxford University Press, 1978), 165–168, 234–235, 293–295; Eugene D. Genovese, *Roll, Jordan, Roll: The World the Slaves Made* (New York: Vintage, 1976), 204–209, 261–271.

15. A. W. Pegues, *Our Baptist Ministers and Schools* (Springfield, Mass.: Willey, 1892), 113–117, 319–321, 526–539; Wheeler, *Uplifting*, 75, 82, appendix.

16. William H. Cooper, "Fowl Town (Col.) Baptist Association," *The Christian Index*, 23 November 1876, 8. Warren also declined "an offer of $3,000 cash, for his influence in carrying an election." See G. H. Dwelle, "History of the Colored Baptists of Georgia," in Love, *History*, 227; Raboteau, *Slave Religion*, 141, 214–215, 220, 307–308; J. P. Tustin, "Andrew Marshall," in William B. Sprague, ed., *Annals of the American Pulpit*, vol. 6 (New York: Robert Carter, 1865), 258, 259. Marshall was also arrested for preaching without proper legal license, but the jury acquitted him (John Krebs, "From the Rev. John M. Krebs, D.D.," in Sprague, *Annals*, 263–264).

17. [Robert Ryland], "Reminiscences of the First African Church, Richmond, Va., by the Pastor, No. 4," *American Baptist Memorial* 14 (1855): 354.

18. *Minutes*, Washington Baptist Association, 1866, 10; *Minutes*, Western Baptist Association, 1866, 6; *Minutes*, Rehoboth Baptist Association, 1866, 11; *Minutes*, New Sunbury Baptist Association, 1874, 20.

19. See Ralph Luker, *Social Gospel in Black and White: American Racial Reform, 1885–1912* (Chapel Hill: University of North Carolina Press, 1991), 12–13. The Freedman's Bureau also spent several million dollars and cooperated closely with the missionary boards. Southern white support was modest: Southern Methodists established the Paine Institute in Augusta, Georgia, in 1884; the Southern Baptist Convention finally gave up its effort to establish a black college; Texas Baptists helped purchase land for Bishop Baptist College in Marshall, Texas; Memphis whites supported the industrial department of the Baptist Bible and Normal Institute. See Luker, *Social Gospel*, 23; Wheeler, *Uplifting*, 101; Pegues, *Our Baptist Ministers*, 588–589, 608, 620; Rufus Spain, *At Ease in Zion: Social History of Southern Baptists, 1865–1900* (Nashville: Vanderbilt University Press, 1967), 84–93; John Eighmy, *Churches in Cultural Captivity: A History of the Social Attitudes of Southern Baptists* (Knoxville: University of Tennessee Press, 1972), 32–40; George Sale, "Atlanta Baptist Seminary," *The Christian Index*, 10 May 1894, 1; *Minutes*, Southern Baptist Convention, 1873, 56. The SBC's Home Mission Board supported students at other schools as well (*Minutes*, Southern Baptist Convention, 1874, 46–47; ibid., 1875, 31).

20. *Minutes*, Southern Baptist Convention, 1867, 14, 49–51, 79; ibid., 1868, 20–21, 62; ibid., 1869, 19–20; ibid., 1870, 25–26; ibid., 1871, 23, 55; ibid., 1872, 56; ibid., 1873, 25–26; ibid., 1879, 46; ibid., 1880, 67; *Minutes*, Georgia Baptist Convention, 1880, 39.

21. David Shaver, "A Movement Well-Timed," *The Christian Index*, 18 November 1869, 178; T. C. Boykin, "The Colored Institute: The Index," *The Christian Index*, 16 December 1869, 194; W. T. Brantly, "Institute for Colored Ministers," *The Christian Index*, 23 December 1869, 198; E. W. Warren, "The Macon Institute," *The Christian Index*, 6 January 1870, 2; E. W. Warren, "Institute for Colored Ministers," *The Christian Index*, 22 December 1870, 198; George Sale, "Atlanta Baptist Seminary," *The Christian Index*, 10 May 1894, 1; *Minutes*, Georgia Baptist Convention, 1895, 44–46.

22. Church Book, Washington First Baptist Church, Washington, Ga., 6 February 1869, MU.

23. J. J. D. Renfroe, "More Alabama Items," *The Christian Index*, 21 October 1869, 162; P. F. Burgess, "The Goshen (Colored) Baptist Church," *The Christian Index*, 2 March 1876, 2. Three newly constituted African-American churches in Coweta County, Georgia, retained the services of white preachers (H., "Colored Churches Constituted," *The Christian Index*, 22 October 1868, 178). White pastor E. W. Warren requested his church to permit some members of the black Baptist church to attend services, since "a few of our old colored brethren had expressed a desire to visit our church & hear him preach occasionally." The church left the matter to Warren's discretion (Church Book, Macon First Baptist Church, Macon, Ga., 1 March 1889, MU).

24. Church Book, Bethesda Baptist Church, Greene County, Ga., 17 July 1897, MU.

25. Foner, *Reconstruction*, 158–161.

26. A. T. Holmes, "The Colored People," *The Christian Index*, 17 June 1869, 93; H. H. Tucker, "Liberia—Kansas—The Exode—The Elect of God," *The Christian Index*, 28 August 1879, 4; Sylvanus Landrum, "A Colored Association—Public Schools—Churches on the Seaboard," *The Christian Index*, 2 August 1866, 122. See also *L*, "Negro Association—Man with a Gun," *The Christian Index*, 22 October 1868, 166; D. G. D., "Zion Association (Col'd)," *The Christian Index*, 12 November 1874, 5.

27. Church Book, Athens First Baptist Church, Athens, Ga., 7 April 1867, MU.

28. *Minutes*, Georgia Baptist Association, 1865, 5–6; *Minutes*, Rehoboth Baptist Association, 1866, 11. The only group I discovered to counsel separation was the Western Baptist Association, which resolved that "we recommend to our colored brethren within the bounds of this Association the propriety of constituting churches of their own" (*Minutes*, 1866, 7).

29. Edward A. Freeman, *The Epoch of Negro Baptists and the Foreign Mission Board, National Baptist Convention, U.S.A., Inc.* (Kansas City, Kan.: Central Seminary Press, 1953), 51, 81–84. Walter H. Brooks, a prominent African-American Baptist pastor, based cooperation on denominational unity: "Yet whatever their differences, Negro Baptists and white Baptists in America constituted one family until after the Civil War. Indeed there has never been any formal separation of the two groups. Each has simply followed the race instinct, in an age of freedom, while one group cooperates with the other, North and South" ("The Evolution of the Negro Baptist Church," *Journal of Negro History* 7 [1922]: 11–22).

30. S. A. McNeal, "Baptist Doctrine," in Love, *History*, 224; G. H. Dwelle, "History of the Colored Baptists of Georgia," in Love, *History*, 230.

31. W. H. Tilman, "Baptist Church History," in Love, *History*, 233; Levi Thornton, "The History of the Baptists," in Love, *History*, 237; William J. White, "More about Easter," *The Georgia Baptist*, 19 April 1900, 4.

32. G. S. Johnson, "The Relation of the White and Colored Baptists in the Past, Now, and as It Should Be in the Future," in Love, *History*, 259; T. J. Hornsby, "The Relation of the White and Colored Baptists," in Love, *History*, 256–257.

33. Harry Toulmin, *The Western Country in 1793: Reports on Kentucky and Virginia*, ed. Marion Tinling and Godfrey Davies (San Marino, Calif.: Castle Press, 1948), 30; "Letters Showing the Rise and Progress of the Early Negro Churches of Georgia and the West Indies," *Journal of Negro History* 1 (1916): 73; James M. Simms, *The First Colored Baptist Church in North America* (Philadelphia: Lippincott, 1888), 80–81; J. P. Tustin, "Andrew Marshall," in *Annals of the American Pulpit* (New York: Robert Carter, 1865), 6: 259; Charles Lyell, *A Second Visit to the United States of North America* (New York: Harper, 1849), 2:14–15; J. L. Kirkpatrick, *Presbyterian Herald*, Louisville, 17 July 1856, quoted in Kenneth K. Bailey, "Protestantism and Afro-Americans in the Old South: Another Look," *Journal of Southern History* 41 (1975): 469 (the phrase "doctrines of grace" was an alias for Calvinist soteriology). See Genovese, *Roll, Jordan*, 243, 244, 263.

34. A. P. Hill, *The Life and Services of Rev. John E. Dawson, D.D.* (Atlanta: J. J. Toon, 1872), 68–69, 97.

35. Charles Octavius Booth, *Plain Theology for Plain People* (Philadelphia: American Baptist Publication Society, 1890), 95, 96, 109.

36. Baptist Missionary Convention [Mississippi], *Minutes*, 1870, quoted in Patrick Thompson, *The History of Negro Baptists in Mississippi* (Jackson, Miss.: R. W. Bailey, 1898), 72.

37. Jerry Freeman, "Colored Western Association," *The Christian Index*, 11 August 1870, 122; W. J. Mitchell, "Constitution and Ordination—Colored," *The Christian Index*, 25 May 1871, 82; Uniontown Baptist Association [Alabama], *Minutes*, 1897, 13; ibid., 1903, 31–32.

38. *Minutes*, Cabin Creek Baptist Association, 1891; *Minutes*, Chattahoochee River Missionary Baptist Association, 1893; *Minutes*, Zion Baptist Association, 1868, 18.

39. Manuscript minutes, Sarepta Baptist Association, 1830, 123, MU. See also manuscript minutes, Tugalo Baptist Association, 1824, 23, MU; manuscript minutes, Chattahoochee Baptist Association, 1871, 76, MU; *Minutes*, Flint River Baptist Association, 1829, 2; *Minutes*, Western Baptist Association, 1833, 5–6; *Minutes*, Stone Mountain Baptist Association, 1853, 10–11. For examples of ordination candidates rejected, see the church books of these Georgia churches: Poplar Springs Baptist Church, Stephens County, 21 December 1832, MU; Kiokee Baptist Church, Columbia County, 15 February 1795, MU; Washington First Baptist Church, 8 January 1870.

40. Newspaper clipping, Church Book, Atlanta First Baptist Church, Atlanta, 17 January 1892, GDAH. For a rare instance noting the length of an ordination examination, see Church Book, Indian Creek Baptist Church, Morgan County, Ga., 14 January 1835, quoted in A. P. Hill, *Life*, 38.

41. Church Book, Macon First Baptist Church, 29 June 1855; A. J. Kelly, "Colored Church and Ministers," *The Christian Index*, 28 May 1868, 87.

42. Church Book, Springfield African Baptist Church, 21 December 1887, 21 March 1888, MU. See ibid., 18 January 1882.

43. R. H. Simmons, "Ordination," *The Georgia Baptist*, 8 September 1898, 3; D. C. Bracy, "Morgan County Notes," *The Georgia Baptist.*, 6 October 1898, 3.

44. First Saints Baptist Missionary Association (Mississippi), *Minutes*, 1869, in Thompson, *History of Negro Baptists*, 49; Union Baptist Association [Alabama], *Minutes*, 1904, 20. See E. K. Love, "Regeneration," in *The Negro Baptist Pulpit: A Collection of Sermons and Papers on Baptist Doctrine and Missionary and Educational Work* (Philadelphia: American Baptist Publication Society, 1890), 66, 76–77; W. H. Tilman, "Baptist Church History," in Love, *History*, 235.

45. Hornsby, "Relation," 253; Johnson, "Relation," 258, 259.

46. Church Book, Springfield African Baptist Church, 14 May 1899 ("All Standing mod[erator] ask[ed] clerk to read the church Discipline or Covenant"), 10 April 1898, 15 March 1899.

47. *Minutes*, Cooper Baptist Association, 1887, 7.

48. See Church Book, Springfield African Baptist Church, 17 February 1886, 20 January 1886, 13 May 1882.

49. Ibid., 15 July 1885, 20 January 1886, 16 September 1885.

50. Ibid., 21 January 1885, 17 November 1886.

51. Ibid., 11 December 1898, 18 January 1899, 16 August 1899.

52. Ibid., 16 May 1882. Various other formulas applied to fornication: "a State unfit for church membership and not Being Married" (13 August 1882); "disorderly living and not Being Married" (17 September 1884).

53. Ibid., 17 November 1886. Springfield had 52 trials per 10,000 members for offenses against the church; antebellum churches had 50 per 10,000.

54. On slave theft, see Genovese, *Roll, Jordan*, 599–609. Springfield had 12 trials per 10,000 members for property crimes; antebellum churches had 35 trials of black members per 10,000 black members.

55. Adeline Jackson, in George P. Rawick, ed., *The American Slave: A Composite Biography*, vol. 3, *South Carolina Narratives* (Westport, Conn.: Greenwood, 1972), pt. 3, 3, quoted in Raboteau, *Slave Religion*, 224; Church Book, Springfield African Baptist Church, 21 December 1887, 16 January 1901, 10 February 1901. The antebellum white churches prosecuted blacks for engaging in worldly amusements at a rate of 4 per 10,000 members annually. The antebellum black churches prosecuted at a rate of 10 per 10,000. The postbellum white churches prosecuted members for worldly amusements at a rate of 14 per 10,000; the postbellum black churches, 30 per 10,000. Before emancipation they excluded the accused 32 percent of the time; after emancipation, 71 percent of the time.

Chapter 6

1. Church Book, Athens First Baptist Church, Athens, Ga., 15 August 1840, MU.

2. H. H. Tucker, "Mistaken, Yet Accepted," *The Christian Index*, 28 January 1885, 8. Early Baptist churches typically identified themselves as "the Church of Christ—Buckhead—Burke Co." or "the Baptist Church of christ at New hope." See Church Book, Buckhead Baptist Church, Burke County, Ga., p. 4 (at the front of church book whose first entry is in 1878), MU; Church Book, New Hope Primitive Baptist Church, Carroll County, Ga., 25 October 1840, MU; Church Book, Penfield Baptist Church, Greene County, Ga., 11 May 1839, MU.

3. Samuel Henderson, "Doctrinal Preaching," *The Christian Index*, 14 November 1878, 1; F. M. Hawkins, "Circular Letter," *Minutes*, Hightower Baptist Association, 1881, 7; Samuel S. Law, "Circular Letter," *Minutes*, Sunbury Baptist Association, 1825, 13; Jesse Mercer, "Address to the Baptists of Georgia," *The Christian Index*, 8 December 1836, 754.

4. David E. Butler, "Doctrinal Sermons," *The Christian Index*, 8 November 1877, 4; J. H. Harris, "Orthodoxy," *The Christian Index*, 27 March 1884, 2.

5. Jesse Mercer, *The Christian Index*, 14 September 1833, 1; Mercer, *The Christian Index*, 12 October 1833, 54; [Samuel Boykin,] *History of the Baptist Denomination in Georgia* (Atlanta: Jas. P. Harrison, 1881), part 2, 391, 528; Shaler G. Hillyer, *Reminiscences of Georgia Baptists* (Atlanta: Foote & Davies, 1902), 123; Julia Sherwood, *Memoir of Adiel Sherwood* (Philadelphia: Grant & Faires, 1884), 167; James McDonald, "Florida Correspondence," *The Christian Index*, 21 January 1847, 27. Mercer recorded subscriptions for sixteen sets in his account book (10 June 1823, MU). See Thomas J. Nettles, *By His Grace and for His Glory: A Historical, Theological, and Practical Study of the Doctrines of Grace in Baptist Life* (Grand Rapids, Mich.: Baker Book House, 1986), 73–107.

6. Church Book, Bethesda Baptist Church, Greene County, Ga., 15 April 1826, MU; Church Book, Macon First Baptist Church, Macon, Ga., 1 June 1878, MU.

7. Church Book, Antioch Baptist Church, Oglethorpe County, Ga., 9 August 1841, GDAH; Church Book, Crooked Creek Primitive Baptist Church, Putnam

County, Ga., 11 May 1822, MU. Antioch Church also granted John Hendrick "liberty . . . to exercise his Gift in Prayer Exhortation &c." (7 March 1829). "Liberty" and "license" were different, the former granting permission, the latter granting both a more formal permission and a written certificate that petitioned other churches to recognize the licensee's gifts in preaching.

8. Church Book, Phillips Mill Baptist Church, Wilkes County, Ga., 27 July 1829, 25 October 1829, MU; Church Book, Powelton Baptist Church, Hancock County, Ga., 1 February 1805, 2 March 1805, 31 July 1829, 31 July 1835, MU.

9. Church Book, Powelton Baptist Church, 30 December 1791.

10. Church Book, Powelton Baptist Church, 31 August 1792, 2 November 1793, 4 July 1801 (two cases). Silas Mercer planted this church and was a warm champion of John Gill, whose view of the atonement Fuller modified.

11. Andrew Gunton Fuller, "Memoir," in *The Complete Works of the Rev. Andrew Fuller*, ed. Joseph Belcher (Philadelphia: American Baptist Publication Society, 1848), 1:9; J. H. Spencer, *A History of Kentucky Baptists from 1769–1885* (Cincinnati: J. H. Spencer, 1885), 1:355–356; Robert B. Semple, *History of the Baptists in Virginia* (1810; reprint, Lafayette, Tenn.: Church History Research and Archives, 1976), 83–84; Church Book, Broad Run Baptist Church, Fauquier County, Va., quoted in John S. Moore, *A History of Broad Run Baptist Church, Fauquier County, Virginia, 1762–1987* (n.p., 1987), 49.

12. Samuel Law, "Circular Letter," *Minutes*, Sunbury Baptist Association, 1825, 11–12.

13. Jesse Mercer, "Anabaptism," *The Christian Index*, 25 August 1836, 513. See also H. H. Tucker, "Methodist Success," *The Christian Index*, 4 June 1885, 8; *Minutes*, Hightower Baptist Association, 1848, 4; Jeremiah Clark and Mark Cooper, "Strictures on Some Parts of the Ocmulgee Circular," *The Christian Index*, 4 February 1834, 17; H. H. Tucker, "Bitter Fruit of the Rebaptism Excitement," *The Christian Index*, 4 July 1889, 9.

14. Jesse Mercer, "Address to the Baptists of Georgia," *The Christian Index*, 8 December 1836, 754, 755.

15. H., "Peace of the Church," *The Christian Index*, 20 August 1841, 538; "Christian Union," *The Christian Index*, 3 January 1839, 13. See David Butler, "Division in Progress," *The Christian Index*, 9 October 1874, 1.

16. I. R. Branham, "More Samples," *The Christian Index*, 1 October 1891, 8.

17. J. C. McMichael, "Close Communion," *The Christian Index*, 2 March 1893, 4; F. G. Ferguson, "The Baptists, Anti-American," *South-Western Baptist*, 31 May 1855, 6; David Butler, "Tendencies," *The Christian Index*, 13 June 1878, 4.

18. J. C. McMichael, "The Exclusiveness of Christianity," *The Christian Index*, 14 June 1894, 4; Jesse Mercer, "Address to the Baptists of Georgia," *The Christian Index*, 15 December 1836, 775; Executive Committee of the Georgia Baptist Convention, *The Christian Index*, 15 January 1841, 43. See Melancthon [Adiel Sherwood], "Is Discipline an Internal Right of the Church," *The Christian Index*, 14 September 1833, 2; Joseph S. Baker, "Confessions of Faith, &c.," *The Christian Index*, 16 February 1844, 3.

19. H. H. Tucker, "Has the Time Come?" *The Christian Index*, 9 July 1885, 8.

20. Samuel Boykin, "Queries in Reference to Discipline," *The Christian Index*, 12 September 1860, 2.

21. Church Book, Kiokee Baptist Church, Columbia County, Ga., 15 November 1795, MU; Church Book, Powelton Baptist Church, 4 July 1801;

Church Book, Savannah First Baptist Church, Savannah, Ga., 22 February 1811, MU.

22. Church Book, Phillips Mill Baptist Church, 6 November 1789; Church Book, Powelton Baptist Church, 5 December 1789, 3 October 1789, 31 August 1792, 2 November 1793. See Church Book, Powelton Baptist Church, 4 July 1801; Church Book, Phillips Mill Baptist Church, 9 September 1871.

23. Church Book, Penfield Baptist Church, 12 April 1879; Church Book, Newnan First Baptist Church, Newnan, Ga., 2 June 1868, MU; Church Book, Atlanta Second Baptist Church, Atlanta, 4 September 1889, 9 October 1889, GDAH; Church Book, Greensboro First Baptist Church, Greensboro, Ga., 4 July 1880, 6 November 1880, 1 December 1880, 6 February 1881, 1 January 1882, GDAH.

24. Church Book, Penfield Baptist Church, 11 May 1860, 9 June 1860.

25. *Minutes*, Hightower Baptist Association, 1877, 3; Melancthon [Adiel Sherwood], "Exclusion the Only Door out of the Church," *The Christian Index*, 14 May 1840, 309.

26. Church Book, Newnan First Baptist Church, 24 July 1842; Church Book, Phillips Mill Baptist Church, 8 June 1816. See J. B. Jeter, "Distinctive Baptist Principles," in *Baptist Principles Reset*, ed. R. H. Pitt (Dallas, Tex.: Standard, 1902), 116. A young Unitarian summed up this attitude: "Surely it would be very sinful for me to continue in a church whose doctrines I cannot believe" (Mary S. Blunt, Kingston, R.I., Letter to Rev. J. F. Schroeder, Flushing, N.Y., 30 August 1843, privately held by Mike Wilkinson, Atlanta).

27. Church Book, Savannah First Baptist Church, 31 March 1873 (James Blackshear made a similar request at the same meeting, having changed his "views on church government"); *Minutes*, Hightower Baptist Association, 1878, 3; Church Book, Newnan First Baptist Church, 23 September 1838.

28. Manuscript minutes, Chattahoochee Baptist Association, 1826, 17, MU; *Minutes*, Ebenezer Baptist Association, 1831, 2.

29. Church Book, Vernon Baptist Church, Troup County, Ga., 1 October 1842, 6 July 1844, MU.

30. Church Book, Bethesda Baptist Church, 20 November 1847; Church Book, Savannah First Baptist Church, 4 May 1871, 29 May 1871; Church Book, Beaverdam Baptist Church, Wilkes County, Ga., 19 February 1842, MU; A. J. Kelly, "Excluding Members," *The Christian Index*, 1 June 1876, 2. See Church Book, Penfield Baptist Church, 14 December 1852, 13 December 1856; Church Book, Bethesda Baptist Church, 17 October 1846; Church Book, Bethsaida Baptist Church, Fayette County, Ga., 21 February 1874, MU.

31. Church Book, Antioch Baptist Church, 2 December 1854. See Church Book, Atlanta Second Baptist Church, 10 December 1875; Church Book, Athens First Baptist Church, 1 April 1877; Church Book, Macon First Baptist Church, 2 February 1855; Church Book, Savannah First Baptist Church, 4 March 1869.

32. Church Book, Macon First Baptist Church, 2 March 1855; Church Book, Athens First Baptist Church, 31 May 1873; Church Book, Newnan First Baptist Church, 22 September 1855; Church Book, Savannah First Baptist Church, 27 August 1832.

33. Church Book, Savannah First Baptist Church, 27 May 1833; Church Book, LaGrange First Baptist Church, LaGrange, Ga., 13 November 1842, MU.

34. Church Book, Newnan First Baptist Church, 27 November 1858, 22 December 1860, 22 September 1855, 27 October 1855. See also 22 September 1860, 24 July 1852, 22 June 1844.

35. Ibid., 21 October 1854, 21 October 1854.

36. Ibid., 25 May 1867; Church Book, Benevolence Baptist Church, Crawford County, Ga., 24 August 1878, MU; Church Book, Powelton Baptist Church, April 1882; Church Book, Crawfordville Baptist Church, Taliaferro County, Ga., 13 November 1897, MU. For other instances, see the church books of: Beaverdam Baptist Church, 1890, 1892, 1900; and Crawford Baptist Church, Oglethorpe County, Ga., 1897, MU.

37. Church Book, Atlanta Second Baptist Church, 8 July 1896; Church Book, Athens First Baptist Church, 1 April 1877; Church Book, Atlanta Second Baptist Church, 9 December 1881.

38. See Walter B. Posey, *Religious Strife on the Southern Frontier* (Baton Rouge: Louisiana State University Press, 1965); Jesse Mercer, "Religious Controversy," *The Christian Index*, 13 July 1837, 445.

39. J. J. O'Connell, *Catholicity in the Carolinas and Georgia: Leaves of Its History* (New York: D. & J. Sadlier, 1879), 494–495, 499; James Jenkins, *Experience, Labours, and Sufferings of Rev. James Jenkins, of the South Carolina Conference* (n.p., 1842), 84, 99–100, 108, 135, 154–155, 166–167; William Carey Crane, "Universalism," *The Christian Index*, 5 April 1838, 199; James Holmes, *"Dr. Bullie's" Notes: Reminiscences of Early Georgia and of Philadelphia and New Haven in the 1800s*, ed. Eugene Presley (Atlanta: Cherokee, 1976), 164–166.

40. J. M. Pendleton, *Church Manual, Designed for the Use of Baptist Churches* (Philadelphia: American Baptist Publication Society [1867]), 21.

41. Church Book, Savannah First Baptist Church, 13 April 1822.

42. Melancthon "Exclusion," 309–310.

Chapter 7

1. *Minutes*, Flint River Baptist Association, 1851, 4–5; ibid., 1852, 4–6.

2. Conference minutes of Tirzah Baptist Church, Flint River Baptist Association, quoted in "Rev. Willis Jarrill," *The Christian Index*, 7 July 1853, 106.

3. *Minutes*, Flint River Baptist Association, 1852, 9–10. The minutes listed 82 delegates this year (p. 23). Jarrill subsequently denied answering the questions negatively ("Willis Jarrill," *The Christian Index*, 3 March 1853, 34).

4. "Report of the Committee Appointed on the Resolutions Withdrawing from Teman Church, and Portions of Tirzah and Holly Grove Churches," in *Minutes*, Flint River Baptist Association, 1853, 13–17; also published in "Report of the Committee," *The Christian Index*, 27 October 1853, 170. See also W. H. C. [William H. Clarke], "Flint River Association," *The Christian Index*, 20 October 1853, 166; Moderator, "Reply to W. H. C.," *The Christian Index*, 24 November 1853, 186.

5. Some Baptists argued that only the joint authority of church and ministers was sufficient to ordain ministers. See Jesse Mercer, "Circular Letter," Georgia Baptist Association, 1821, in Mercer, *History of the Georgia Baptist Association* (Washington, Ga., 1838), 249–250; Mercer, *The Christian Index*, 6 July 1837, 417–419.

6. Church Book, Bethesda Baptist Church, Greene County, Ga., 20 June 1818, MU.

7. Church Book, LaGrange First Baptist Church, LaGrange, Ga., 9 August 1834, 11 October 1834, MU.

8. Church Book, Penfield Baptist Church, Greene County, Ga., 8 November 1845, 7 February 1846, MU; Church Book, LaGrange First Baptist Church, 13 May 1865.

9. Joseph Baker, "Notices of Publications," *The Christian Index*, 3 May 1844, 3; See Church Book, Sharon Primitive Baptist Church, Monroe County, Ga., 13 September 1887, MU.

10. Jesse Mercer, *The Christian Index*, 9 June 1835; Jesse Mercer, *The Christian Index*, 28 October 1834. See Hugh Wamble, "The Concept and Practice of Christian Fellowship: The Connectional and Interdenominational Aspects Thereof, among Seventeenth Century English Baptists" (Th.D. dissertation, Southern Baptist Theological Seminary, 1955), 301–307; and Walter Shurden, "Associationalism among Baptists in America, 1707–1814" (Th.D. dissertation, New Orleans Baptist Theological Seminary, 1967), 1–13.

11. Georgia Baptist Association, "Abstract and Decorum," in Jesse Mercer, *History of the Georgia Baptist Association*, 33; manuscript minutes, Tugalo Baptist Association, 1818, 4, MU; *Minutes*, Washington Baptist Association, 1836, 4. See also manuscript minutes, Echaconnee Primitive Baptist Association, 1829, 5, MU.

12. *Minutes*, Hightower Baptist Association, 1848, 4; ibid., 1850, 2; ibid., 1882, 5, 7 (the association asserted that the minister's baptisms were valid, "whether he was a bad man or a good man"); *Minutes*, Ocmulgee Baptist Association, 1830, 4 (Cyrus White, who published a treatise advancing Arminian views of the atonement, was an ordained preacher in this church); *Minutes*, Middle Baptist Association, 1893, 8.

13. Manuscript minutes, Sarepta Baptist Association, 1843, 213, MU; ibid., 1844, 220; *Minutes*, Sarepta Baptist Association, 1850, 4.

14. Chattahoochee [Joseph S. Baker], "Church Polity," *The Christian Index*, 5 August 1842, 493.

15. David Shaver, "Independency," *The Christian Index*, 9 May 1872, 74; Chattahoochee [Baker], "Church Polity," *The Christian Index*, 5 August 1842, 492. H. H. Tucker made the same point: "We believe in the doctrine of religious liberty; we hold that the so-called Second Baptist church of St. Louis is an independent body, subject to no ecclesiastical tribunal; and that if it should practice infant baptism, or the baptism of bells in the name of the Trinity, or if it should deny the Trinity altogether, . . . no one has the right to molest them or to interfere with them in any way whatever. But we claim the same liberty for ourselves that we accord to others. If we say we have no fellowship with that church, we have a right to do so" ("The St. Louis Church," *The Christian Index*, 9 October 1879, 4).

16. See John T. McNeill, *The History and Character of Calvinism* (New York: Oxford University Press, 1954), 263–265.

17. See Frederick L. Wiley, *Life and Influence of the Rev. Benjamin Randall: Founder of the Free Baptist Denomination* (Philadelphia: American Baptist Publication Society, 1915), 63–77; Robert Torbet, *A History of the Baptists* (Philadel-

phia: Judson Press, 1950), 273–278; Frank Mead, *Handbook of Denominations in the United States,* seventh edition (Nashville: Abingdon, 1980), 49.

18. J. M. Stillwell, "Social Circle, Stone Mountain, Indian Creek," *The Christian Index,* 27 November 1873, 2. See *Minutes,* Georgia Baptist Convention, 1846, 27; "Statistical Table of the Denomination in Georgia," in *Minutes,* Georgia Baptist Convention, 1870. In Virginia, where Arminian Baptists were the strongest, a large minority of the Separate Baptists there in the eighteenth century, Arminianism waned markedly at the end of the century, due to effective polemics by Calvinists and to the fall of two of the Arminian leaders. See Robert B. Semple, *A History of the Rise and Progress of the Baptists in Virginia* (1810; reprint, Richmond, Va.: Pitt & Dickinson, 1894), 83–84, 99–101, 107–110. Around 1790, Jeremiah Walker, a popular Baptist preacher in Virginia, established an evanescent Arminian Baptist contingent in Georgia.

19. Joseph Baker, "Brother Costello's Reply," *The Christian Index,* 27 May 1847, 174.

20. Church Book, Hopeful Baptist Church, Burke County, Ga., March 1819 (recorded prior to 1815 minutes), MU.

21. Church Book, Greensboro First Baptist Church, Greensboro, Ga., 9 June 1821, GDAH. See William Lumpkin, *Baptist Confessions of Faith* (Valley Forge, Pa.: Judson, 1969), 144–149, 235–240, 348–349; letter to Rev. John Asplund, 30 November 1793, Polhill Family Papers, SBTS.

22. Church Book, Phillips Mill Baptist Church, Wilkes County, Ga., 10 June 1785, MU; Church Book, LaGrange First Baptist Church, 12 April 1828. The phrases "everlasting love of God" and "covenant of grace," which recur frequently in Baptist creeds, refer to specific Calvinist doctrines: the first to God's eternal purpose to save the elect and the second to the covenant made before creation between the Father and the Son to redeem the elect. Particular redemption was another expression for the doctrine of the limited extent of the atonement—Christ died to redeem the elect and the elect only.

23. *Minutes,* Centennial Baptist Association, 1884, 3; manuscript minutes, Sarepta Baptist Association, n.d., 8; *Minutes,* Flint River Baptist Association, 1824, 4. See Jesse Mercer, *History,* 29–30; manuscript minutes, Sarepta Baptist Association, n.d., 8–9 (apparently transcribed in 1817 from the 1799 minutes); *Minutes,* Ebenezer Baptist Association, 1828, 6; *Minutes,* Bethel Baptist Association, 1838, 8; manuscript minutes, Echaconnee Primitive Baptist Association, 1829, 2; manuscript minutes, Savannah River Baptist Association (South Carolina and Georgia), 1802, MU.

24. W. H. Stokes, "Our Old Confession of Faith," *The Christian Index,* 7 November 1839, 710; Jesse Mercer, "Unanimity of Sentiment among the Baptists," *The Christian Index,* 16 December 1834, 3.

25. Samuel Boykin and Sylvanus Landrum, "Salutatory," *The Christian Index,* 6 July 1859, 2; T. P. Bell, "To the Baptists of Georgia," *The Christian Index,* 30 January 1896, 4. See, for example, Jesse Mercer, "Doctrines of Grace Stated and Proved," *The Christian Index,* 14 June 1838, 374; "Predestination," *The Christian Index,* 4 November 1852, 177; C., "We Believe in Eternal Election," *The Christian Index,* 27 January 1858, 1; Edwin S. Atkinson, "The Nature of the Atonement," *The Christian Index,* 4 July 1895, 2; S. G. Hillyer, "The Doctrines of Grace," *The Christian Index,* 20 July 1899, 1.

26. "Minutes" (ministers' and deacons' meeting), in *The Christian Index*, 6 August 1841, 508; "Minutes" (ministers' and deacons' meeting of the third district of the Ebenezer Baptist Association), in *The Christian Index*, 17 September 1841, 606.

27. *Minutes*, Hightower Baptist Association, 1852, 6. Imputation and depravity were ideas central to Calvinism.

28. *Minutes*, Central Baptist Association, 1842, 3; manuscript minutes, Chattahoochee Baptist Association, 1871, 76, MU; manuscript minutes, Sarepta Baptist Association, 1830, 123.

29. *Minutes*, Flint River Baptist Association, 1829, 2; manuscript minutes, Tugalo Baptist Association, 1824, 23; *Minutes*, Western Baptist Association, 1833, 5–6; manuscript minutes, Tugalo Baptist Association, 1831, 52; I. R. Branham, "More Samples," *The Christian Index*, 1 October 1891, 8.

30. Church Book, Savannah First Baptist Church, Savannah, Ga., 2 May 1812, MU; letter of dismission, Hopewell Baptist Church, location unknown, in Church Book, Long Run Baptist Church, Jefferson County, Ky., flyleaf of 1804–1817 volume, SBTS; Salt River Baptist Church, Anderson County, Ky., 1805, in ibid.

31. Jesse Mercer, "To Correspondents and Patrons," *The Christian Index*, 9 January 1840, 19; Joseph Baker, "Rev. C. A. Parker's Reply," *The Christian Index*, 2 February 1844, 3. See Mercer, "Queries Answered," *The Christian Index*, 28 February 1839, 133; Baker, *The Christian Index*, 10 March 1843, 151–152; Joseph Baker, "Remarks on the Preceding," *The Christian Index*, 28 July 1843, 470. Mercer rejected fellowship with any church that denied unconditional election, if after receiving instruction it refused to reform ("An Article of Faith," *The Christian Index*, 15 September 1836, 561).

32. See Joseph Baker's articles in *The Christian Index*: "Associational Record," 9 June 1843, 363; "Associational Record," 16 June 1843, 376; "Associational Record," 1 December 1843, 762. Cyrus White and Barnabas Strickland, leaders of Georgia's Arminian Baptists, argued against effectual calling (Robert Fleming, "Effectual Calling," *The Christian Index*, 20 May 1834, 79; Barnabas Strickland, *The Christian Index*, 23 September 1834, 3). White argued also for a general, nonsubstitutionary atonement and free will (Jesse Mercer, *Ten Letters, Addressed to the Rev. Cyrus White, in Reference to his Scriptural View of the Atonement* [Washington, Ga.: News Office, 1830], 1–2, 36–38). See the confession of faith of the Sharon Baptist Church, a member of the United Baptist Association (Arminian): Sharon Baptist Church, "Confession of Faith," *The Christian Index*, 13 May 1834, 75.

33. Joseph Baker, "Discussions about Creeds, &c.," *The Christian Index*, 22 April 1847, 135. John W. Wilson explained the two views of salvation from the Calvinist perspective: "Arminians maintain the doctrine of a conditional election, and that faith is the condition. Predestinarians hold forth the doctrine of unconditional election, and that faith is the evidence" ("Election—Arminian and Predestinarian Views of It," *The Christian Index*, 28 January 1847, 33).

34. J. S. Lawton, "Differences of Opinion," *The Christian Index*, 12 February 1874, 4.

35. An Old Man, "Mercer's Memoirs, &c.," *The Christian Index*, 11 November 1847, 362; William H. Holcombe, *The Christian Index*, 21 January 1836, 21; Watcher, "The Efficacy of Divine Grace, No. 1," *The Christian Index*, 26 May 1858,

1; David Butler, "Preaching the Doctrines," *The Christian Index*, 22 November 1877, 4. Jesse Mercer criticized one Baptist church for leaning toward Methodism: They upbraided their pastor's preaching for having "too much election in it, the doctrine was too strong" (Mercer, "From Correspondents," *The Christian Index*, 7 November 1839, 710). David Shaver noted some slippage of Baptist commitment to Calvinism ("Calvinism," *The Christian Index*, 26 October 1871, 166).

36. Sharon Baptist Church, "Confession of Faith," *The Christian Index*, 13 May 1834, 75. See John M. Costello, *The Christian Index*, 27 May 1847, 169.

37. Mary Fitzgerald, quoted in P. H. Mell Jr., *Life of Patrick Hues Mell* (1895; reprint, Harrisonburg, Va.: Gano, 1991), 58–59; R. W. F., "What I Saw and Heard on the Line of the Georgia Railroad," *The Christian Index*, 16 February 1871, 26.

38. J. H. Campbell, "Rev. Alford Buckner," *The Christian Index*, 13 September 1855, 147; Mercer, *History*, 24–28; Sylvanus Landrum, "New Sunbury Association," *The Christian Index*, 28 October 1880, 2; *Minutes*, Middle Baptist Association, 1854; ibid., 1855, 7; ibid., 1856, 8–9; manuscript minutes, Chattahoochee Baptist Association, 1843, 141; *Minutes*, Sarepta Baptist Association, 1847, 4. The Middle Association was an exception: By 1870 the articles of faith had been amended to the ambiguous "Election and Predestination as taught in the Bible."

39. H. H. Tucker, "Methodist Success," *The Christian Index*, 4 June 1885, 8; Jesse Mercer, "Doctrines of Grace," *The Christian Index*, 29 March 1838, 132; church letter, Phillips Mill Baptist Church, in Mercer, *History*, 141, 140–141, 142; David Shaver, "Unsound Doctrine and Scepticism," *The Christian Index*, 9 January 1868, 6; Silas, "Church Discipline," *The Christian Index*, 14 July 1853, 110. See also David Shaver, "Calvinism," *The Christian Index*, 26 October 1871, 166; Shaver, "'Calvinism' and Policy," *The Christian Index*, 10 September 1868, 142; David E. Butler, "Preaching the Doctrines," *The Christian Index*, 22 November 1877, 4; A. B. Vaughan Jr., "The Doctrine of Election," *The Christian Index*, 23 May 1895, 1.

40. G. T. Wilburn, "Texas Baptists," *The Christian Index*, 2 April 1874, 2; "The Religious Press," *The Christian Index*, 27 March 1890, 1.

41. *Minutes*, New Sunbury Baptist Association, 1900, 8.

42. For a different view, see Nathan O. Hatch, *The Democratization of Christianity* (New Haven, Conn.: Yale University Press, 1989), 97–101.

43. Elias Hibbard, *The Christian Index*, 22 July 1834, 113; Elias Hibbard, *The Christian Index*, 3 December 1833, 82; Isaac C. Perkins, "State of Mississippi," *The Christian Index*, 13 May 1834, 74–75; Joseph Baker, "Confessions or Declarations of Faith," *The Christian Index*, 7 June 1844, 2.

44. Joseph Baker, "Confessions of Faith, &c.," *The Christian Index*, 16 February 1844, 3. See M., who similarly wrote that although churches did not require candidates to subscribe to their creeds, "no candidate will apply for admission that has any special objection to them" (*The Christian Index*, 4 April 1850, 54). See also Baker, "The Rights of the Churches," *The Christian Index*, 6 March 1861, 1.

45. Church Book, Newnan First Baptist Church, Newnan, Ga., 26 August 1837, 26 June 1847, MU. Newnan also "received sister Nancy Dixon upon a certificate of her christian character and an acknowledgement of our Faith" (27 May 1843).

46. *Minutes*, Tallapoosa Baptist Association, 1854, 1; ibid., 1853, 2; *Minutes*, Stone Mountain Baptist Association, 1908, 48; *Minutes*, Ebenezer Baptist Association, 1831, 2; *Minutes*, Western Baptist Association, 1833, 2. See also *Minutes*, Western Baptist Association, 1843, 3; *Minutes*, Hephzibah Baptist Association, 1842, 2; *Minutes*, Georgia Baptist Association, 1794, 6; Manuscript Minutes, Sarepta Baptist Association, 1807, 31; *Minutes*, Stone Mountain Baptist Association, 1900, 6. The Stone Mountain Association resolved that "we recommend to all our churches, severally, to adopt the Constitution of the Rock [Stone] Mountain Association in substance, as their Constitutions" (*Minutes*, 1848, 3).

47. H. H. Tucker, "New Association," *The Christian Index*, 26 February 1880, 4; C. D. Campbell, "The Gillsville Association," *The Christian Index*, 25 March 1880, 4. See also Peace, "Gillsville Association," *The Christian Index*, 18 March 1880, 2; Lumpkin, *Baptist Confessions*, 360–367.

48. *Minutes*, Georgia Baptist Convention, 1846, 4; James McDonald, "Of Creeds, Florida Correspondents, and the N.H. Confession," *The Christian Index*, 21 January 1847, 27.

49. James McDonald, *The Christian Index*, 11 March 1847, 81; Baker, "Florida Association—New Hampshire Confession of Faith," *The Christian Index*, 25 September 1846, 3; *Minutes*, Florida Baptist Association, 1847, 2; John M. Costello, *The Christian Index*, 27 May 1847, 169. In 1847, the West Florida Association constituted and adopted a standard southern creed, that of the Georgia Association (D. P. Everett, "Association Constituted," *The Christian Index*, 9 December 1847, 394). See also Joseph Baker, "Discussions about Creeds, &c.," *The Christian Index*, 22 April 1847, 135.

50. Francis Wayland, *Notes on the Principles and Practices of Baptist Churches* (New York: Sheldon, Blakeman, & Co., 1857), 13; Henry Keeling, "Editorial Note," *The Baptist Preacher* n.s. 9 (1850): 217; A. S. Worrell, *Review of Corrective Church Discipline* (Nashville: Southwestern, 1860), 207, footnote.

51. Jesse Mercer, "Principle More Than Words," *The Christian Index*, 14 July 1836, 117.

52. See Nathan Hatch, *The Democratization of American Christianity* (New Haven, Conn.: Yale University Press, 1989), 97–101; Robert G. Torbet, *A History of the Baptists* (Philadelphia: Judson, 1950), 24–25; Leon McBeth, *The Baptist Heritage* (Nashville: Broadman, 1987), 686–687; Walter Shurden, "John E. Steely . . . On Being Baptist," *Perspective in Religious Studies* 20 (1993): 434–435.

53. *Minutes*, Georgia Baptist Association, 1808, 2; ibid., 1810, 2; Jesse Mercer, "Unanimity of Sentiment among the Baptists," *The Christian Index*, 16 December 1834, 3.

54. Jesse Mercer, "Unanimity," 3; William W. Gardner, "An Essay on Creeds as Used by the Baptists," in *Church Fellowship* (Charleston, S.C.: Southern Baptist Publication Society, 1858), 46–55.

55. W. H. Stokes, "Implicit Faith," *The Christian Index*, 1 April 1842, 202; Wm. J. H—d [Hard], "To the Georgia Baptists—Greeting," *The Christian Index*, 18 January 1838, 24.

56. E. R. Carswell, "Circular Letter—Shall Our Churches Live?" *Minutes*, Hephzibah Baptist Association, 1873, 8; Asa Chandler, "Circular Letter," *Minutes*, Sarepta Baptist Association, 1849, 15. Erastianism is the view that the state rightly exercises authority over church matters.

57. W. H. Stokes, "Bond of Union," *The Christian Index*, 13 May 1842, 298; Stokes, "Implicit Faith," *The Christian Index*, 1 April 1842, 202.

58. W. H. Stokes, *The Christian Index*, 29 July 1842, 473; Stokes, "Our Old Confession of Faith," *The Christian Index*, 7 November 1839, 710.

59. James Armstrong, "Circular Letter," *Minutes*, Savannah River Baptist Association, 1811, 5 (Armstrong wrote the circular, but the association ordered it revised at points with the help of W. B. Johnson and C. O. Screven); Joseph Baker, "Confessions or Declarations of Faith," *The Christian Index*, 3 May 1844, 2; M., *The Christian Index*, 4 April 1850, 54.

60. "Abstract and Decorum" of the Georgia Baptist Association, in Mercer, *History*, 29; Church Book, Little Ogeechee Baptist Church, Screven County, Ga., June 1823, MU.

61. W. H. Stokes, "Our Old Confession of Faith," *The Christian Index*, 7 November 1839, 710; *Minutes*, Tallapoosa Baptist Association, 1868, 5; Posey Maddox, "Marietta Baptist Church," *The Christian Index*, 4 January 1855, 2.

62. Conference minutes of Tirzah Baptist Church, in "Rev. Willis Jarrell," *The Christian Index*, 7 July 1853, 106; Moderator, "Reply to W. H. C.," *The Christian Index*, 24 November 1853, 186.

63. Eli Ball, "The Substance of Two Addresses Delivered at the Flint River Association on Creeds," *Minutes*, Flint River Baptist Association, 1852, 10, 18–22.

64. J. C. McMichael, *The Christian Index*, 26 January 1893, 4; James Willson, *The Christian Index*, 16 February 1837, 102; Jesse Mercer, *The Christian Index*, 16 February 1837, 103; James Wilson, *The Christian Index*, 23 November 1837, 752.

65. Testis [Adiel Sherwood], "Reminiscences of Georgia, No. 6: Uniformity in Discipline," *The Christian Index*, 25 July 1860, 2; David Shaver, "Glimpses of the Times," *The Christian Index*, 28 February 1867, 38; Shaver, "Creeds," *The Christian Index*, 2 December 1869, 186; Shaver, "Credophobia," *The Christian Index*, 9 June 1870, 90; Shaver, "Enemies of Creeds Returning to Them," *The Christian Index*, 30 April 1868, 70; Shaver, "No Longer Necessary (?)," *The Christian Index*, 27 January 1870, 14. S. G. Hillyer rebutted the notion that "Christianity is not a creed, but a life," arguing that "Christianity is in the highest sense a creed" and that Christianity is a life "only because it is a creed,—something to be believed" ("Christianity Is Not a Creed; But a Life," *The Christian Index*, 5 May 1892, 1).

66. Asa Chandler, "Circular Letter," *Minutes*, Sarepta Baptist Association, 1849, 15–16.

67. T. P. Bell and I. J. Van Ness, "Two Sorts of Creeds," *The Christian Index*, 3 February 1898, 6.

68. Asa Chandler, "Circular Letter," *Minutes*, Sarepta Baptist Association, 1849, 15.

Chapter 8

1. J. A. Bell, "State of Religion," *Minutes*, Western Baptist Association, 1910, 27; J. F. Jackson, "State of Religion," *Minutes*, Ebenezer Baptist Association, 1915, n.p.

2. These figures are based on an examination of the published annual minutes of sixty associations in Connecticut, Delaware, Indiana, Maine, Massa-

chusetts, New Hampshire, New Jersey, New York, Ohio, Pennsylvania, Rhode Island, and Vermont.

3. Six circulars of the Georgia Baptist Association urged faithfulness in exercising church discipline 1803–1816 (1803, 1806, 1807, 1809, 1814, 1816). See also Reedy River Association (South Carolina), "Circular Letter," *The Christian Index*, 1 December 1835, 1; W. H. Stokes, "Church Discipline," *The Christian Index*, 29 October 1840, 692.

4. A Missionary, "Faults of the Baptists," *The Christian Index*, 19 July 1849, 228; Observer, "Faults of the Baptists," *The Christian Index*, 2 August 1849, 244; (Delegates from several churches in the Western Baptist Association), "Preamble and Resolutions," *The Christian Index*, 28 August 1851, 138; A. L. Moncrief, "A Disorderly Church," *The Christian Index*, 12 June 1861, 1; Joseph Baker, "Games of Hazard, &c.," *The Christian Index*, 16 October 1846, 2.

5. H. B. McCallum, "Indifference," *The Christian Index*, 11 July 1878, 1; Samuel Henderson, "Church Discipline," *The Christian Index*, 16 October 1879, 1; B. (Huntsville), "Lax Discipline—Some of Its Causes," *The Christian Index*, 28 August 1873, 3; *Minutes*, Ebenezer Baptist Association, 1878, 9; *Minutes*, Georgia Baptist Association, 1873, 7; J. A. Stradley, quoted in David Shaver, "Church Growth," *The Christian Index*, 20 November 1873, 4. See also, *Minutes*, Bethel Baptist Association, 1878, 9.

6. Church Book, Athens First Baptist Church, Athens, Ga., 3 June 1894, MU; E. W. Warren, letter to committee on discipline of LaGrange First Baptist Church, in Church Book, LaGrange First Baptist Church, LaGrange, Ga., 28 September 1890, MU. See also F. M. Law, "Church Discipline," *The Christian Index*, 19 January 1893, 2; J. C. Solomon, "Church Discipline for 1894," *The Christian Index*, 8 February 1894, 2.

7. Edward Ayers, *The Promise of the New South: Life after Reconstruction* (New York: Oxford University Press, 1992), 9, 19–20, 20–22. See also C. Vann Woodward, *Origins of the New South, 1877–1913* (Baton Rouge: Louisiana State University Press, 1971), 107–141.

8. Quoted in Ayers, *Promise*, 21. Not all southerners welcomed the New South. See Charles Reagan Wilson, *Baptized in the Blood: The Religion of the Lost Cause, 1865–1920* (Athens: University of Georgia Press, 1980), 79–99.

9. W. W. Barnes, *The Southern Baptist Convention, 1845–1953* (Nashville: Broadman, 1954), 306–307; Roger Finke and Rodney Stark, *The Churching of America, 1776–1990: Winners and Losers in Our Religious Economy* (New Brunswick, N.J.: Rutgers University Press, 1992), 146–147.

10. "Preamble and Resolutions," *The Christian Index*, 28 August 1851, 138; E. V. Baldy, "Salvation Army," *The Christian Index*, 27 March 1890, 2. See also *Minutes*, Western Baptist Association, 1851, 7; "Prompt Discipline," *The Christian Index*, 12 August 1852, 129; "Report on the State of Religion," *Minutes*, Hephzibah Baptist Association, 1851, 7; Church Book, LaGrange First Baptist Church, 28 September 1890; Persis, "Christ's Church Discipline," *The Christian Index*, 21 December 1876, 2; Finke and Stark, *The Churching of America*, 163–166.

11. David Butler, "The Method of Receiving Candidates for Baptism," *The Christian Index*, 6 June 1878, 4; Stokes, "Church Discipline," *The Christian Index*, 29 October 1840, 692; Benjamin Roberts, "Circular Letter," *Minutes*, Washington Baptist Association, 1829, 5; J. C. Solomon, "Church Discipline for 1894,"

The Christian Index, 8 February 1894, 2. See B. H. Whilden, "State of Religion," *Minutes*, Rehoboth Baptist Association, 1870, 17.

12. Church Book, Penfield Baptist Church, Greene County, Ga., 7 October 1854, MU; Basil Manly Jr., Letter to Rev. M. B. Wharton, 1 February 1873, Manly Collection, SBTS. See Church Book, LaGrange First Baptist Church, 12 December 1863, 12 March 1864.

13. Benjamin Roberts, "Circular Letter," *Minutes*, Washington Baptist Association, 1829, 17; Stokes, "Church Discipline," *The Christian Index*, 29 October 1840, 692; Church Book, Powelton Baptist Church, Hancock County, Ga., 4 January 1845, 1 and 28 February 1845, 3, 30, and 31 May 1845, 3 July 1845, MU.

14. Layman, *The Christian Index*, 27 September 1844, 1.

15. "Prompt Discipline," *The Christian Index*, 12 August 1852, 129; Samuel Henderson, "Beloved for the Father's Sake," *The Christian Index*, 6 August 1885, 2; Julia Sherwood, *Memoir of Adiel Sherwood* (Philadelphia: Grant & Faires, 1884), 128–129.

16. B., "Lax Discipline—Some of Its Causes," *The Christian Index*, 28 August 1873, 3; A. L. Moncrief, "A Disorderly Church," *The Christian Index*, 12 June 1861, 1.

17. L., "Conference Meetings," *The Christian Index*, 28 September 1871, 149.

18. Jesse Mercer, quoted in G. E. Thomas, "Rev. Jesse Mercer and His Ecclesiastical Court," *The Christian Index*, 13 July 1863, 4; Zurich statute quoted in Steven E. Ozment, *The Reformation in the Cities* (New Haven, Conn.: Yale University Press, 1975), 33.

19. See Joseph E. Marks, *America Learns to Dance: A Historical Study of Dance Education in America before 1900* (New York: Dance Horizons, 1957), 17–18, 45–60, 94–95; Frances, "Is the Tuition of a Dancing Master Necessary?" *The Christian Index*, 20 April 1837, 254.

20. Church Book, Phillips Mill Baptist Church, Wilkes County, Ga., 9 May 1794, MU; Church Book, Savannah First Baptist Church, Savannah, 24 February 1835, MU; *Minutes*, Washington Baptist Association, 1837, 4.

21. Church Book, Powelton Baptist Church, 10 August 1799; Church Book, Kiokee Baptist Church, Columbia County, Ga., 20 November 1824, MU; Church Book, Long Creek Baptist Church, Warren County, Ga., 16 January 1790, MU; *Minutes*, Ocmulgee Baptist Association, 1818, 4. See Church Book, Long Creek Baptist Church, 23 April 1836; Church Book, Phillips Mill Baptist Church, 10 May 1806; *Minutes*, Ebenezer Baptist Association, 1816, 4–5.

22. Peter Cartwright, *Autobiography of Peter Cartwright* (1856; reprint, New York: Abingdon Press, 1956), 61; manuscript minutes, Hopewell Presbytery, 8 September 1808, Presbyterian Historical Society, Montreat, N.C.; Sally Elmore Taylor, "Memoir 1910," Southern Historical Collection, University of North Carolina at Chapel Hill, typescript, quoted in Mary Fulton Green, "A Profile of Columbia in 1850," *South Carolina Historical Magazine* 70 (1969): 118; Eliza Frances Andrews, *The War-time Journal of a Georgia Girl, 1864–1865*, ed. Spencer Bidwell King (Macon, Ga.: Arcadian, 1960), 382.

23. George Whitefield, *George Whitefield's Journals* (1741; reprint, Carlisle, Pa.: Banner of Truth, 1960), 444; Nelson Mount, Letter to William Sidney Mount, 1837, Mount Family Correspondence, Library of the Museums at Stony

Brook, Stony Brook, N.Y., quoted in Jack Larkin, *The Reshaping of Everyday Life, 1790–1840* (New York: Harper & Row, 1988), 243; Dorothy Shorter, *The Christian Index*, 9 December 1834, 3.

24. Church Book, Newnan First Baptist Church, Newnan, Ga., 24 July 1858, MU. When Thomas Mullin was tried for "playing at fives at the court house," he confessed that the charge was true and "that he then thought no harm of it but now thinks it was harm" (Church Book, Poplar Springs Baptist Church, Stephens County, Ga., 27 June 1818, MU). When Brother Holtzclaw confessed to playing cards with no betting, he admitted that he was "now satisfied as to the impropriety of such an amusement" (Church Book, Penfield Baptist Church, 12 November 1853, MU). See also Church Book, Poplar Springs Baptist Church, 27 February 1819.

25. V. S., "Greensboro' vs. the Theatre: The Devil Foiled for Once," *The Christian Index*, 13 July 1837, 439; Bar-Samuel [Robert Fleming], "Worthy of Notice," *The Christian Index*, 2 July 1841, 427.

26. Quoted in Thomas Cary Johnson, *The Life and Letters of Benjamin Morgan Palmer* (Carlisle, Pa.: Banner of Truth Trust, 1987 [1906]), 93–96. See Session Records, Indiantown Presbyterian Church, South Carolina, 28 April 1834, quoted in Margaret Burr DesChamps, "The Presbyterian Church in the South Atlantic States, 1801–1861" (Ph.D. dissertation, Emory University, 1952), 120.

27. Moses M. Henkle, *Primary Platform of Methodism; Or, Exposition of the General Rules* (Louisville, Ky.: Southern Methodist Book Concern, 1853), 10.

28. L. L. V., "Drunkenness Increasing," *The Christian Index*, 30 August 1866, 137.

29. *Minutes*, Ebenezer Baptist Association, 1868, 6; Church Book, Penfield Baptist Church, 8 June 1866.

30. For a discussion of Southern Baptists and civil religion, see Rufus Spain, *At Ease in Zion: A Social History of Southern Baptists, 1865–1900* (Nashville: Vanderbilt University Press, 1967); John Eighmy, *Churches in Cultural Captivity: A History of the Social Attitudes of Southern Baptists* (Knoxville: University of Tennessee Press, 1972).

31. Church Book, LaGrange First Baptist Church, 8 May 1857; Church Book, Penfield Baptist Church, 12 March 1859.

32. Church Book, Beaverdam Baptist Church, Wilkes County, Ga., 17 March 1866, MU; Church Book, Powelton Baptist Church, 25 January 1878, 27 October 1894, April 1871, May 1871, 27 July 1878, 23 August 1878.

33. Dancing offenses include dancing; hosting, attending, or patronizing a dance or ball; abetting dancing; fiddling for dancing; and patronizing a dancing school. Simple dancing was the most common charge, accounting for 82% of all dancing offenses. From 1785 to 1860, 49.5 percent of those accused of dancing offenses were excluded; from 1861 to 1880, 23.8 percent.

34. Church Book, LaGrange First Baptist Church, 8 February 1857; Church Book, Washington First Baptist Church, Washington, Ga., 2 January 1864, MU; Church Book, Athens First Baptist Church, 2 July 1864; Church Book, Atlanta First Baptist Church, Atlanta, 3 March 1866, GDAH; Church Book, Newnan First Baptist Church, 25 July 1869; *Minutes*, Middle Baptist Association, 1860, 5; *Minutes*, Hightower Baptist Association, 1930, 8; ibid., 1931, 6.

35. *Minutes*, Rehoboth Baptist Association, 1851, 3; Church Book, LaGrange First Baptist Church, 11 April 1874; Church Book, Greensboro First Baptist

Church, Greensboro, Ga., 2 July 1870, GDAH; Church Book, Poplar Springs Baptist Church, 23 July 1814; Church Book, Newnan First Baptist Church, 21 July 1860, 26 September 1846; Church Book, Kiokee Baptist Church, 9 June 1894, 7 July 1894.

36. Church Book, Crawfordville Baptist Church, Taliaferro County, Ga., 7 May 1898, 11 June 1898, MU; *Minutes*, Middle Baptist Association, 1878, 3; Church Book, Powelton Baptist Church, 24 July 1880; Church Book, Antioch Baptist Church, Oglethorpe County, Ga., 10 November 1883, 8 December 1883, GDAH; Church Book, Powelton Baptist Church, 24 August 1877; *Minutes*, Hightower Baptist Association, 1860, 5. A. S. Wheeler confessed attending a dancing party, but "did not know it to be a dance" (Church Book, Powelton Baptist Church, 25 January 1878). See also Church Book, Phillips Mill Baptist Church, 10 February 1883; Ted Ownby, *Subduing Satan: Religion, Recreation, and Manhood in the Rural South, 1865–1920* (Chapel Hill: University of North Carolina Press, 1990), 120.

37. Church Book, Little Ogeechee Baptist Church, Screven County, Ga., May 1838, MU; G. E. Thomas, "Jesse Mercer and His Ecclesiastical Court," *The Christian Index*, 13 July 1863, 4; *Minutes*, Georgia Baptist Association, 1865, 6; Church Book, LaGrange First Baptist Church, 28 September 1890; Church Book, Barnesville Baptist Church, Lamar County, Ga., 21 February 1892, MU; Church Book, Washington First Baptist Church, 4 November 1886.

38. Church Book, Atlanta Second Baptist Church, Atlanta, 6 January 1871, 10 February 1871, GDAH.

39. Church Book, Crawford Baptist Church, Oglethorpe County, Ga., 23 December 1876, 26 July 1885, MU; Church Book, Newnan First Baptist Church, 27 December 1856, 24 January 1857, 21 February 1857, 27 March 1858, 24 April 1858, 25 July 1869, 15 March 1885.

40. Church Book, Powelton Baptist Church, 23 October 1878; Church Book, LaGrange First Baptist Church, 3 April 1895. The LaGrange church was deeply divided over disciplinary action against amusements and endured a good deal of conflict over it. The most important resolution against "dancing, card playing, and attending theatres" passed on 11 April 1874.

41. Church Book, Powelton Baptist Church, 26 May 1877; *Minutes*, Georgia Baptist Association, 1865, 6; Church Book, LaGrange First Baptist Church, 12 December 1863, 12 March 1864, 13 May 1864.

42. Church Book, Phillips Mill Baptist Church, 10 February 1883; Church Book, Savannah First Baptist Church, 1 October 1877. Antebellum average annual dancing-related trials per 10,000 church members was 8.4; the 1890s rate was 5.4. Antebellum average annual dancing-related exclusions per 10,000 members was 4.2; 1890s rate was 1.2.

43. Ayers, *Promise*, 55–65.

44. Ibid., 72–80; Finke and Stark, *Churching*, 203–207.

45. Mercer, "Baptist Church in Mobile," *The Christian Index*, 12 March 1840, 164.

46. See E. Brooks Holifield, *The Gentlemen Theologians: American Theology in Southern Culture, 1795–1860* (Durham, N.C.: Duke University Press, 1978), 15–23. Antebellum urban Southern Baptist preachers were paid $1,000 to $1,500; rural preachers earned about $100 or $200 (Anne Loveland, *Southern Evangelicals and the Social Order, 1800–1860* (Baton Rouge: Louisiana State Uni-

versity Press, 1980), 58; Finke and Stark, *Churching*, 81–82). The national average wealth of a free white male in 1860 was $2,580; the average wealth of urban Southern Baptist clergy in 1860 was $9,778 (E. Brooks Holifield, "The Penurious Preacher? Nineteenth-Century Clerical Wealth: North and South," *Journal of the American Academy of Religion* 58 [1990]: 23–24).

47. Letter to J. L. Reynolds, 21 August 1849, in Basil Manly Sr., "A Letter of the Late Dr. Manly," *The Christian Index*, 18 March 1869, 41; Jesse Mercer, in a speech delivered before the 1841 Triennial Baptist Convention, quoted in Charles Dutton Mallary, *Memoirs of Elder Jesse Mercer* (New York: John Gray, 1844), 213; Nathan, "Georgia Baptist Convention (Colored)," *The Christian Index*, 21 June 1877, 3.

48. *Minutes*, Western Baptist Association, 1868, 10.

49. S. G. H. [S. G. Hillyer], "The Responsibility of City Churches," *The Christian Index*, 1 April 1869, 49.

50. Of 482 urban church trials 1861–1900 (excluding 95 trials of unknown or indefinite charges), fully 272 involved offenses against the church. Of these 272, 153 cases involved members who joined the Methodists, Presbyterians, Episcopalians, Campbellites, or an unspecified denomination. Twenty-one others joined the Roman Catholic or Christian Science Church.

51. F. M. Law, "Church Discipline," *The Christian Index*, 19 January 1893, 2; J. B. Gambrell, "Southern and Northern Baptists," *The Christian Index*, 11 May 1893, 1.

52. S. G. H. [S. G. Hillyer], "The Responsibility of City Churches," *The Christian Index*, 1 April 1869, 49.

53. M., "Baptist Harmony—Amusements," *The Christian Index*, 28 August 1884, 3.

54. Rural and village churches from 1861 to 1900 had 203 cases involving worldly amusements of 1,101 cases (excluding 174 cases of indeterminate charges); urban and town churches had 24 of 482 (excluding 95 cases of indeterminate charges). Urban and town churches from 1785 to 1860 had 8.82 trials for dancing per 10,000 members annually and 3.78 exclusions per 10,000; from 1861 to 1900, they had 3.83 trials and 1.41 exclusions. Rural and village churches from 1861 to 1900 had 31.3 trials for dancing annually per 10,000 members and 7.36 exclusions per 10,000; urban churches (excluding town churches) had 1.37 trials and 0.64 exclusions.

55. See E. Brooks Holifield, "Toward a History of American Congregations," in James W. Lewis and James P. Wind, eds., *American Congregations* (Chicago: University of Chicago Press, 1994), 1:23–53.

56. Church Book, Atlanta Second Baptist Church, 23 January 1872.

57. Church Book, Savannah First Baptist Church, 13 January 1873; Church Book, Athens First Baptist Church, 3 August 1867; *Minutes*, Georgia Baptist Association, 1872, 6.

58. Church Book, Barnesville Baptist Church, 28 August 1887; Church Book, Newnan First Baptist Church, 21 April 1897. See also the notice of the resignation of Newnan pastor F. M. Daniel, "who has zealously, faithfully and efficiently served" (26 September 1869).

59. For examples of interior refinements, see Church Book, Newnan First Baptist Church, 26 February 1853; Church Book, Long Creek Baptist Church, 23 October 1858; Church Book, Atlanta Second Baptist Church, 11 Novem-

ber 1865; Church Book, Greensboro First Baptist Church, 3 September 1882; Church Book, Phillips Mill Baptist Church, 9 December 1899.

For examples of the introduction of organs, see Church Book, Savannah First Baptist Church, 29 November 1855; Church Book, Macon First Baptist Church, Macon, Ga., 3 August 1860, MU; Church Book, LaGrange First Baptist Church, 8 October 1864; Church Book, Greensboro First Baptist Church, 1 June 1867; Church Book, Newnan First Baptist Church, 22 March 1868; Church Book, Atlanta First Baptist Church, 14 July 1869; Church Book, Little Ogeechee Baptist Church, September 1869, 10 July 1880; Church Book, Washington First Baptist Church, 30 April 1870; Church Book, Crawford Baptist Church, 22 March 1873; Church Book, Antioch Baptist Church, 3 December 1887; Church Book, Mount Vernon Baptist Church, Butts County, Ga., 4 November 1893, MU.

For examples of adoption of professional musicians and choirs, see Church Book, Savannah First Baptist Church, 29 November 1855, 30 October 1889, 29 November 1893, 31 October 1894; Church Book, Macon First Baptist Church, 19 October 1884, 3 August 1888, 3 October 1900; Church Book, Atlanta Second Baptist Church, 11 March 1881, 8 December 1882, 7 July 1886; Church Book, Athens First Baptist Church, 3 March 1889.

Savannah First Baptist Church set the 1868 salary of Sylvanus Landrum at $3,000, as did Macon First for E. W. Warren in 1869, as did Atlanta First for Landrum in 1870, and as did Atlanta Second for Henry McDonald in 1881 (Church Book, Savannah First Baptist Church, 4 November 1867; Church Book, Macon First Baptist Church, 1 October 1869; Church Book, Atlanta First Baptist Church, 1 September 1870; Atlanta Second Baptist Church, 9 December 1881). Town churches generally paid their pastors between $1,000 and $2,000: Church Book, LaGrange First Baptist, 6 March 1881 ($970); 30 January 1887 ($1,284); 1 October 1895 ($1,429); Church Book, Newnan First Baptist Church, 27 October 1860 ($1,000) 26 September 1866 ($800); Church Book, Washington First Baptist Church, 1 January 1866 ($1,500); 4 April 1874 ($1,200); Church Book, Greensboro First Baptist Church, 12 November 1870 ($1,000).

60. Church Book, Atlanta First Baptist Church, 31 October 1888, 2 April 1890, 1 June 1887, 30 October 1889.

61. H. H. Tucker, "An Interesting Service," *The Christian Index*, 15 January 1885, 8; Church Book, Barnesville Baptist Church, 22 January 1882.

62. Urban churches sometimes employed pew rents, at times simultaneously with the envelope system. Savannah First Baptist Church probably rented pews almost from the start and continued them into the twentieth century (Church Book, Savannah First Baptist Church, 17 January 1812, 9 March 1824, 3 February 1909). Atlanta First Church adopted pew rents prior to 1872, retaining the practice at least until 1897 (Church Book, Atlanta First Baptist Church, 29 February 1872, 2 December 1896). Atlanta Second Church adopted pew rents in 1865 (Church Book, Atlanta Second Baptist Church, 13 September 1865). Macon First Baptist Church adopted pew rents in 1866, abandoned them in 1868, renewed them in 1872, and abandoned them again in 1874 (Church Book, Macon First Baptist Church, 17 April 1866, 2 October 1868, 5 September 1872, 27 September 1874). One finance committee recommended an assessment of church members at 1 percent on property and 5 percent on income

above a certain amount (Church Book, Atlanta First Baptist Church, 1 May 1869). Atlanta First Church assessed $1 annual dues and paid a "collector" (Church Book, Atlanta First Baptist Church, 8 May 1888). See also Church Book, Crawford Baptist Church, 18 August 1894, 16 March 1895, 17 October 1896, 18 March 1899.

63. William Henry Strickland, "Circular Letter," *The Christian Index*, 3 November 1870, 169.

64. Church Book, Macon First Baptist Church, 4 April 1877; David E. Butler, "Plan of Church at Work," *The Christian Index*, 4 October 1877, 4; Butler, "Church Work," *The Christian Index*, 21 February 1878, 4; W. J. Dotson, "The Importance of Exercising Church Discipline," *The Christian Index*, 14 July 1887, 2. See Church Book, Newnan First Baptist Church, 22 January 1879; Church Book, Atlanta First Baptist Church, 1 March 1883; Church Book, Atlanta Second Baptist Church, 9 November 1883; Church Book, LaGrange First Baptist Church, 31 August 1892; Church Book, Ebenezer Baptist Church, Wilkes County, Ga., 21 July 1894, MU; Church Book, Beaverdam Baptist Church, 3 August 1894.

65. X., "Church Work—The Right Theory," *The Christian Index*, 26 July 1877, 8.

66. *Minutes*, Hightower Baptist Association, 1915, 8; *Minutes*, Flint River Baptist Association, 1901, 15.

67. J. B. Gambrell, "Our Supreme Problem," *The Christian Index*, 22 February 1894, 2. Ted Ownby argued a similar point: "As churches were losing interest in disciplining the behavior of their members, they were trying to reform the behavior of all Southerners" (*Subduing Satan*, 207).

68. "An Eastern Texas Wedding," *The Christian Index*, 9 January 1851, 6; H. C. C., "Progressive Christianity," *The Christian Index*, 3 September 1891, 1; Provence, "Creeds," *The Christian Index*, 13 March 1884, 2. See also Student, "Dancing Christians," *The Christian Index*, 6 December 1849, 386; W. H. Stokes, "Getting Religion," *The Christian Index*, 16 September 1842, 585; J. B. Gambrell, "Our Supreme Problem," *The Christian Index*, 22 February 1894, 2.

69. *Minutes*, Flint River Baptist Association, 1900, 13; *Minutes*, Georgia Baptist Association, 1897, 9; *Minutes*, Middle Baptist Association, 1914, 17. See also *Minutes*, Georgia Baptist Association, 1896, 11; *Minutes*, Middle Baptist Association, 1909, 16; *Minutes*, Flint River Baptist Association, 1898, 15–16.

70. *Minutes*, Georgia Baptist Convention, 1870, 8, 24–25; ibid., 1880, 40–43; ibid., 1895, 44, 51–52; Church Book, LaGrange First Baptist Church, 26 December 1886.

71. Church Book, LaGrange First Baptist Church, 28 September 1890; *Minutes*, Ebenezer Baptist Association, 1868, 6; *Minutes*, Georgia Baptist Association, 1897, 10. See *Minutes*, Central Baptist Association, 1893, 6.

72. "Historical Sketch of the Baptist Church at Sardis," in Church Book, Sardis Baptist Church, Wilkes County, Ga., 1888 (at the front of the third church book), MU; Church Book, Savannah First Baptist Church, 30 October 1871.

73. J. H. Fortson, "State of Religion," in *Minutes*, Georgia Baptist Association, 1896, 11; [Basil Manly Sr.], "Circular Letter," *The Christian Index*, 24 March 1843, 179 (Joseph Baker ascribes authorship to Manly on p. 188). See Fortson, "State of Religion," *Minutes*, Georgia Baptist Association, 1891, 9; J. W. Ellington, "State

of Religion," *Minutes*, Georgia Baptist Association, 1892, 8; "Church Discipline," *The Christian Index*, 10 December 1841, 789–790.

74. J. C. McMichael, "Wayside Jottings," *The Christian Index*, 15 February 1894, 4; McMichael, "Church Discipline," *The Christian Index*, 13 September 1894, 4.

75. J. B. Parrott, "Have Baptist Churches Too Many Organizations?" *The Christian Index*, 13 December 1894, 1; W. J. Dotson, "The Importance of Exercising Church Discipline," *The Christian Index*, 14 July 1887, 2.

76. M. J. Webb, "Discipline," *The Christian Index*, 11 April 1889, 5; David Shaver, "The Right and Duty of Excommunication," *The Christian Index*, 27 January 1870, 14; B., "Lax Discipline—Some of Its Causes," *The Christian Index*, 28 August 1873, 3.

77. B., "Lax Discipline—Some of Its Causes," *The Christian Index*, 28 August 1873, 3; Wharton, "The Lives of Our Fathers—The Inspiration of Their Sons," in *Centennial Year Book of Georgia Baptists*, ed. M. B. Wharton (Atlanta: Jas. P. Harrison, 1884), 56.

78. J. L. D. Hillyer, "Distinctive Principles of Baptists," *The Christian Index*, 26 January 1893, 2; B., "Lax Discipline—Some of Its Causes," *The Christian Index*, 28 August 1873, 3.

79. Church Book, Washington First Baptist Church, 3 October 1897.

Conclusion

1. John Dewey, *Reconstruction in Philosophy* (New York: Henry Holt, 1920), 48.

2. Basil Manly Sr., letter, 9 September 1856, quoted in Joseph Walker, "Dr. Manly of Charleston, on Pedobaptist Immersions," *The Christian Index*, 24 June 1857, 99.

Index

Abrams, Joseph, 72
abuse, 39
accusation, 21, 37–38
  and gender, 38
  and race, 38
acknowledgment of guilt, 40–41
acquittals, 22
  and egalitarianism, 62
  frequency of, 39
  rates of, compared by race, 65
activism, 133–134, 136
admission to church membership, 19
admonition. *See* rebuke
adultery, 37, 59, 66, 81–82, 120, 140
aid, to poor of church, 44, 62–63, 132
alcohol-related offenses, 100
  excommunication rates for, compared by gender, 55–56
  excommunication rates for, compared by race, 66
  See also drunkenness
alien immersion, 6, 89, 101
  and individualism, 140
  and urban churches, 129
Allen, Thomas, 71
Anabaptists, 42
Andrews, Eliza, 122
Anglican Church. *See* Church of England
annihilationism, 90
anticreedalism. *See* confessions of faith: opposition to
antinomianism, 77, 114
Antioch Baptist Church, 107, 110
anxious bench, 34
appeals, of church verdicts, 24
Arianism, 114
Arminianism, 59, 77, 91, 96, 101, 103, 105–109, 114
  and church discipline, 87
  and heresy, 90
  history of, 102–103
  and New Hampshire Confession, 110
  and ordination, 78
  and Separate Baptists, 87
Arminius, Jacob, 102
Armstrong, James, 112
Asplund, John, 14, 15

associations
  and black representation, 64–65
  and church discipline, 32–33
  and confessions of faith, 109–110
  origins of, 100–101
atheism, 90, 114
Athens First Baptist Church, 16, 75, 94, 110, 125, 131
Atlanta First Baptist Church, 21, 24, 57, 125, 132
Atlanta Second Baptist Church, 90, 94, 126, 131, 132
atonement, doctrine of, 6–7, 78–79, 85–87, 103–107
Augusta First Baptist Church, 112
Augusta Theological Institute, 73
authority, associational, 98–99, 101
authority, ecclesiastical, 11–12, 21, 37, 39, 48
  and admission of members, 19–20
  and biblical interpretation, 109
  in black Baptist churches, 69, 80–83
  and democracy, 5, 29
  and doctrine, 87–88
  and freedom, 4
  and fundamentalist-moderate controversy (Southern Baptist Convention), 3–4
  and individualism, 137
autonomy, church, 20, 29, 32–33, 88, 102
  and associations, 101–102
autonomy, individual, 14–15, 33, 111

backgammon, 125
Backus, Isaac, 32
Bairds Baptist Church, 100
Baker, Joseph, 34–35, 100, 103, 106–107, 109, 110, 117
Baldy, E. V., 118
Ball, Eli, 114
balls, 121–122, 125–126
baptism, 15–16, 106
Baptist Foreign Mission Convention, 70
baptistries, indoor, 16
Baptists
  aspirations for respectability, 50–51
  southern gentry's views of, 13, 44, 50
  views of cities, 128–129
Baptists, African-American. *See* black Baptists
Baptists, English, 6–7, 100–101
Baptists, Freewill. *See* Freewill Baptists
Baptists, General. *See* General Baptists
Baptists, Georgia
  demographics, 8, 36, 67
Baptists, northern, 72, 74, 95, 108, 117
Baptists, Particular. *See* Particular Baptists
Baptists, Primitive. *See* Primitive Baptists
Baptists, Separate. *See* Separate Baptists
Baptists, United States
  demographics, 8, 14, 36, 118
  origins, 7
Baptist successionism, 75–76, 142n9
Baptist usages, 88
Barnesville Baptist Church, 132
baseball, 125
Battle Hill Baptist Church, 109
Beecher, Henry Ward, 85
Bell, J. A., 116
Bell, T. P., 105
Benevolence Baptist Church, 24, 94
benevolent societies, 32–33, 57, 61
Bethel Baptist Church, 36
Bethesda Baptist Church, 15–16, 24, 54, 74, 86
Bethlehem Baptist Church, 98–99
Beza, Theodore, 102
biblical interpretation, freedom of, 112
billiards, 82, 122, 125
black Baptists
  and Baptist identity, 75
  and Calvinism, 76–80
  and church discipline, 80–83
  and individualism, 68

persecution of, 72, 76
relationship to white Baptists, 63–64, 69–70, 72, 74
white Baptist views of, 60–61, 72–76
black Baptists, Georgia
demographics, 67
blacks
excommunication rates of, 60
role in church discipline, 38, 54
role in social hierarchy, 60
standing in civil courts, 38
See also slaves
blasphemy, 81
Boothe, Charles O., 77
Botsford, William, 7
Boykin, Samuel, 90, 105
Bracy, D. C., 79
Branham, I. R., 89
Brantly, Benjamin, 43, 45
Brantly, William T., 57
Broad Run Baptist Church, 87
Brown, Joseph E., 126
Browne, Robert, 85
Bryan, Andrew, 63, 72, 76
Bull Run Baptist Church, 46
Burgess, P. F., 73
Butler, David E., 71, 85, 89, 119

Callaway, Enoch, 86
Callaway, J. S., 74
Calvin, John, 13, 102
Calvinism, 6–9, 17, 19–20, 34, 59, 90, 95, 105, 109–110
and black Baptists, 76–80
and church discipline, 17, 87, 102
and confessions of faith, 103–105, 115
history of, 102–103
neglect of, 77, 85, 107
opposition to, 98–99
Campbell, Alexander, 28, 72, 93, 96, 112
Campbell, C. D., 110
camp meetings, 34, 95
card playing, 24, 82, 122, 125–127, 130
Carey, William, 57, 86–87
Carter, E. R., 71
Cartwright, Peter, 121
Central Baptist Association, 105
Chandler, Asa, 112
Chattahoochee Baptist Association, 92, 105
chess, 125
choirs, 132
Christian Church (Campbellite), 96
Christian Science, 90, 95
church, offenses against
black and white churches compared, 82
excommunication rates for, compared by gender, 55
excommunication rates for, compared by race, 66
trial rates for, compared by gender, 59
church censures, 30
and publishing, 42–43
rebuke, 11, 22, 31, 41
suspension, 40, 47–48, 148n12
See also excommunication
church conferences, 18–21
for black membership, 53, 64
in urban churches, 132
church covenants, 20–21, 80, 86
church discipline
black and white practice compared, 81–83
decline of, 9, 20, 35, 117–119, 135–136
and efficiency, 135
and exclusivism, 5
formative vs. corrective, 135–136
and gender, 54–56, 59
as mark of true churches, 13, 142n4
Methodist, 23, 42, 121–123
neglect of, 35–36, 117, 132
northern Baptist, 6, 117
obstacles to, 22, 48–49, 119–120
Presbyterian, 22–23, 42, 122–123
resistance to, 42, 46–49, 123–124
and revival, 8, 27–28, 33–36
role of, 8, 17–18, 30–31
and social control, 9
church growth, 35

church membership, 17, 29, 44–45, 109
  rates of, 67
  withdrawal from, and ecclesiastical authority, 47–48
Church of England, 28, 32, 63
church records, black Baptist, 68
church seating, 63
church trials, 11–12, 21, 23–25
  open to public, 14, 42
circus, 82–83, 122, 124–125
cities, 128
civil law suits, 22, 48
civil religion, 123, 133
Civil War, 64, 123
close communion, 6, 89, 105, 129
committees, church, 133
common fame, accusation by, 38
Compere, Lee, 109
confessing sin, 21, 40, 81
confessions of faith, 20, 108–113, 115
  assent required, 92
  in black associations, 77–78
  and Calvinism, 103–105, 113
  and individual freedom, 111
  opposition to, 98–99, 111, 113–115
  and theological controversy, 86
congregation, 14–15
Congregationalists, 5, 28, 61, 63
conscience, liberty of, 33, 47–48, 87, 108
contempt, of church, 11–12, 43, 81
controversies, 7, 88, 95, 98–99
conversion
  and church membership, 5, 19–20, 29, 92–93, 111
  and exclusivism, 5
conversion narrative, 19–20, 62
cooperation
  Baptist, 99–100
  evangelical, 95
councils, interchurch, 24, 99–100, 120
County Line Baptist Church, 100
Crane, William C., 57, 95
Crawford Baptist Church, 126
Crawfordville Baptist Church, 94, 133
creeds. *See* confessions of faith
cursing, 48

Dagg, John F., 65
Dagg, John L., 33, 57
dancing, 27, 31, 40, 54, 81, 100, 135, 137
  in American culture, 121
  Baptist views of, 26, 121–127, 130
  and black Baptists, 82–83
  and conversion, 16
  and decline of church discipline, 121–127, 129, 131
  evangelical opposition to, 121–123
  excommunication rates for, 56, 124, 127
  hosting a dance, 26
  trial rates for, 124
  and urban churches, 130–131
  and youth, 125–126
dancing games, 125
dancing schools, 121–122, 125
Davis, Jonathan, 16
Dawson, John E., 16, 77
deacons, 19, 22, 64, 81, 86
decorums, church, 20, 22–23, 58
defections, from Baptist churches, 91–97
Deism, 87, 90
democracy, church
  and biblical interpretation, 29
  and confessions of faith, 111
  and ecclesiastical authority, 5–6, 137, 139
depravity, doctrine of, 76–79, 86–87, 103–106, 110
desertion, 38, 43
Dewey, John, 140
Dexter Avenue Baptist Church, 77
dice, casting, 82
discipline, interchurch, 100–102
disestablishment, 32
disobedience, 24
doctrine, role of, 84–88, 168n26
Dover Baptist Association, 51

drunkenness, 38–39, 42, 44, 53–54, 59, 81, 120, 123, 129, 135
 trial rates for, compared by gender, 59
due process, 24–25
dues, church, 132

Easter, 76
Ebenezer Baptist Association, 92, 109–110, 116, 123, 135
ecclesiology, Baptist, 28–30
education, of blacks, 72–75
Edwards, Jonathan, 86
Edwards, Morgan, 7
efficiency, church, 131–134
 and church discipline, 134–138
 and toleration, 137
egalitarianism, 9, 50, 61–63
elders, Baptist, 155n4
election, doctrine of, 17, 77–79, 91, 103–108, 110, 113, 172n33
envelope system, 132–133
Episcopal Church, 22, 28, 94, 112, 122, 128
erasure, from membership roll, 91–95
evangelism, 4, 35, 88, 133
evidence, 23
exclusion. *See* excommunication
exclusivism, Baptist, 6, 84, 89, 129–130
 and confessions of faith, 113, 115
 and fundamentalist-moderate controversy (Southern Baptist Convention), 3–4
 persistence of, 137–138
exclusivism, evangelical, 5
excommunication, 12, 18, 21–22, 30–31, 40–45, 48, 102, 132, 136
 history of, 12–13, 42
 ritual of, 12, 42–44
excommunication, rates of, 22–23
 chronological comparisons, 117
 compared by gender, 54–56
 compared by race, 66, 68
 urban and rural compared, 129–130
exhortation, gift of, 86
expulsion. *See* excommunication

falsehood, 87
familiar address, and church membership, 44–45
family, 55
family worship, 62
fiddling, 26–27, 82, 121, 125
Fifth Street Baptist Church, 68
fighting, 40, 41, 81, 129
finances, church, 19, 57, 131–133
Finney, Charles G., 34
First London Confession, 104
Fleming, Robert, 56–57
Flint River Baptist Association, 98–99, 113
Florida Baptist Association, 110
Ford, J. W., 134
Foreign Mission Baptist Convention, 75
forgiveness, 22, 39–40
fornication, 18, 23, 81, 119
Fortson, J. H., 135
fortune telling, 24
Franklin Covenant Baptist Church, 65
fraud, 46, 132
Frazier, Garrison, 71
Freedmen's Bureau, 71, 74
freedom, church, 32–33, 88, 102
freedom, individual, 6, 21, 33, 46, 68, 102, 137
 and biblical interpretation, 87–88, 109
 and confessions of faith, 108
 and ecclesiastical authority, 4, 46
Freewill Baptists, 80, 90, 103, 106, 110
Friendship Baptist Church, 71
Fuller, Andrew, 86–87, 102
fundamentalist-moderate controversy (Southern Baptist Convention), 3–4, 137–138

gambling, 13, 31, 39, 122, 129
Gambrell, J. B., 130, 133
Gano, John, 7
gender. *See* men; women
General Baptists, 6–7, 87, 90, 103

Georgia Baptist Association, 7, 14, 30, 57, 65, 101, 104, 108, 111, 114, 127, 131, 135
Georgia Baptist Convention, 26, 110
Gill, John, 77, 85–86, 102
Gillfield African Church, 68
Gillsville Baptist Association, 110
Goshen Colored Baptist Church, 73–74
gospel steps, 24–25, 30
Grady, Henry, 118
Graves, J. R., 8
Grayson, William, 13
Great Awakening, 5, 7, 33–34, 122
Greensboro First Baptist Church, 45, 53, 61, 90, 104, 125
Green Street Baptist Church, 68

Hall, J. H., 132
Hard, William J., 112
Harmony Baptist Church, 71
Harris, J. H., 85
Hartford Baptist Church, 109–110
Hawthorne, J. B., 57, 59
helps. *See* councils, interchurch; presbyteries, Baptist
Henderson, Samuel, 85, 120
Henkle, Moses, 123
Hephzibah Baptist Association, 24, 52, 65
heresy, 30, 87, 90–91, 93–94, 97, 99, 113–114, 119, 123
Hightower Baptist Association, 91, 92, 101, 105, 125
Hillyer, J. L. D., 137
Hillyer, S. G., 55, 62, 129, 130
Holcombe, Henry, 11, 12, 16, 47, 51–52
Holcombe, William, 107
Holiness movement, 82, 118–119
Holly Grove Baptist Church, 99
Holmes, A. T., 55, 71
Home Mission Board, Southern Baptist, 73
homicide, 24, 30, 47, 122
homosexuality, 140
honor, southern ideal of, 37, 48–49
Hopeful Baptist Church, 40, 104
Hornsby, T. J., 80
horse racing, 122–123, 125
hyper-Calvinism, 87, 107

idolatry, 30
individualism, 3–4, 21, 33, 137
inerrancy, 3–4
infant baptism, 5–6, 20, 29, 89, 95–96, 111
investigating committees, 21–22, 48, 100, 120
Ivey, F. H., 75

Jarrill, Willis, 98–99, 113–115
Jenkins, James, 95
Johnson, Andrew, 74
Johnson, E. P., 79
Johnson, W. B., 26, 43, 46–47
Jones, Charles Colcock, 61
Jordan, F. B., 79
Judson, Adoniram, 57, 153n29
jurisdiction, church, 24, 46

Keach, Elias, 104
Keeling, Henry, 111
Kilpatrick, J. H., 35
Kiokee Baptist Church, 54
Kirkpatrick, J. L., 77
Klugh, D. S., 79

LaGrange First Baptist Church, 54, 93, 100, 118, 124, 126, 127, 133, 134, 135
Landmarkism, 7–8, 95, 142n9
Landrum, Sylvanus, 31, 35, 51, 105
Law, F. M., 129
Law, Josiah, 61
Law, Samuel, 85, 88
Lawton, J. S., 107
Leland, John, 33
Liele, George, 63, 77
Little Ogeechee Baptist Church, 54
Long Run Baptist Church, 87
Lord's Supper, 15, 44
Love, E. K., 70, 71, 75, 162n9
Luther, Martin, 13
Lyell, Charles, 77
lynching, 70

Macon First Baptist Church, 73, 133
majority, democratic, 30

Mallary, C. D., 16
Manly, Basil, Jr., 18, 70, 119
Manly, Basil, Sr., 57, 128, 135, 140
Marietta First Baptist Church, 113
Marshall, Andrew, 63, 72, 76, 77
Marshall, Daniel, 7, 34
Mars Hill Baptist Church, 120
Martin, Thomas D., 91
Masonry, 46
masters, 61–62
McDonald, James, 110
McMichael, J. C., 89, 136
McTyeire, H. N., 55
Mell, P. H., 107–108
men
  Baptist views of, 58–59
  excommunication rates of, 54–56
  trial rates of, 59
Mercer, Jesse, 14, 19–20, 26–27, 57, 60, 128
  and Arminian Baptists, 106
  and associational authority, 33
  on Baptist ecclesiology, 28–29
  and Calvinism, 105, 108
  on church discipline, 23, 31, 34–36
  on confessions of faith, 111, 114
  on dancing, 26, 121
  on individual freedom, 33
  on moral philosophy, 59
  on need for purity, 31
  on orthodoxy, 85
  on role of women, 56
  on social equality of races, 162n6
  theological views of, 85–86
  on unity, 32, 88
  on women voting, 51, 58
Mercer, Silas, 32, 108
Methodists, 5, 8, 13–14, 20, 56, 58, 67, 69, 77, 89, 107–108, 111–112, 119, 121–123
  and Baptist cooperation, 95
  Baptist defections to, 92–94, 96
  doctrine of, 96, 103
  growth of, 118
  and heresy, 90, 94
Middle Baptist Association, 101, 134
Missionary Baptist Convention (Georgia), 76
missions, 4, 27, 32, 34, 45, 57, 101, 132–134
modernism, 116, 137
Moncrief, A. L., 120
Morehouse College, 73
Mormonism, 90, 95
Mount Olive Baptist Church, 39, 101
Mount Zion Baptist Church, 100
musical instruments, 57, 93, 132

Nails Creek Baptist Church, 101
National Baptist Convention, 75
New Hampshire Confession, 110
Newnan First Baptist Church, 43, 90, 92–94, 109, 122, 125, 126, 132, 133
New Orleans First Presbyterian Church, 42
New South, 116, 118, 127–128
Newton, John, 102
novel reading, 56–57

Ocmulgee Baptist Association, 101
O'Connell, J. J., 95
offenses
  abuse, 39
  adultery, 37, 59, 66, 81–82, 120, 140
  blasphemy, 81
  classes of, 30
  contempt of church, 11–12, 43, 81
  cursing, 48
  desertion, 38, 43
  disobedience, 24
  drunkenness, 38–39, 42, 44, 53–54, 59, 81, 120, 123, 129, 135
  falsehood, 87
  fiddling, 26–27, 82, 121, 125
  fighting, 40–41, 81, 129
  fornication, 18, 23, 81, 119
  fortune telling, 24
  fraud, 46, 132
  gambling, 13, 31, 39, 122, 129
  heresy, 30, 87, 90–91, 93–94, 97, 99, 113–114, 119, 123
  homicide, 24, 30, 47, 122
  homosexuality, 140

offenses (*continued*)
  idolatry, 30
  Masonry, 46
  profanity, 12
  resisting authority, 41, 48
  running away, 24, 38, 44
  Sabbath breaking, 13, 27, 53
  slander, 24, 43, 46, 120
  spying, 37
  swearing, 12–13
  theft, 24, 30, 40, 48, 66, 82
  See also dancing; sexual offenses; worldly amusements
open communion, 80, 92, 102
opera, 82–83, 123, 130
ordination, 78–79
organs, 57, 93, 132
orthodoxy, 29, 78–79, 84–87, 133
  and exclusivism, 5, 89
  and fundamentalist-moderate controversy (Southern Baptist Convention), 3–4
Owen, John, 85

Paine, Robert, 42
Paley, William, 59
Palmer, Benjamin Morgan, 42, 122–123
Parrott, J. B., 136
Particular Baptists, 6–7, 100–101, 104
penance, medieval practice of, 13
Pendleton, James M., 95
Penfield Baptist Church, 22, 43, 90, 100, 123–124
Perryman, James, 18
perseverance, doctrine of, 17, 77, 79, 90, 96, 103–104, 110
pew rents, 132
Philadelphia Baptist Association, 7, 14, 101, 104
Phillips Mill Baptist Church, 86, 90, 92, 121
pietism, 139
pleas, 39
Pope, W. H., 61
Poplar Springs Baptist Church, 22–23
populism, 6, 33–34, 39, 112, 115
Powelton Baptist Church, 19, 24, 26, 46, 52, 86–87, 90, 94, 120–121, 124–126
preaching
  and church purity, 17
  and orthodoxy, 86
  by slaves, 40–41
predestination, doctrine of, 17, 76–79, 102, 106–108, 113–114
Presbyterians, 5, 8, 13–14, 20, 28, 42, 56, 61, 69, 111–112, 122–123, 128, 140
  and Baptist cooperation, 95
  Baptist defections to, 93–94
  doctrine of, 96
  and heresy, 90
presbyteries, Baptist, 15, 86, 99–100
priesthood of believers, 4
Primitive Baptists, 7, 32–33
  black, 77–78
primitivism, 28
private offenses, 24, 30, 41
profanity, 12, 123, 132
progress, ideal of, 133–134
prohibition, 71
property offenses
  excommunication rates for, compared by gender, 56
  excommunication rates for, compared by race, 66, 82
  trial rates for, compared by gender, 59
protracted meetings, 34. *See also* revivals
Provence, S. M., 134
public offenses, 30, 41
Puritans, 13, 20–21, 28, 63, 139
purity, church
  changing role of, 131
  and church discipline, 23–24, 31
  and exclusivism, 17
purity, doctrinal, 90–91, 93

Quarles, Frank, 128

race issue, 80
raffles, 130
Randall, Benjamin, 103, 110
rebuke, 22, 30–31, 41

Reconstruction, 69–71
refinement, 27, 93, 132
regeneration. *See* conversion
Regular Baptists, 7, 29, 103
Rehoboth Baptist Association, 107, 125
Rehoboth Baptist Church, 43
religious liberty, 6, 32–33, 68, 87–88, 102
Renfroe, J. J. D., 73
repentance, 40
resisting authority, 41, 48
respectability, Baptist aspirations for, 13–14, 128
restoration, 45–46
  rates of, 65
Restorationism, 28
retrials, 24
revivals, 33–34
  and baptism, 16
  and church discipline, 27–28, 31, 33–36
  and worldly amusements, 122
Rhodes, Thomas, 100
Rice, Luther, 57
Richland Baptist Church, 48
Richmond First African Baptist Church, 72
Ripley, Henry J., 17
Rippon, John, 77
Robert, Joseph T., 73
Roberts, Benjamin, 31, 119
Rocky Ford Baptist Church, 101
Roman Catholicism, 76, 90, 95, 99, 110
running away, 24, 38, 44
Ryland, Robert, 72

Sabbath breaking, 13, 27, 53
salaries, ministerial, 45, 132, 134, 179n46
Salvation Army, 119
Sardis Baptist Church, 135
Sarepta Baptist Association, 52, 101
Savannah First African Baptist Church, 63, 70–71, 77
Savannah First Baptist Church, 11, 43, 46–47, 52–53, 58, 92–93, 106, 121, 127, 131–132, 135
Savannah Second Baptist Church, 52–53
schisms, 86–87, 100, 115
Screven, Benjamin, 48
Second London Confession, 5, 104–105, 110–112, 115
segregation, racial, 69
self-accusation, 21, 38–39
self-vindication, 41
Separate Baptists, 7, 87
separation from the world, 10, 13–14, 17, 21, 31, 36, 123, 129–130
sexual offenses, 30
  excommunication rates for, compared by gender, 56
  excommunication rates for, compared by race, 66, 81
  trial rates for, compared by gender, 59
  trials rates for, compared by race, 81
shaming rituals, 41
Sharon Baptist Church, 107
Shaver, David, 102, 114
Sherman, William T., 71
Sherwood, Adiel, 29, 62, 91, 96, 114, 120
shooting matches, 125
singing, 15, 44, 62, 86
singing societies, 15
slander, 24, 43, 46, 120
slave laws, 63–64
slaves
  evangelism of, 60–61
  moral duties of, 60
  testimony of, in church trials, 24
  voting privileges of, 51, 53–54
social equality
  black Baptist views of, 76, 162n9
  white Baptist views of, 61, 69–71, 162n6
social hierarchy, 9, 31, 50, 55
social reform, 10
soul liberty, doctrine of, 3–4, 137
Southern Baptist Convention, 3, 26, 58, 61, 73

speech offenses
  excommunication rates for, compared by race, 66
  trial rates for, compared by gender, 59
Spiritualism, 90
Springfield African Baptist Church, 16, 63, 68, 80–82
spying, 37
Stanton, Edwin M., 71
Stearns, Shubal, 7, 34
Stocks, Thomas, 57
Stokes, William H., 15–16, 19, 112–113
Stone, J. Barton, 28
Stone Mountain Baptist Association, 35, 109, 133
Stout, T. H., 36
Stradley, J. A., 117
strife, religious, 5, 88, 95
Sturgis, C. F., 60
submission to church, 17, 20, 39–41, 45–46, 48–49, 69, 81
subscription, of church contributions, 132
suffering, and black Baptist identity, 76
Sunbury Baptist Association, 53, 61, 65, 95, 108
Sunbury Baptist Church, 61
swearing, 12–13
Swedenborg, Emanuel, 91
Swedenborgianism, 90–91, 95
Synod of Dort, 103

Tallapoosa Baptist Association, 109, 113
Teague, E. B., 70
Teman Baptist Church, 99
temperance societies, 32, 56–57, 61
theater, 82, 122–126, 130
theft, 24, 30, 40, 48, 66, 82
theology, Baptist, 3, 5, 76–78, 102–106
Tilman, W. H., 76
Tirzah Baptist Church, 99
tobacco, use of, 56, 59
Toer, J. W., 71
toleration
  of doctrinal differences, 94, 106–107
  and ecclesiastical authority, 137–138
  and fundamentalist-moderate controversy (Southern Baptist Convention), 3–4, 137
Toplady, Augustus, 85
Torbet, Robert G., 4
Toulmin, Harry, 76
trials, church
  rates of, compared by gender, 65–66
  rates of, compared by race, 65–66, 68
  rates of, urban and rural compared, 129–130
Triennial Convention, 27, 32, 57–58
Tucker, H. H., 56, 70, 89–90, 132
Tugalo Baptist Association, 23, 106
Turretin, Francis, 102

unanimity, in voting, 30, 47
union, of Protestant churches, 89–90
Unitarianism, 114
United Baptist Association, 105, 107
unity, ideal of, 30, 32, 88
  and confessions of faith, 109, 113
Universalism, 87, 90, 95, 114
University of Georgia, 121
urbanization, 118, 127–131

violence, 37, 47, 66, 69–70
  excommunication rates for, compared by gender, 56
  excommunication rates for, compared by race, 66
  as response to church discipline, 42, 48–49
  trial rates for, compared by gender, 59
violins, 125. *See also* fiddling
voluntary societies. *See* benevolent societies
voting practices, egalitarian aspects of, 51

Waddell, Moses, 121
Walker, Jeremiah, 108
Warren, E. W., 73
Warren, Willis, 72
Washington Baptist Association, 45, 101, 121
Washington First Baptist Church, 60–61, 125
Watterson, Henry, 118
Wayland, Francis, 110
wealth, 120, 130, 136
Webb, M. J., 136
Webb, Richard, 92
Wesley, Charles, 103
Wesley, John, 103
Western Baptist Association, 52, 110, 116, 129
Westminster Confession of Faith, 104
Wharton, M. B., 136
Whilden, B. H., 17
White, Cyrus, 103
White, William J., 71, 76
Whitefield, George, 122
white preaching, to blacks, 71, 73–74
Williams, Roger, 7
Williams, Thomas, 46–48
Willingham, R. J., 132
Willson, James, 114
withdrawing, from Baptist church, 92–93
witnesses, 23
women
 Baptist views of, 56–59
 and benevolent societies, 57–58
 demands of piety for, 56–57
 education of, and southern evangelicalism, 56
 excommunication rates of, 54–56
 keeping silence, 38
 membership rates of, 54
 ordination of, 140
 role in church discipline, 38, 54, 58–59
 trial rates of, 59
 voting privileges of, 51–53
worldly amusements, 16, 121–127, 130
 backgammon, 125
 balls, 121–122, 125–126
 baseball, 125
 billiards, 82, 122, 125
 card playing, 24, 82, 122, 125–127, 130
 chess, 125
 circus, 82–83, 122, 124–125
 dice, casting, 82
 excommunication rates for, compared by race, 66, 82
 horse racing, 122–123, 125
 novel reading, 56–57
 opera, 82–83, 123, 130
 shooting matches, 125
 theater, 82, 122–126, 130
 trial rates for, compared by gender, 59
 See also dancing
Worrell, A. S., 51, 111
Wyer, H. O., 31
Wynne, J. A., 52

youth, and worldly amusements, 125–126